T0129115

Military Paternalism, Labour, and the Rideau Canal Project

Robert W. Passfield

For my mother, the late Gertrude Violet Passfield,
and my daughter, Mary Barnes

AuthorHouse™ LLC
1663 Liberty Drive
Bloomington, IN 47403
www.authorhouse.com
Phone: 1-800-839-8640

© *2013 Robert W. Passfield. All rights reserved.*

No part of this book may be reproduced, stored in a retrieval system, or transmitted by any means without the written permission of the author.

Published by AuthorHouse   10/10/2013

ISBN: 978-1-4817-5569-6 (sc)
ISBN: 978-1-4918-3010-9 (hc)
ISBN: 978-1-4918-2376-7 (e)

Library of Congress Control Number: 2013918217

Any people depicted in stock imagery provided by Thinkstock are models, and such images are being used for illustrative purposes only. Certain stock imagery © Thinkstock.

This book is printed on acid-free paper.

Because of the dynamic nature of the Internet, any web addresses or links contained in this book may have changed since publication and may no longer be valid. The views expressed in this work are solely those of the author and do not necessarily reflect the views of the publisher, and the publisher hereby disclaims any responsibility for them.

Cover Design: Craig Passfield. Illustration: "Brewer's Lower Mill: Masonry of the Lock nearly completed, Excavation for Canal in progress, 1831-2". Thomas Burrowes, watercolour, (Archives of Ontario).

-Rideau Canal labour
-Canal workers
-Royal Engineers
-Military paternalism
-Lt. Col. John By
-Anglican toryism

Summary

This book comprises a revisionist history of the labour situation on the Rideau Canal construction project, 1826-1832. In previous studies, Labour historians have focused on the suffering and supposed exploitation of the canal workers, and have posited that the military deployed troops to suppress labour unrest and were indifferent to the suffering of the workers. This book provides a contrary assessment from a different perspective. It places the military canal project within its natural and physical environment in analyzing the living and working conditions under which the canal workers laboured, and takes cultural factors into account in examining how the workers of different ethnic groups responded to the demands of living and working in a wilderness environment. It also assesses to what extent, if any, the Commanding Royal Engineer, Lt. Col. John By, responded to the suffering of the canal workers.

Through examining the Rideau Canal project within a broader framework, a totally different view emerges with respect to the causes of the suffering experienced by the canal workers, and the role of the military on the canal project. Moreover, the paternalism of Lt. Col. John By is revealed in his efforts to alleviate the suffering of the canal workers, and to promote their physical, material and moral well-being. In addition, the character, education and upbringing of Lt. Col. By is examined to gain an understanding of his character, cultural values and worldview, and a wider view of military paternalism is taken through examining the founding of the Rideau Military Settlement in Upper Canada prior to the construction of the Rideau Canal.

Lastly, within an Appendix, a critique is offered of the Marxist interpretation of the labour situation on the Rideau Canal project, and the practice of paternalism. In its stead, a cultural values interpretation, based on Anglican toryism, is preferred.

Anglican toryism is also differentiated from Lockean liberal cultural values in addressing the currently prevailing view that the Province of Upper Canada had an all pervasive Lockean-liberal political culture.

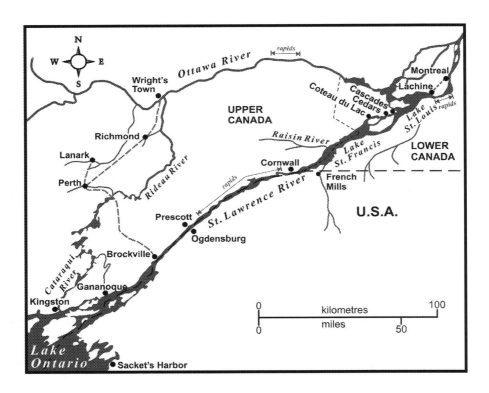

Figure 1. "St. Lawrence River Waterway ca. 1826". Map showing the towns and rapids of the St. Lawrence River navigation, and the Rideau Military Settlement towns of Perth, Richmond and Lanark, in the interior. (Ken W. Watson, 2013).

Contents

Preface   xi

Acknowledgements   xv

Part One: Military Paternalism on the Rideau Canal Project
    Introduction   3
    Obtaining a Workforce   4
    Getting the Project Underway   17
    The Irish Catholic Pauper Immigrants   20
    Health Care   23
    The Sickness Factor   31
    Origins, Circumstance, and Acculturation   41
    The Provisioning System   51
    Wage Rates   57
    Maintaining Order   63
    Conclusion   68
    Endnotes   72

Part Two: Lt. Col. John By, Commanding Royal Engineer, Rideau Canal
    Introduction   105
    Biographical Sketch: The Early years   106
    Character and Worldview   118
    Endnotes   121

Part Three: Military Paternalism and the Rideau Military Settlement
    Introduction   133
    Strengthening the British Character of Upper Canada 134
    Implementing a Military Settlement Strategy   137
    The Assisted Emigration Scots   142
    The Rideau Military Settlement   145
    The Perth Settlement   146
    The Richmond Settlement   158
    The Lanark Settlement   164

The Irish Catholic Poor-Relief Immigrants   180
Conclusion   189
Endnotes   190

Bibliography   209

Appendix: Marxism, Cultural Values, and Military Paternalism
Marxist Canal Historians   219
Cultural Values   226
Anglican toryism   230
Lockean liberalism   237
Endnotes   250

A Note about the Author   261

Rideau Canal publications by the Author.   263

Index   269

Illustrations

Figure 1. "St. Lawrence River Waterway ca. 1826". (Ken W. Watson, 2013).

Figure 2. "Rideau-Cataraqui Waterway in 1827". (Ken W. Watson, 2013).

Figure 3. "Maitland's Rapids, Rideau [Kilmarnock], 19 Augt. 1830", Lt. Col. James Pattison Cockburn, Royal Artillery, watercolour. (Royal Ontario Museum).

Figure 4. "First Camp, Bytown; September 1826", attributed to Lt. Col. John By, Royal Engineers or his staff, watercolour. (McCord Museum).

Figure 5. "Rideau Canal, Long Island on the Rideau River: August 1830", Lt. Col. James Pattison Cockburn, Royal Artillery, watercolour. (Royal Ontario Museum).

Figure 6. "Royal Sappers & Miners, Uniform & Working Dress, 1825", George B. Campion, Drawing Master, Royal Military Academy, Woolwich, coloured lithograph. (T.W. Connolly, *The History of the Corps of Royal Sappers and Miners* (London: Longman, Brown, Green and Longmans, 1855, Volume 2, Plate 13).

Figure 7. "Near Old Sly's, Rideau; August 1830", Lt. Col. James Pattison Cockburn, Royal Artillery, watercolour. (Library and Archives Canada).

Figure 8. A Settlement on Long Island on the Rideau River, Upper Canada, 17 Augt. 1830". Lt. Col. James Pattison Cockburn, R.A., watercolour. (Royal Ontario Museum).

Figure 9. "Places Associated with John By in England". (Ken W. Watson, 2013).

Figure 10. "Lt. Col. John By", n.d. Photograph of a portrait by "C.K" (Royal Engineers' Museum, Chatham, England).

Figure 11. "The Rideau Military Settlement Townships". (Ken W. Watson, 2013).

Figure 12. "Bush farm near Chatham, ca. 1838", Lieutenant Philip John Bainbrigge, Royal Engineers, watercolour. (Library and Archives Canada.)

Note: In this publication, the watercolour images have been reproduced in grey tones.

Preface

The Rideau Canal was constructed by the Corps of Royal Engineers to provide a secure, uninterrupted water communication by which British Army troops, ordnance, equipment and supplies could be moved inland in wartime from the ocean port of Montreal to Lake Ontario through the interior of Upper Canada (Ontario), without being exposed to attack in wartime by American forces on the upper St. Lawrence River. Although historians have agreed that the construction of the Rideau Canal, in 1826-1832, was an outstanding engineering achievement, differences exist concerning the conditions under which the canal workers laboured.

In studying working conditions during the construction of the Rideau Canal, Labour historians have seen but yet another example of a major canal construction project on which workers suffered from "poverty, distress and disease", and lived in squalor. The canal workers are depicted as having been poorly paid, exploited by company stores, and controlled by troops employed in curbing labour unrest.[1] Yet from the commencement of construction on the Rideau Canal project the Commanding Royal Engineer, Lt. Col. John By, professed a paternalistic concern to maintain a healthy and robust workforce in the wilderness environment through which the canal was being constructed – a paternalism that embraced both the psychological and physical wellbeing of the canal workers, as well as their protection from rapacious contractors.[2] Given such a divergence, was military paternalism an abject failure during the construction of the Rideau Canal, or have Labour historians erred in their interpretation of working conditions on the Rideau Canal and the role of the military?

To provide a more balanced and comprehensive assessment of the labour situation on the Rideau Canal project, several questions need to be addressed. First, to what extent was the suffering experienced by the Rideau Canal workers but part of living and working in the swamps and marshes of the backwoods in Upper

Canada where disease was rife, and the threat of injury and death always present for anyone working in that environment? Secondly, did military paternalism contribute to alleviating the particular afflictions suffered by labourers on the Rideau Canal project as it evolved? And lastly, to what extent was the degree of suffering experienced by the canal workers on the Rideau Canal project a product of the differing levels of well-being and acculturation among the various ethno-religious immigrant groups in responding to the imperatives of living and working in that environment?

More generally, this examination of working conditions and the treatment of canal workers on the Rideau Canal project presents an interesting multi-cultural study in that the workforce comprised large numbers of men of different ethno-religious identities and loyalties. The workforce was drawn from among the pioneer settlers of Upper Canada, from the older settled areas of Lower Canada, and from immigrants but newly-arrived in Canada. As such, the labour force was comprised largely of Irish Catholics, Irish Protestants (Anglo-Irish and Scots-Irish), and French Canadians, with a significant component of Presbyterian Scots amongst the artificers, as well as English, Irish Protestant and Scots soldier-artificers of two companies of the Corps of Royal Sappers and Miners who were assigned to the Rideau Canal project. Moreover, the civilian contractors comprised Scots-Canadians, Anglo-Canadians, English immigrants, several Americans, and a French-Canadian; all of whom were under the supervision of English officers of the Corps of Royal Engineers. As such, all of the ingredients for ethnic and religious strife, and – according to some Labour historians – even of class conflict, were present on the Rideau Canal project; yet that never materialized.

In sum, Part One of this book constitutes a revisionist treatment of the history of the canal workers on the Rideau Canal project. It rejects the prevailing interpretation, forged by Labour historians, that the canal workers were exploited on the Rideau Canal project under a military class indifferent to their suffering; and that labour unrest was suppressed by military force and/or by the threat of military force.

Part Two of this book, "Lt. Col. John By, Commanding Royal Engineer, Rideau Canal", comprises a brief biographical sketch of Lt. Col. By prior to his appointment to superintend the construction of the Rideau Canal. It is included to illuminate the political culture in which Lt. Col. By was raised, and the influences – religious, family, educational, and military – that played a role in the formation of the character, cultural values, and worldview of the 'paternalist authority' on the Rideau Canal project.

Part Three, "Military Paternalism and the Rideau Military Settlement", treats the prior establishment of the Rideau Military Settlement, and examines the extent to which the officers of the Commissariat of the British Army, went beyond their prescribed duties in providing aid to the settlers when in need. It has been included to attest that the paternalism practiced by Lt. Col. By on the Rideau Canal project was not simply a product of his personal character, but rather was an attribute of the character and cultural values of the officers of the British Army during that period of history.

Herein, 'paternalism' is conceptualized in terms of its traditional meaning: viz. the practice of promoting, in a fatherly manner, the well-being of those under one's authority, and doing so by going well beyond the prescribed duties and responsibilities of one's position. To the contrary, modern definitions of 'paternalism' and the present usage of the term in political science, philosophy, and sociology, carry a negative connotation in denoting an unwarranted government interference or meddling in the lives of citizens.[3]

The Appendix – "Marxism, Cultural Values, and Military Paternalism" – addresses an historiographical concern with respect to Labour historians who have adopted a Marxist framework for interpreting the labour situation on the Rideau Canal project. In sum, it addresses the proclivity of Labour historians to view the canal project through a Marxist lens in seeing only worker exploitation, class conflict, and an emerging class consciousness, and of Marxist historians to set forth a strictly economic explanation for the paternalism which was practiced by 'those who ruled' during that era. To the contrary, a culturally- based explanation is posited for the paternalism practiced by Lt. Col. John By and his fellow military officers.[4]

Robert W. Passfield
Ottawa, Ontario
June 2013

Endnotes

1. See William N.T. Wylie, "Poverty, Distress, and Disease: Labour and the Construction of the Rideau Canal, 1826l832, *Labour/Le Travailleur*, Vol. 11, Spring l983, 729; and H. Clare Pentland, *Labour and Capital in Canada, l650-l860* (Toronto: James Lorimer & Co., l981), 52 & 190. For an historical overview of the Rideau Canal construction project, see: Robert W. Passfield, *Building the Rideau Canal: A Pictorial History* (Don Mills, Ontario: Fitzhenry & Whiteside/Parks Canada, 1982), and Robert F. Legget, *Rideau Waterway* (Toronto: University of Toronto Press, 1967).

2. Library and Archives Canada (LAC), RG8, Series C, Vol. 42, reel C-2617, 103, Lt. Col. By to Major General Darling, Military Secretary to the Commander-in-Chief, 2 October 1826; and John Mactaggart, *Three Years in Canada: An Account of the Actual State of the Country in 1826-7-9 comprehending its resources, productions, improvements, and Capabilities and including Sketches of the State of Society, Advice to Emigrants, etc.* London: Henry Colburn, 1829, Vol. I, 159-162.

3. Simon Clarke, "A Definition of Paternalism", *Critical Review of International Social and Political Philosophy*, vol. 5, No. 3, Spring 2002, pp. 81-91.

4. From 1791 to 1841 Canada comprised the provinces of Upper Canada (southern Ontario) and Lower Canada (southern Quebec), which were often referred to as the Canadas.

Acknowledgements

Part One of this book, "Military Paternalism on the Rideau Canal", comprises a recasting of an unpublished earlier research paper, "All Will Succeed" (1984), which the author prepared almost thirty years ago while employed by the Parks Canada Agency. Additional material has been worked up from more recent research to further support and extend the original argument. The principal sources consulted were the microfilm reels of the War Office records (WO 44 and WO 55), and the British Military and Naval Record Group (RG 8, Series C) at the Library and Archives Canada. These records contain the progress reports of the Commanding Royal Engineer of the Rideau Canal project, Lt. Col. John By, and his correspondence with the Board of Ordnance in London, England, as well as his correspondence with the Commanding Royal Engineer for Canada, Colonel Elias Durnford, and with the Commander-in-Chief/Governor-in-Chief for British North America, Lord Dalhousie and his successor, Lt. General Sir James Kempt.

The archival records of several contemporaries who were associated with the construction of the Rideau Canal were also consulted, as well as contemporary travelogues which were published by visitors to the Rideau Canal project, and several contemporary newspapers articles. Additional research was pursued in more recent secondary sources.

For the most part the extant historical records convey the views, values, and outlook of the engineering staff on the Rideau Canal project; and that of contemporary observers of some means who took pen in hand. With the exception of a single petition, the voice of the workers is absent.

One of the challenges that an historian faces in writing about the history of particular cultural groups from the records left by persons of a different ethnicity or class, is the cultural biases and prejudices of the sources, as well as the disconcerting knowledge that the recorded observations and judgements might not always be palatable to one's contemporaries. To which one might add that when an historian expounds upon a particular view of events as seen through the eyes of the witnesses who left a record, it does not mean that the historian necessarily shares their views or prejudices.[1]

The present work is not a social history written from 'the bottom up', rather it is a history of the labour situation on the Rideau Canal construction project as seen largely from the viewpoint of the engineering establishment, principally the Commanding Royal Engineer, Lt. Col. John By, and the Clerk of Works, John Mactaggart, the latter of whom published a two-volume work focusing on his three years of service on the canal project. Where Lt. Col. By is concerned, his principal objective, and assigned duty, was to construct the canal as expeditiously and economically as possible. Consequently, the labour situation – as conveyed in his reports and correspondence – was framed by what he observed and what he concluded was needed to forge a robust workforce, to keep labour costs at a reasonable level, and to maintain labour peace. In sum, the labour situation on the Rideau Canal was perceived from the viewpoint of the needs of a major canal engineering project; yet that commitment was tempered by a genuine concern for the health and well-being of the workforce on the part of Lt. Col. John By.

As such, the surviving archival records of the Rideau Canal project abound with material on the provisioning of the canal workers, the contracting of the work, engineering decisions, the progress of construction, and construction problems, as well as efforts to reduce the suffering of the workers from 'lake fever and ague' (malaria). However, the multi-cultural composition of the workforce did not evoke any considerable or meaningful comment. The only time any particular ethnic group was mentioned was if, and when, they posed a particular labour problem which needed to be addressed to facilitate an expeditious completion of the canal.

Acknowledgements

Most of the members of the various ethno-religious groups who worked on the Rideau Canal posed no particular problem to the engineering establishment, and are almost completely absent from the historical record. They came to the Rideau project, did their work without complaint, received their pay, and moved on to settle elsewhere in Upper Canada or in the United States. On the other hand, one particular ethnic group, or more correctly a sub-group within a particular ethno-religious group – the Gaelic-speaking, Irish Catholic pauper immigrants – initially posed a major labour problem on the Rideau Canal project, and needed a great deal of support to cope with the demands of living and working in a wilderness environment. Hence, they appear frequently in the historical record of the canal project.

As a result, the contributions of the various different ethnic groups to the construction of the Rideau Canal are not clearly defined and delineated in the historical record, and hence not fully known or appreciated in terms of their respective numbers and particular achievements. Over time that situation has led to a misconception amongst the public in terms of the perceived ethnicity of the canal workers as a whole on the Rideau Canal project. In sum, there is a widespread belief that the canal was constructed primarily by Irish Catholic immigrant workers. Herein that misconception is redressed; although it has not proven possible to identify the exact numbers of the members of each ethnic group who were employed on the canal construction project or, with any accuracy, the precise contribution of each group to the particular canal works.

In treating the labour situation on the Rideau Canal project, a particular effort has been made to provide a thoroughly comprehensive treatment which brings into play the many different factors that had an impact on the canal labourers. Among the factors taken into account are military planning, engineering decisions, the climate, topography and environment, the provisioning and equipping of the workforce, wage rates on the canal project and in the province, the accommodation of the workers, the impact of disease, the problem of ethnic animosities, the emigration experience of the canal workers, and the economic circumstances, health, and condition of the different ethnic groups upon their arrival on the canal project.

Part Two of this book comprises a biographical sketch of Lt. Col. John By prior to his appointment to construct the Rideau Canal. The sketch is based largely on secondary sources which were supplemented through research in archival records and online searches for genealogical information.

Part Three treats the founding of the Rideau Military Settlement prior to the construction of the Rideau Canal. It is based on research in the microfilm copies of the War Office and Colonial Office records in the Library and Archives Canada, and pertinent secondary sources. This piece was undertaken to determine whether, and to what extent, military paternalism was practiced in responding to the needs of the discharged soldier settlers, and the assisted-emigration settlers, in the Rideau Military Settlement. In the treatment of the Rideau Military Settlement, there is some minor overlap with the information provided on the military settlement in Part One. However, the treatment of that subject is a requisite element in the argument being pursued in both pieces. No apology is offered for any minor repetition in the two texts.

The Appendix, "Marxism, Cultural Values, and Military Paternalism", is based on an analysis of several works by Labour historians that interpret the labour situation on the Rideau Canal project from a Marxist perspective; and that attribute strictly economic motives to the phenomenon of paternalism on canal projects in early 19th Century Canada. Herein, a different approach to the writing of history is set forth. It is advocated that the historian, in seeking a better understanding of human conduct in interpreting historical events, ought to enter into the minds of his subjects "for the thought behind their acts" (E.H. Carr, *What is History*). In effect, the historian must develop an understanding of the character, cultural values, and worldview of the main actors in any historical event, as well as an understanding of their immediate situation as perceived and conceptualized within their own particular metal framework. This different approach to the writing of history is set forth for consideration as a potential enrichment of the orthodox Marxist interpretation of labour history, which is based on economic factors, class interest, and economic determinism.

Where the history of Upper Canada is concerned, there were two major political interests in conflict in the post-War of 1812 period over their respective efforts to establish the future political culture of the Province of Upper Canada. The members of each political interest believed in the superiority of their particular political culture and embodied a different character and cultural values, and held a distinctly different worldview. To aid historians in seeking to enter into an imaginative understanding of the character, cultural values and worldview of the two major political interests present in the body politic of Upper Canada, the political philosophies of Anglican corporate toryism and Lockean-liberal individualism are sketched in the Appendix as well. The political philosophy sketches are based largely on George Sabine (*A History of Political Theory*), the author's readings in political theory over a number of years and, if truth be told, several thoughtful articles posted online in wikipedia.org. What is proferred is not a political treatise, but a personal statement.

On a more personal level, a debt of gratitude is owed to my nephew, Craig Passfield, for designing and preparing the book covers, to Carla Morse and Judith Dufresne of Parks Canada for assistance in securing the illustrations, and to a good friend, Ken Watson, for preparing the maps. My brother, John Passfield, perused the text and offered helpful suggestions for improving the clarity of the writing. A special debt is owed to Susan James for her understanding and support as my retirement years continue to be devoted to a demanding muse – Clio – in writing of history.

A further debt is owed to the Parks Canada Agency, which maintains and operates the Rideau Canal World Heritage Site under a heritage conservation and interpretation mandate bestowed by the Canadian government. For thirty years the author single-mindedly pursued his career as a public historian at Parks Canada during which time he had the good fortune to be assigned a number of research projects pertaining to the history and heritage of the Rideau Canal. Nonetheless, that being said, the historical interpretations and judgements which are presented in this book, are solely the responsibility of the author, and do not necessarily represent either the views or values of the Parks Canada Agency.

Terminology

Where terminology is concerned, the officers of the Royal Engineers referred to the unskilled canal workers simply as "labourers" and, surprisingly, did not use the British term "navvies". The tradesmen who served in the Corps of Royal Sappers and Miners were referred to as "artificers", and the skilled civilian workers were referred to as either "artisans" or "artificers" . In the latter case, the term "soldier-artificer", or "military artificer", served to distinguish the Royal Sappers and Miners from their civilian counterparts. Initially, Lt. Col. By expressed his intention to employ 'labourers, excavators, and artisans' to construct the canal, with excavators presumably being men skilled in excavating canals.

Thereafter the term 'excavator' was dropped, and subsequently the skilled worker were generally referred to by their particular trade – smiths, stone masons, stone cutters, carpenters, sawyers, tinsmiths, harness makers, quarrymen, etc. – as in advertisements for skilled workers, canal construction progress reports, and lists of wage rates. A generic term, 'dayworker', was used to describe both the skilled workers and the labourers who were hired directly on the military canal establishment and paid a daily wage. In this book, a similar practice has been followed in employing the term 'labourers' for unskilled workers, 'artificers' for skilled civilian workers – unless citing a specific reference to 'artisans' or to a particular trade – and 'dayworkers' to denote canal workers employed directly by the Royal Engineers on the military canal establishment as distinct from the canal workers employed by the contractors.

Endnotes

1. The author's approach to the writing of history, and the issue of cultural bias, is set forth in another work: Robert W. Passfield, *Phips' Amphibious Assault on Canada — 1690* (Amazon.com, 2011), Acknowledgements, xiii-xvii.

Part One

Military Paternalism
on the
Rideau Canal Project

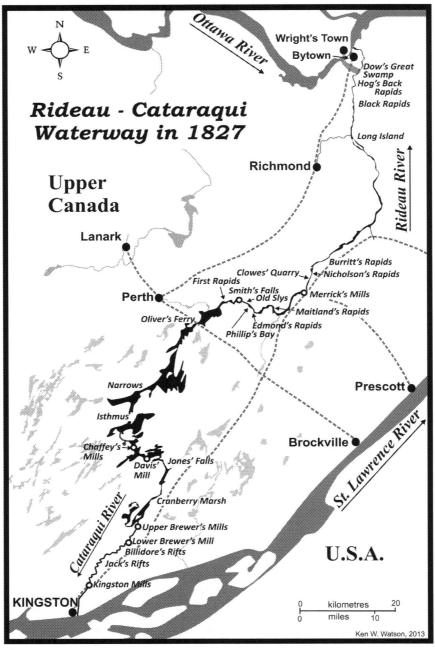

Figure 2. *"Rideau-Cataraqui Waterway in 1827". Map showing the rapids, and several hamlets and mill sites along the waterway, the outlying towns, and the new Bytown townsite. (Ken W. Watson, 2013).*

Military Paternalism
on the
Rideau Canal Project

Introduction

In the spring of 1826, the Board of Ordnance in Britain decided to undertake the construction of the Rideau Canal by contract, under the supervision of officers of the Corps of Royal Engineers; and Lt. Col. John By, R.E., was appointed to command the project. The Erie Canal (1817-1825) in New York State, and the Lachine Canal (1821-1825) at Montreal, had been constructed by contract, and a major perceived advantage of the contract system was that only a small engineering establishment would need to be supported by the Ordnance. Contractors would be responsible for carrying out the work, and for the housing, provisioning, and well-being of the canal workforce. Moreover, the Ordnance would be free of the heavy cost of maintaining a large workforce of military artificers in barracks during the six-month winter season; civilian artisans and labourers could simply be dismissed by the contractors at the end of each summer work season.[1]

Based on an earlier survey by a provincial land surveyor, the canal was to be constructed along the Rideau River flowing northward into the Ottawa River, and the Cataraqui River flowing southward into Lake Ontario, with a 1 ½ mile-long canal channel to be excavated at the Isthmus summit level to connect the two waterways. The preliminary plan called for the excavation of canal channels to bypass rapids and waterfalls, with stone masonry locks to step from one navigable river stretch to another, and the erection of low-head dams to flood out shallows in the rivers with an adjacent lock to bypass each low-head dam. All told, it was initially expected that 53 locks, and a total of roughly 28 miles of canal channel excavation – mostly in rock – would be required to ascend 269 feet on the Rideau River to its Rideau Lake headwaters, and to descend 154 feet from the Mud

Lake headwaters of the Cataraqui River to Kingston Bay on Lake Ontario, on a 125 mile-long waterway.[2]

Obtaining a Workforce

At the commencement of work in the fall of 1826, it was estimated that anywhere from 4,000 to 6,000 labourers, and as many as 1,000 masons, would be required to construct the Rideau Canal.[3] This was a phenomenal number of men at a time when the largest town in Upper Canada, Kingston, at the southern terminus of the projected canal, had a population of 2,849 persons, and the next largest town, York (Toronto) on Lake Ontario, a population of only 1,677. Wright's Town, which was situated across the Ottawa River from the Entrance Valley for the canal, had only 800 inhabitants. How such a large workforce was to be assembled, provisioned and housed by the contractors presented a major challenge in a veritable wilderness.

Along the planned canal route, the forest cover was broken only by several hamlets at waterfalls where a saw mill, or a grist mill, served a seeming handful of settlers who were scattered on small isolated clearings throughout the heavily-forested interior. There the settlers lived by a subsistence agriculture, growing wheat, corn and the dietary staple potatoes, and securing a cash income by cutting timber for floating out on the spring floods of the Rideau and Cataraqui rivers to Wright's Town on the Ottawa River and Kingston on Lake Ontario, respectively, where the timber sticks were assembled for rafting to Quebec for export.[4]

In May 1827, on his first reconnaissance trip by canoe, Lt. Col. By found that the proposed canal waterway was dotted with cedar swamps, rapids, and lakes, and that the settlers on their isolated clearings in the bush and the inhabitants of several hamlets along the waterway had little communication with the outside world. They could be reached only by canoe in portaging around the numerous rapids and waterfalls along the rivers, or by walking on bridle paths that wound for miles through the heavily forested interior in branching off from the two overland access routes that penetrated directly inland from the St. Lawrence River front: the Prescott Trail that ran over twenty miles inland from Prescott to the hamlet of Merrick's Mills on the upper Rideau River; and the Brockville Road that ran inland for thirty miles to Oliver's Ferry on Rideau Lake and beyond the lake to the new settlement of Perth deep in the bush. However, both access routes were impassable for weeks on end during the rainy season, and the bush roads were difficult to traverse by heavy cart at the best of times.[5]

To facilitate the provisioning and housing of the workers, Lt. Col. By initially intended to establish three major work camps, each capable of accommodating 2,000 men. The camps were to be located at either end of the waterway – at the Entrance Valley on the Ottawa River, at Kingston on Lake Ontario, and, centrally, on the Isthmus summit level.[6] However, at the commencement of construction, only the Bytown work camp was established owing to the lack of a ready access into the interior by water or by road. In such a situation, the Royal Engineers were forced to undertake the construction of a total of 26 miles of bush road to connect up the navigable river stretches along the entire waterway to open a communication and supply line linking the projected canal work sites.

Once assured of access to the interior, contractors submitted reasonable bids for the excavation and masonry work, and established mini-workcamps at their separate work sites. Thereafter, supplies, tools, equipment, and materials were forwarded inland by the contractors during the winter months over the snow-covered bush road and along the ice on the frozen river sections.

To secure the large number of labourers and artisans which were required by the contractors, Lt. Col. By took the initiative and placed advertisements in Montreal and New York newspapers to spread the word that employment could be had at good wages on the Rideau Canal project. At the same time, he forwarded a

Figure 3. "Maitland's Rapids, Rideau, 19 Augt. 1830", Lt. Col. James Pattison Cockburn, Royal Artillery, watercolour. A scene typical of a number of isolated clearings in the bush along the Rideau River. (Royal Ontario Museum).

request to the Ordnance that four companies of Royal Sappers and Miners be sent out from England to undertake the more demanding lock gate and lock sill masonry construction work.[7] However, first impressions had been deceiving.

The settlement and labour situation in Upper Canada was undergoing a dramatic transformation, and was continuing to evolve in a direction favourable to the Rideau Canal project. Moreover, a May 1827 decision by Lt. Col. By to adopt a slackwater system of construction, wherein high dams were to be constructed to flood out rapids and shallows, greatly reduced the potential labour demand through eliminating the need to excavate long canal cuts in a rocky terrain.

On first contemplating the construction of a navigable waterway through the interior Rideau wilderness during the War of 1812, the military had been stymied by the problem of how to secure the men and draught animals required to construct the waterway, and how to provision and provide fodder for a major construction project in a heavily-forested wilderness.[8] Once peace was restored, a Military Settling Department was established to assist discharged soldiers to settle in compact settlements at strategic locations in Canada. One location chosen for a military settlement was in the wilderness to the rear of the proposed Rideau waterway route over forty miles inland from the St. Lawrence Front settlements which were vulnerable to attack in wartime.

The Rideau Military Settlement was intended to serve as nuclei for the growth of settlement to provide workers, draught animals, food and fodder for the future canal construction project, and a loyal militia for its defence against marauders in wartime. New townships were surveyed deep in the bush, and commissariat depots were established at two new townsite surveys: at Perth (1816) and Richmond (1818), on tributaries of the Rideau River. To provide the new settlers with access to their land grants, the British Army hired axemen to cut bush roads inland 42 miles from the St. Lawrence River Front to Perth (the Brockville Road), and 21 miles inland from the Ottawa River to Richmond (the Richmond Road).

The first of the soldier-settlers were placed on lots in the back townships to the rear of the Rideau River in 1816. They were the officers and men of the Glengarry Light Infantry of Fencibles, the Canadian Fencibles, and the De Watteville Regiment, discharged in Canada. They were settled compactly in the newly-surveyed townships around the commissariat depot at the Perth townsite. Subsequently, they were joined by veterans of British Army regiments who had fought in Canada during the War of 1812.

In 1818, a total of 167 soldiers of the 99th Regiment (former 100th), who chose to be discharged in Canada following at the close of the war, were settled in the newly-surveyed townships around the Richmond depot. They were joined by veterans of other regiments, and, subsequently, in 1819-1820, free land grants were also given to discharged veterans of Canadian militia units who wished to settle in the back townships of the Rideau Military Settlement.

Under the Military Settling Department programme, the military paid for the land surveys, the opening of the bush roads into the back townships, and provided transport for the discharged soldiers – and, if married, their families and baggage – to their location on the land. Axemen were hired to construct cabins for the new soldier-settlers, who were provided with agricultural implements, domestic utensils, and seed, free of charge. Once located on their land, the soldier-settlers and their family members were issued military ration each month from their local commissariat depot to sustain them in the bush until their first crops were harvested. In addition, the army veterans discharged in Britain received free ocean passage on naval transports, and free transportation inland from the ocean port of Montreal by military batteaux brigades and by horse and wagon to their settlement location in the interior, with provisions provided en route. The military land grants were made according to rank, ranging from 100 acres for a private to 1,200 acres for a Lt. Colonel.

At the same time, the population of the Rideau Military Settlement was augmented through several assisted-emigration programmes which were instituted by Lord Bathurst, the Secretary of State for War and the Colonies, to relieve postwar economic distress in Scotland. Under the initial scheme, families willing to emigrate, and able to pay a £16 deposit for each adult member – refundable after two years of settlement – were provided with free ocean transport, transport to their location, and medical care en route, as well as a free grant of 100 acres of land, an axe, farm implements and domestic utensils. Military rations were to be provided for each family member for six months; and salaries were paid by the Colonial Office for the employment of a clergyman and schoolmaster at Perth. Delays in getting settled on the land, and crop failures – which were caused by killing frosts during the summer of 1816 – ultimately resulted in the military rations system being maintain for almost two years.

The first assisted-emigration settlers who arrived in the fall of 1815, were the families of a Scots tenant farmers and tradesmen from Perthshire. The members of that party, comprising 337 persons in total, were accommodated in military barracks during the winter; and placed on their land in the spring of 1816 in the Perth settlement survey. The first party of Scots settlers was soon joined by a second influx of Scots who emigrated under a far less generous Colonial Office assisted-emigration program. Each family paid a single, £10 deposit, and received a free ocean passage and free land grant, but otherwise were responsible for feeding and equipping themselves for living and farming in the bush. They were followed in turn by Irish Protestants of some means, who were fleeing the postwar economic dislocation and discontent in Ireland, and who emigrated unassisted.

In 1820, a new townsite, Lanark, was established on the Clyde River on an adjacent watershed to the rear of the Rideau Military Settlement, and the surrounding townships were surveyed. The newly-opened lands were settled initially by over 160 families of weavers from Lanark and Renfrewshire in Scotland, who were suffering from the postwar depression in the textile industry. They were aided to emigrate by Emigration Societies, and were promised free land in Upper Canada by the Colonial Office. Once in Upper Canada, the Scots weavers were settled on their land by the Military Settling Department, and received military rations issued from a Commissariat depot established at Lanark, as did a number of discharged soldiers who were placed in the Lanark settlement. Axemen were hired by the military to cut a road through the bush a distance of fourteen miles from Perth to the new Lanark settlement depot, and subsequently, a 30 mile long road was cut by the military through the bush from Richmond to Perth.

Lastly, in a poor-relief experiment by the British government, over 500 destitute Irish Catholics, comprising mostly displaced tenant farmers from the southern counties of Ireland, were placed in the Rideau Military Settlement in 1823. The heads of families were selected for being literate in English, knowing the rudiments of arithmetic, and having good character references. Each family was granted 70 acres of land, with an option to purchase an adjacent 30 acres for a nominal sum after fulfilling their settlement duties. That requirement was intended to act as an incentive for the Irish Catholic immigrants to clear their new land, rather than simply subsist on a small clearing. Given the impoverished condition of the Irish poor-relief emigrants, they were not required to pay a deposit to emigrate. Moreover, each family was given two bolts of cotton serge and flannel, as well as a cow, and had a cabin erected for them on their new plot of land.[9]

As of the commencement of the Rideau Canal project, the military settling program and the various postwar assisted-emigration schemes of the British government had been discontinued for several years. Nonetheless, these government programs had succeeded in placing as many as 10,700 settlers in the back townships to the rear of the projected Rideau Canal in the Rideau Military Settlement. Among their number were 3,570 males, including 1,300 discharged soldiers.

Some settlers had anywhere from 30 to 50 acres cleared in the bush, and possessed a yoke of oxen as well as several cows and pigs. The military settlement was also producing a significant surplus crop of potatoes, grain and turnips, lacking only a market to encourage them to further production.[10] Yet on commencing work on the Rideau Canal, there was no way of knowing to what extent the Rideau Military Settlement could contribute to the provisioning of the workforce, or whether the thousands of wage labourers required for heavy excavation work could be procured or employed at reasonably moderate wage rates.

Despite widespread economic distress in postwar Britain, emigration in the immediate postwar period had been limited by the high cost of ocean passage. However, that had changed in 1817 when timber ships returning in ballast to Quebec began to offer drastically reduced ocean passage rates for emigrants. For the first time, displaced tenant farmers and tradesmen of some means were able to emigrate unassisted.[11] Subsequently, a heavy tide of British emigration had flowed into Canada, far outstripping direct emigration to the United States. Over the decade prior to the commencement of the Rideau Canal project, anywhere from 9,000 to 13,000 emigrants departed from the British Isles – Ireland, Scotland and England – in any given year for the British North American provinces. During the postwar decade, the Irish immigrants arriving in Canada were mostly Protestants – Anglo-Irish Anglicans and Scotch-Irish Presbyterians – from Ulster and the adjoining northern commercial counties, who had the means to emigrate and were prone to do so to better their economic situation.

These British immigrants might have been expected to have formed a permanent wage labour force in Upper Canada, but such had not happened. Many of the immigrants – estimated as high as sixty percent – took advantage of the lower ocean fares to sail for British North American ports, and then continued on their journey into the United States.[12] Of the immigrants who remained in Canada, the ready availability of land in Upper Canada had served to accommodate them without difficulty. The situation was such that a labour scarcity existed in Upper Canada, and wage rates were at what was considered a very high rate.[13] Yet there was one new factor. As of 1826, large numbers of destitute Irish Catholic immigrants began arriving in the ports of Lower Canada; and in the early spring of 1827 several hundred arrived at the site of the Rideau Canal project on the Ottawa River in search of work.[14]

A significant number of labourers were also attracted to the Rideau Canal project from among settlers but newly placed on their land. In the first years of settlement, money was scarce for settlers engaged in subsistence farming in the bush. Canal projects offered one of the few opportunities for steady employment at good rates of pay as a means of obtaining the cash required to purchase agricultural implements, cooking utensils, pigs, a cow, and even an ox, to facilitate the development of a farm. Consequently, the women and children were commonly left to plant the first crops – in sowing the ground around the stumps standing in the cleared areas – while the fathers and grownup sons went off to seek work on canal projects at great distances.

Once work commenced on the Rideau project, men came from settlements as far as 150 miles away seeking work, with even a small number arriving from the United States. Most of the Canadian settlers were from the older settled regions of Upper Canada and the Rideau Military Settlement.[15] Subsequently, they were joined by French Canadians migrating to the Rideau Canal project from Lower Canada.

By the mid-1820's, Lower Canada was deep in the throes of an agricultural crisis. Most of the readily accessible agricultural land in the settled areas had been occupied, the population was increasing rapidly, and soil exhaustion in the older areas of settlement caused wheat production to stagnate, if not decline, resulting in rising prices. A large surplus labour force crowded into the towns and villages of Lower Canada with men seeking seasonal work on farms during the summer and in the timber trade during the winter.[16] In 1806, Philemon Wright, the

founder of Wright's Town, had started the timber trade on
the Ottawa Valley in sending rafts of squared timber down
the Ottawa and St. Lawrence rivers to Quebec for export to
Britain; and within two decades up to 2,000 men, largely French
Canadians, were engaged each winter in the timber trade on
the Ottawa River. However, the early years of the Rideau Canal
construction project, 1827 through 1829, coincided with the
beginning of a long depression in the timber trade.

As a result of the depressed economy, a large number of French
Canadian shantymen were available not only for working on
the canal during the summer months, but the winter months
as well if needed. This was likewise the case with the English,
Scots, and Irish Protestant bush farmers, who lived by subsistence
farming on clearings in the bush, and hired out as axemen or
teamsters with their draught animals during the winter to cut
and haul the timber to the rivers for the spring river-drive. All
of these men were highly skilled with the axe, adept at felling
trees, and accustomed to working outside during the bitter cold
of a Canadian winter, as well as in the bush in clearing trees and
farming during the summer heat.[17]

To facilitate the surveying and laying out of the canal works,
axemen were employed in clearing the Rideau Canal work sites
during the spring and summer of 1827, and by the summer
of 1828 large numbers of French Canadian labourers had
begun arriving in Lower Bytown seeking work on the canal.[18]
The French Canadians worked for the contractors from Lower
Canada, and at their work sites made up from twothirds to
threequarters of the labour force. The settlers from the military
settlement tended to predominate, probably to the same degree,
at the several interior work sites where the work was under
contract to men from the Rideau Military Settlement.

Through drawing on such diverse sources of manpower, no
shortage of labourers was experienced on the Rideau Canal
project. A sufficient number of skilled artisans was also obtained,
despite earlier fears to the contrary. They were drawn from among

the British immigrants who were arriving in Canada, from among the settlers in the older settled areas of Canada, and from the new settlers in the Rideau Military Settlement. French Canadian, Scots and Irish Protestant artificers were also brought to the Rideau Canal project by Montreal contractors who had previously worked on the Lachine Canal (1821-1825) project. The ethnic composition of the artificers employed in the workforce varied from work site to work site. Scots, Irish Protestants, and French Canadians, and to a lesser extent Englishmen, appear to have been well represented among the various trades of quarrying, stonecutting, masonry, smithing, carpentry, cooperage, and harnessmaking. The artificers were hired from among newly-arrived immigrant tradesmen, and from among Canadian tradesmen – both English and French speaking – from Lower Canada, primarily Montreal.[19]

Overall, the Rideau Canal project may well have employed upwards of 4,000 men annually at the peak of construction. Of that number as many as 2,700 were newly-arrived immigrants who were directed to the Rideau project each spring and summer by Emigrant Societies in the ocean ports of Quebec and Montreal. Each year, new immigrant workmen replaced the itinerant canal workers of the previous season – both artificers and labourers – who had left to purchase land elsewhere in Upper Canada or in the United States, as well as the men who died from disease or injury.

Most immigrants, who possessed some capital, were able to settle directly on the land, but others of more limited means would work on a canal project for several months, or a summer work season, before moving on the settle on the land. Canal work not only replenished family financial resources, but accustomed the immigrant to hard work, taught him how to use a felling axe, and enabled him to gain the knowledge of the country that was needed to successfully settle in the bush.[20]

The five major years of summer construction work on the Rideau Canal project, – 1827 through 1831, inclusive – were years of a heavy British emigration to Canada during which the number of immigrants arriving at the port of Quebec grew steadily from 12,648 in 1827 and 12,084 in 1828, to 15,945 in 1829 and 28,000 in 1830, and soared to 50,254 in 1831.[21] Of that total – for the years 1829 through 1831, inclusive, for which information has been found – the number of the immigrants arriving in Canada from England fluctuated between 20% and 24%, the number from Ireland (inclusive of both Protestants and Catholics) increased from 61% to 68%, and the number from Scotland declined from 16% to less than 9%, in round numbers.[22]

Given such numbers, it is understandable that many Irish immigrants were hired as workers on the Rideau Canal project; however, the relative numbers of Irish Protestant to Irish Catholic canal workers remains unknown. What is known is that the timber ship immigrants were the least well off immigrants arriving in Canada; that most managed to settle on the land during the 1820s -1830s period, with a significant number seeking wage labour for a summer before doing so; and that 2/3s of the timber ship immigrants were Irish Protestants during that period.

Nonetheless, no conclusion can be drawn concerning the relative balance of Irish Protestant and Irish Catholic canal labourers on the Rideau Canal, based on their respective immigration numbers. On the one hand, there was a major out-migration of Irish Catholic immigrants who passed through Quebec on their way to settle in the United States; yet, on the other hand, the Irish Catholic immigrants generally lacked the financial resources of the Irish Protestant immigrants, and were more inclined to seek wage labour. The Irish Catholics did so either on a temporary basis before settling on the land, or on a permanent basis in the established towns and villages of Lower Canada, on farms in older settled areas, or on canal projects.[23]

All one can say is that there was no shortage of labour on the Rideau Canal project; that both Irish Protestants and Irish Catholics immigrants were represented in large numbers among the canal labourers; and that the Irish Protestants and

Figure 4. "First Camp, Bytown; September 1826", attributed to Lt. Col. John By, Royal Engineers or his staff, watercolour. The initial camp of Lt. Col. By and his engineering staff, with the French Canadian voyageurs who manned the canoes, under canvas in a beaver meadow at the head of the proposed canal entrance valley. (McCord Museum).

Irish Catholics, together with the French Canadians migrant workers from Lower Canada, constituted by far the three largest identifiable labour groups employed.[24]

Getting the Project Underway

From the time of the establishment of his first camp in late September 1826 – in a beaver meadow on the future site of Bytown – Lt. Col. By and his engineering staff were particularly concerned about the problem of maintaining a healthy, well-motivated workforce in a wilderness environment. That concern embraced the workers psychological, as well as physical wellbeing, as it was noted that there was "a melancholy" peculiar to working and living in the Canadian bush that had to be combatted. To that end, Lt. Col. By was prepared to ensure that the workers were furnished with provisions, spirits, clothing and accommodation at a fair price at each of the three workcamps which were planned for construction, and to protect them from being cheated of their wages by unscrupulous contractors and company stores.

Although the military was not responsible for providing health care for the canal workers, Lt. Col. By was determined to do so. It was known that "the swampy wilderness, and swampy waters, may sometime create distempers". Thus, at the very commencement of the project, the Commander-in-Chief was informed that Lt. Col. By intended to station a staff surgeon at each of the three projected main camps to administer to the sick and the injured among the canal workers.[25]

To provision the workers, arrangements were made with the Commissariat Department in Montreal to let tenders on competitive bids for barrels of salted pork and flour and puncheons of rum to be forwarded to the canal project for sale in bulk to the contractors.[26]

Lt. Col. By had no responsibility for providing accommodation for the canal workers; yet he was prepared to make land available for the housing of his Clerks, Overseers, and canal artisans, as well as for labourers. However, his initial objective was to set up a workcamp at the Entrance Valley, to provide access to the site from the Ottawa River, and to erect the support buildings needed for storing equipment and provisions for undertaking the construction of the canal.

During the fall of 1826, the Entrance Valley was surveyed, cleared, and grubbed, two wharfs were constructed, and four support buildings of a log construction were erected: an engineers' office; a storehouse for tools and supplies; a blacksmith shop; and a carpentry shop.[27] During the following spring, contracts were let for the construction of five substantial stone masonry buildings: a Commissariat Stores building and a Royal Engineers' Office in the Entrance Valley; and three barracks on the high ground to the west overlooking the Entrance Valley. The barracks buildings were intended to accommodate the engineering officers, and the requested four companies of Royal Sappers and Miners, as well as a small military detachment which was to guard the military chest and stores, and a small hospital.[28]

The hospital was intended for the benefit of the military establishment personnel who might become seriously sick or injured on the project. However, steps were taken to provide medical care for the sick or injured workers who were employed by the contractors. At the very commencement of the project in the fall of 1826, Dr. Alexander J. Christie, a retired naval surgeon from nearby March Township on the upper Ottawa River, was engaged by Lt. Col. By to provide medical care and medicines for the contractors' artificers and labourers, as needed. Christie was paid 7s. per diem when attending to the sick or injured, and was reimbursed for the cost of the medicines administered to the canal workers. That expense was born by the contingency allowance of the Rideau Canal estimate. Payment was made upon Dr. Christie submitting a monthly report listing each patient treated, the sickness suffered, the total days of treatment, and the results, as well as a statement of the medicines given each day and their cost.[29]

While work proceeded in erecting the workcamp infrastructure, a townsite – Bytown – was surveyed on a block of land surrounding the Entrance Valley, which had been purchased earlier for the government by Lord Dalhousie, the Governor-in-Chief. To provide accommodation for the canal workers, building lots in the townsite survey were to be leased to respectable settlers and merchants for from £1 to £6 per annum, depending on the commercial potential of the location with respect to the proposed canal, as well as to the Clerks, Overseers, and artisans who were employed on the Rideau Canal project. Building lots were also laid out on the opposite side of the canal, in what became known as Lower Bytown, for lease to canal labourers for a rent as low as 10s. per annum.[30]

The civilian Clerks and Overseers were expected to live in Bytown, with the Overseers going on regular tours to oversee the quality of the work being done by the contractors' men. The intent was to have the labourers erect their own cabins in Bytown for working on the nearby work sites, and apparently to do likewise at the other two planned workcamps. Elsewhere, at great distances from the main workcamps, the men were to be accommodated in bunkhouses which were erected at the work site by the contractor. In cases where an immigrant artificer or labourer brought his family to the Rideau Canal project, presumably it was expected that they would remain at their cabin in one of the projected workcamps.

At the very commencement of the Rideau project, Lt. Col. By sought to make clothes, caps, shoes, socks and bedding available to the canal workers. Clothing and bedding purchases represented a major expenditure for a labourer, and were beyond the means of many of the immigrants who were arriving on timber ships. Clothing was very difficult to procure and highly expensive in the Rideau corridor, much more so than in Britain, owing to the dearth of sheep in the newly-settled back townships of the military settlements.[31]

Arrangements were made with the Commissariat for the bedding, blankets, and clothing to be offered to the workers at cost plus transport from Montreal, with easy repayment terms. Workers could pay for these items directly by foregoing an equivalent portion of their wages, or opt for small pay deductions to be made over an extended period of time. Nonetheless, during the spring of 1827 when the first of the immigrant workers – Irish pauper immigrants – began to arrive at the Entrance Valley, they did not receive the benefits of the newly-established supply system. In his haste to get work underway, Lt. Col. By outstripped the transport capacity of the Commissariat Department to forward supplies from Montreal in a situation where a priority had to be given to forwarding provisions to feed the workforce.[32]

Irish Pauper Immigrants

Despite the determination of Lt. Col. By to promote the welfare of his workforce, serious distress and suffering was experienced during the initial phase of construction, due to the haste to get work underway and the impoverished circumstances of a large number of the Irish immigrants who turned up seeking work. As early as March 1827, a contract was let for the excavation of the first 1200 feet of canal in the Entrance Valley; and in April several hundred destitute Irish Catholic immigrants – the socalled "pauper Irish" – arrived at the Entrance Valley. The Irish paupers presented no end of problems at the commencement of construction.

Upon arrival, many of the Irish pauper immigrants were dressed in rags and were suffering from malnutrition and all manner of sickness after enduring a long sea voyage on overcrowded timber ships. Not only did they arrive at the Rideau project in a wretched state, but their situation was made all the worse by the circumstances in which they found themselves. With excavation work just beginning in the Entrance Valley, and still underway in erecting the support buildings for the Rideau Canal project, and settlement yet to commence in the Bytown survey, no shelter was available.[33]

Moreover, the Irish pauper immigrants, in their impoverished state, lacked the means to rent the cheap building lots on which labourers were expected to erect their cabins; nor was it practicable. Upon their arrival, which was totally unexpected, the Lower Bytown site was still largely a cedar swamp, and had yet to be drained. Consequently, the immigrant labourers and their families had to sleep out of doors with no protection from the elements. Fearing for their health with the onset of the spring rainy season, Lt. Col. By permitted them to erect their shelters on the cleared high ground of the Lower Bytown survey and to settle free of charge there and along the canal right of way.[34]

That summer, the Irish pauper immigrants squatted in crude hovels built into hillsides, in mud huts, and in caves which were burrowed into a sandy hill on the outskirts of the Lower Bytown survey. In what became known as "Corktown", the Irish immigrants found themselves in a totally foreign environment. They were on the edge of a cedar swamp, surrounded by a heavily-forested wilderness, and plagued by swarms of black flies and mosquitoes. There the immigrant families huddled together in squalor, drinking the stagnant water in the nearby swamp rather than fetching clear river water from a distance. The result, reportedly, was widespread sickness, fevers, and dysentery, and "much individual disappointment and misery" which was aggravated by heavy drinking.[35]

Although the Irish Catholic pauper immigrants did not bulk large in numbers amongst the labourers who were eventually employed in constructing the Rideau Canal – and constituted only a component of the Irish Catholic immigrant labour force employed on the canal project – their bellicose behaviour, abject poverty, and difficulties experienced in adopting to the Canadian wilderness environment, made them a source of continual concern and expense at the commencement of construction. Not only were they the first large group of workers to arrive on the Rideau Canal project in the early spring of 1827, but they did so before the workcamp was constructed and a supply system organized. Moreover, a good many of them were accompanied by their wives and children.

The contractor for the Entrance Valley excavation, John Pennyfeather, was able to provide employment for several hundred of the Irish pauper immigrants upon their arrival, but experienced no end of difficulties with his workforce. With the large influx of Irish immigrants, and the ready availability of spirits and beer from two distilleries and a brewery across the Ottawa River in Wright's Town, the labourers soon became unmanageable.

During April and May 1827 – while Lt. Col. By was absent in Montreal going over contract tenders for the initial canal works on the first overland section of the canal, and thereafter engaged on his first reconnaissance trip by canoe through the Rideau-Cataraqui waterway – the Entrance Valley work site was in constant turmoil. Widespread drunkenness and fighting occurred amongst the Irish immigrant labourers at all hours of the day and night. Andrew Wilson, the local magistrate who lived twenty miles away on a clearing in the bush, was helpless to maintain order when summoned in a situation where the Irish labourers far outnumbered the settlers in the surrounding townships of Nepean and Gloucester.

Several men were killed in drunken brawls and juries, whether motivated by Irish solidarity or fear of retaliation, rendered hopeless verdicts such as – "died by the visitation of God!" In the absence of any restraining force, the Irish labourers were very belligerent and threatened the life of an overseer who tried to direct their labour. They were led by several of the reputedly worst characters from amongst the Irish Catholic poor-relief immigrants from the Rideau Military Settlement. Disorderly conduct, frequent work stoppages, and demands for higher pay threatened the whole viability of the Rideau Canal project at its very inception.[36]

In the early spring of 1827, Lt. Col. By had been shocked by "the wretched condition of most of the Emigrants applying to

[him] for work", and was concerned to alleviate their suffering, to improve their living conditions, and to prevent the spread of disease. To that end, he had immediately ordered the Commissariat Department to forward a thousand sets of bedding or great blankets from the Montreal depot to comfort and protect the health of the destitute immigrants.[37] Nonetheless, when work stoppages occurred, he refused to be coerced into paying the exorbitantly high wages that the Irish labourers demanded.

On the 1st of June 1827 he arrived at Bytown from Montreal with a 30-man detachment of the 71st Regiment of the Line. To overawe the workers, the detachment was encamped in tents on the high ground to the west of the Entrance Valley. When the 15th Company of Royal Sappers and Miners arrived several days later, they were tented on the high ground to the east.[38] At the same time, a ban was placed on the drinking and sale of intoxicants in the vicinity of the workplace, and enforced by the troops. In that manner, the unruly behaviour of the Irish labourers was checked, and the work proceeded in an orderly fashion as efforts were begun to alleviate their suffering.[39]

Health Care

At the commencement of the preliminary work on the Rideau Canal project in the fall of 1826, there was no indication that sickness would be a major problem. Initially, Dr. Christie provided medical care for the men employed in establishing a workcamp infrastructure at the newly-selected Entrance Valley, and for the men employed in erecting the first two spans of a projected bridge crossing of the islands in the Ottawa River to connect Wright's Town with the new Bytown workcamp. Dr. Christie reported that the men were "remarkably healthy". Moreover, he added that they were surprisingly so, given the severely cold winter working conditions. Only a few minor injuries required treatment, and one man died from injuries which were received in the blasting of a rock.[40] However, that situation changed dramatically with the arrival of the Irish Catholic pauper immigrants during the spring of 1827.

All manner of sickness was widespread amongst the pauper immigrants upon their arrival on the Rideau project. Indigestion was the most common problem, followed closely by bowel disorders – diarrhea, dysentery, and constipation – which were attributed by Dr. Christie to the effect of the sudden change from a vegetable (potato) to a meat (salt pork and beef) diet. The Irish pauper immigrant labourers also suffered in great numbers from various "fevers" – both continued and intermittent. Moreover, all too often the fevers recurred amongst those who had been "cured", which Dr. Christie attributed to the poor clothing, heavy drinking, and the "improvident behaviour" of the new arrivals, and their inadequate shelter.

During the first summer work season – May through November 1827, inclusive – 781 patients were treated by Dr. Christie, and almost all of the patients were Irish immigrants who had come to Bytown in search of work on the canal project. Nine of the patients died, and all of the deaths were attributed to "fever" (probably ship fever/epidemic typhus). Nonetheless, despite widespread suffering amongst the Irish pauper immigrants from indigestion, bowel disorders and fevers, their ability to earn good wages and purchase wholesome food on the Rideau Canal project did improve their health, with their recovery enhanced by the medical care and medicines that were provided for them.

Amongst the families of the Irish immigrant labourers – whom Dr. Christie also treated, but without receiving any remuneration from the canal contingency fund – two women and nine children died. In contrast, the settlers from the Military Settlements, the French Canadian migrant workers and the farmers from the older areas of settlement, who turned up for work on the canal construction project, were in comparatively good health and they did not bring their families with them. They were much more appropriately dressed, erected better shelters for themselves, had better living habits, and for the most part did not suffer from the debilitating fevers and bowel disorders that afflicted the Irish pauper immigrants. More generally, native Canadians were "seasoned" in having built up immunities to many of the fevers suffered by new arrivals, and the Canadians were accustomed to a varied diet that included vegetables, animal protein, and wheat.[41]

Concerned about the numerous sick among the Irish immigrant labourers, whom he was admitting to the military hospital, Lt. Col. By sought, and received, permission from Lord Dalhousie, the Governor-in-Chief/Commander of the Forces, to construct a large hospital at Bytown. Subsequently, the Ordnance acquiesced in that expenditure upon Lt. Col. By asserting that a large hospital was "indispensably necessary". It was built in the fall of 1827. The £700 cost of erecting and equipping the hospital was carried on the canal contingency fund, as was the cost of erecting several wooden civilian barracks to shelter the pauper Irish labourers and their families during the coming winter of 1827-1828.[42]

Both of these initiatives were undertaken in response to a report from Dr. Christie that a greater hospital accommodation was needed to properly care for the sick among the canal workers, and his warning that if the Irish pauper immigrants continued to live crowded together in miserable hovels during the winter months, a major contagion of fever and bowel diseases might well arise.[43]

Fortunately winter work was available for several hundred of the landless Irish labourers at the Hog's Back Rapids where the contractor, Walter Fenelon, was struggling to close up the clay apron of a massive 45-foot high dam before the onset of the 1828 spring floods. At that work site, log bunkhouses were erected by the contractor to house the canal workers, provisions were readily available, and winter clothing and blankets were available for purchase at reasonable prices from the Commissariat depot in Bytown.[44] The pauper Irish immigrants at Bytown, who were unable to secure winter work, were provided with provisions from the Commissariat for their families with repayment to be made from pay deductions in the spring when work would be readily available.[45]

Later, during a tour of inspection of the winter work at the Hog's

Back, Lt. Col. By was appalled at what he found. Several men, who were seriously injured in blasting accidents and from cave-ins, were left untended in unheated bunkhouses to suffer from the freezing cold during the day while their fellow labourers pursued their work out of doors. He immediately ordered the removal of the injured to hospital, even though the Irish immigrants proved loath to enter the hospital.

While in hospital, the sick and injured workers were paid 9 pence (9d.) per day to cover the cost of their hospitalization, medical care and medicines. The payments that were made to the contractors' men were contrary to existing regulations, but as Lt. Col. By explained to the Ordnance: "this was the only means I had of saving the lives of the poor sufferers". Nonetheless he was quick to reassure the Ordnance that only "the most distressing cases" would be removed to hospital.[46]

During the first summer work season on the Rideau Canal project in 1827, the circumstances and condition of the pauper Irish labourers at the Bytown end of the canal improved dramatically, and they were well housed and well fed during the following winter. However, that was not the case for the Irish Catholic immigrants employed during the first work season on the Cataraqui River section of the canal project. The winter of 1827-1828 was the very nadir of their existence.

During a reconnaissance trip through the waterway by canoe in the spring of 1827, Lt. Col. By had let a small contract for the clearing and grubbing of the projected work sites along the Cataraqui River to facilitate the follow-up levelling and layout of the canal works. The clearing and grubbing work was undertaken during the summer months, and in the fall a workforce comprising some eighty men was dismissed by the contractor. The axemen returned to their homes, but the Irish Catholic immigrant labourers erected hovels on the outskirts of Kingston where they suffered an utterly wretched existence.

With the onset of winter, whole families were reported as

suffering terribly from sickness and hunger, and lacking the basic necessities of life. The Irish immigrants had rioted in desperation, and the Kingston military establishment and the local citizenry and clergy – Anglican, Presbyterian, and Roman Catholic (Scots) – had striven to aid the sick and needy in a situation so appalling that even the condemned bedding of the Kingston garrison was made use of to protect the destitute immigrants from the cold.[47] However, during subsequent years once the canal infrastructure was in place, accommodations erected, a provisioning system and medical care established, and winter work became available, the suffering and neglect experienced by the Irish Catholic immigrant labourers at Kingston in the fall of 1827 was not repeated.

One continuing problem posed by the Irish pauper immigrants was not only the diseases that they brought with them, and/or succumbed to in large numbers shortly after their arrival on the Rideau Canal project, but many otherwise healthy individuals arrived in such an emaciated state as to be unemployable. Contractors would not hire men who were incapable of giving a good day's work for their daily wage and, lacking securities, the men were unable to help themselves through subcontracting for work in gangs. To enable these men to earn a sustenance, Lt. Col. By hired them as casual labourers, equipped them with picks, shovels and wheelbarrows, and paid them out of the ten percent contingency allowance of the Rideau Canal estimate.

The casual labourers were employed in excavating the overland section of the canal between Bytown and Dow's Great Swamp at rates per cubic yard of excavation somewhat less than was paid to the contractors. The men were thus able to work at a slower, less demanding pace, and were paid whenever they requested a measurement of their work. When ill or injured, however, the casual labourers and their families were totally dependent on the paternalism of Lt. Col. By and his medical staff for their survival.

As of the summer of 1829, some 600 Irish pauper immigrants were employed as casual labourers under the direction of the engineering officers at the Bytown end of the canal project.

*Figure 5. "Rideau Canal, Long Island on the Rideau River: August 1830", Lt. Col. James
Pattison Cockburn, Royal Artillery, watercolour. An Irish immigrant labourer and his
wife on a bush road. The man is dressed in the distinctive dress of the Gaelic Irish with a
black felt hat, a linen shirt, an older style of breeches and knee stockings, and what appears
to be a 'brat' on his arm. A primitive shelter of piled logs can be seen within a fenced area.
(Royal Ontario Museum).*

A good deal of expense was incurred in providing medical treatment, medicines, and hospitalization for the ill and injured amongst them, as well as financial support for their families to live on while the men were unable to work. Such expenditures were totally unauthorized, and contrary to Ordnance regulations. Lt. Col. By was forced to provide an *ex post facto* justification to the Board of Ordnance for his actions, and did so on humanitarian grounds, a claim of dire necessity, and general references to the future benefits to be gained through aiding the Irish pauper immigrants:

> "attention to these poor men and their families has saved the lives of a great number and their families who are extremely grateful, and will no doubt become good settlers and Loyal Subjects".[48]

Where the provision of health care was concerned, the Ordnance regulations provided that a stoppage of l ½ pence (1 ½ d.) per diem be withheld from the pay of every Foreman and artificer, and 1d. per diem from the pay of each labourer employed as a dayworker by the Royal Engineers' Department. The stoppage fund served to cover the cost of medical care, medical supplies, and hospitalization if needed, for dayworkers who might become seriously ill, and also to reimburse the Ordnance Surgeon for his medical services.

When an individual became thoroughly incapacitated through illness or injury, or required hospitalization, 9d. per day was paid out of the stoppage fund for his medical care and support. For a married man, the 9d. payment was supplemented by an additional payment of the difference between the 9d. sum and the patient's daily rate of pay based on his position. The additional sum was paid to the family of the ill or injured individual during his hospitalization.[49] However, neither the casual workers, nor the canal workers employed by the contractors, were covered by stoppages.

To relieve the canal contingency fund of the expense of paying for the health care and medicines which were provided to the canal workers, Lt. Col. By requested permission from the Board of Ordnance to issue Ordnance medicines to all of the canal workers when ill or injured. He also sought permission to pay the Ordnance Surgeon, Michael Tuthill, an additional 10 shillings (10s) per diem for tending to the sick or injured amongst the canal workers not covered by stoppages, and to reimburse Tuthill for the medicines that he dispersed from his private chest in treating them.

At the Ordnance in London, the Director General of the Medical Department, John Webb, recommended that the Board respond positively to Lt. Col. By's requests in taking into consideration the unusual circumstance of excavating a canal through a wilderness where the men were subject to fevers and marsh influenza and far removed from any other medical assistance. Dr. Webb recommended further that the stoppage system be extended to all the canal workers by deducting 1d. per person, per work day, from the monies paid to the contractors.

Subsequently, the Board authorized a payment of 10s per diem for Surgeon Tuthill when treating sick canal workers, and agreed to reimburse Tuthill for the cost of medicines dispensed to the canal workers. On the other hand, the Board refused to extend the stoppage system to cover the contractors' men as that was contrary to the existing regulations. Moreover, the Board reiterated that the medical care of the workers was the responsibility of the contractors, and suggested that the contractors ought to make some such arrangement to cover the expense of providing medicines and medical care for the canal workers in their employ.

Eventually, the Board of Ordnance did reconsider the matter. An extension of the stoppage system was authorized to cover the casual workers employed by the canal engineering establishment. The extension was authorized on the grounds of "the necessity of adopting an extraordinary means to meet an extraordinary case".[50]

Thus, as of the spring of 1830, the contingency allowance of the Rideau Canal project was relieved of the cost of providing health care and medicines for upwards of 600 casual labourers – the Irish pauper immigrants – who continued to be employed on the Bytown-Hog's Back section of the canal under the direct supervision of the Royal Engineers. The men were placed on stoppage, and when sick their medical expenses and support for their families were covered from their own financial contributions to the stoppage fund. This constituted a major cost savings on the Rideau Canal estimate as health care costs had soared during the previous two summer work seasons due to a severe and recurring sickness problem. However, the stoppage system was not extended to the canal workers who were employed by the contractors. The cost of their medical care, medicines, and hospitalization continued to be borne on the contingency allowance of the Rideau Canal estimate.

The Sickness Factor

On the Rideau Canal project, the construction infrastructure and the provisioning system were well in place by the mid-summer of 1827 on the lower Rideau River section, while surveying continued along the upper Rideau River and Cataraqui River sections in the interior. Once the planning phase was completed, the last of the excavation and masonry contracts for constructing the canal were let by the Commissariat Department on competitive bids, and at reasonable rates, during February 1828. Thereafter, during the winter months, the contractors were reportedly busy in forwarding supplies into the interior on snow roads and the frozen lakes and rivers in preparing to push forward the canal work along the entire waterway during the coming summer work season.[51] What was totally unexpected was the impact of sickness on the project during the 1828 work season.

Initially, a smallpox threat was contained. Upon smallpox breaking out in June 1828 at Bytown, Lt. Col. By sent to the Commissariat depot in Montreal for vaccinating material, and had Surgeon Tuthill vaccinate upwards of 500 of the children of the labourers.[52] In that manner a potential smallpox epidemic was avoided in a period when – amongst unvaccinated individuals, once infected – the mortality rate could reach as high as 70 per cent.[53] In sum, had smallpox spread amongst the canal workers and their families, it would have had a devastating impact.

Two months later, another disease, "lake fever and ague" – malaria – struck the work sites, and had a devastating impact. During the 1827 work season, it was noted that the workers who were employed in clearing and grubbing the work sites along the Cataraqui River, amidst swamps and marshes, were suffering greatly from the "lake fever and ague". Thereafter, in an effort to reduce the amount of excavation work that would be required to deepen the sickly swamps and marshes, Lt. Col. By, as of June 1828, decided to raise the dam at Kingston Mills and construct extensive embanking to flood out the swamps and marshlands and the shallows at Jack's Rifts and Billidore's Rifts immediately upstream.[54] With that work pending, malaria struck the entire Rideau Canal project.

Throughout the early summer of 1828, the Province of Upper Canada had suffered from an intense heat wave – one of the worst ever experienced by the settlers – and the unusually hot weather brought an unprecedentedly severe outbreak of "lake fever and ague."[55] Thereafter, for the better part of almost three months – from mid-August through October, inclusive – temperatures hovered around 90 degrees Fahrenheit in the shade and the ravages of malaria were reported from across the province. In some areas of Upper Canada, whole towns and villages fell sick. In Perth, "every house was like a hospital".[56]

Along the entire canal, only a handful of men remained capable of working at the various work sites. The sickness was particularly virulent in the swamps and marshes along the waterway where the men employed in the excavating work were already suffering greatly from dysentery which was brought on by drinking swamp water.[57] There the mortality rate soared, and at one of the sickliest sites – Kingston Mills – thirteen men out of a 100-man workforce died. Everywhere the work came almost to a complete standstill during the duration of the sickly season.[58] The Ordnance Surgeon, Michael Tuthill, was ordered to do what he could to provide medical care and medicine for the sick workers, in addition to his regular duties in providing medical care for the military establishment on the canal project.[59]

Among the various remedies which were employed by the early settlers, only quinine proved effective in curing the 'lake fever and ague'. However, quinine sold for as high as 1s. 6d. per grain; and it required anywhere from six to ten grains per day to effect a cure.[60] Although quinine could be purchased in Upper Canada, such expenditures were far beyond the means of canal labourers who were earning 2s. 6d. per day, or 1s. 3d. per diem when room and board were provided by the contractor.[61] The labourers were treated by Dr. Christie, as well as by Surgeon Tuthill free of charge, but their stock of medicines was soon exhausted.[62] Thereafter, the workers had little alternative but to suffer and let the sickness take its course. Many of the canal workers were reduced to a debilitated state after a bout with malaria; and it was known that, once caught, the "dreadful disease" would recur each year thereafter, although usually in less severe bouts.[63]

John Mactaggart, the Clerk of Works, was struck by the particular virulence of the strain of 'lake fever and ague' in Upper Canada, and recorded that:

> "The Fever and Ague of Canada are different, I am
> told, from those of other countries; they generally
> come on with an attack of bilious fever, dreadful
> vomiting, pains in the back and loins, general
> debility, loss of appetite, so that one cannot even
> take tea, ... After being in this state for eight or
> ten days, the yellow jaundice is likely to ensue, and
> then fits of trembling.... For two or three hours
> before they arrive, we feel so cold that nothing
> will warm us; the greatest heat that can be applied

is perfectly unfelt; the skin gets dry, and then the shaking begins. Our very bones ache, teeth chatter, and the ribs are sore, continuing in great agony for about an hour and a half, and a profuse sweat ensues, which lasts for two hours longer. This over, we find the malady has run one of its rounds, and start out of bed in a feeble state, sometimes unable to stand, and entirely dependent on our friends (if we have any) to lift us on to some seat or other".[64]

In an effort to eliminate the source of the sickness, Lt. Col. By hired axemen to clear back the trees over 250 feet on each side of the work sites along the waterway, and had the swamps and marshes drained. These efforts were made to increase air circulation to eliminate the stagnant foul air that was hanging over many of the work sites clearings, and the noxious miasma arising from the swamps and marshes.[65]

The removal of the forest cover to let air circulate, and the draining of wet lands, was in keeping with the then-prevailing medical belief concerning the cause of 'lake fever and ague'. A contemporary medical treatise described that as follows:

> "The chief predisposing cause is debility, however induced: but the grand exciting cause [of ague or intermittent fever] is *marsh miasma*, or the effluvia arising from stagnant water, or marshy ground, impregnated with vegetable matter in a state of putrificative decomposition. Dampness, and the night air, are particularly favourable to the full operation of marsh miasma."[66]

Malaria – the name derived from 'mal aria', the Italian phrase for bad air – was present in North America in many swamps and marsh areas. Unbeknownst to contemporary medical practitioners, the disease was transmitted by the bite of the female anopheles mosquito which absorbed the parasites responsible for the disease in taking blood from an infected person, and then passed on the parasites in taking blood subsequently from an uninfected person.[67]

Although the cause of the malaria was misunderstood, the measures undertaken to open the heavily-forested work sites to the wind and sunlight, and to drain the swamps and marshes, no doubt reduced the swarms of mosquitoes that were plaguing the canal workers, and hence the spread of the disease. On the Rideau Canal project, "the sickness" abated in September, at least a month before it did in the military settlement at Perth which was situated in a swampy area on the Tay River tributary of the Rideau River. At Perth, no concerted effort was made by the settlers to improve the air circulation or to drain the surrounding swamps.[68]

Each year, the 'lake fever and ague' returned about the 10th -12th of August, and remained unabated through to the end of September. In subsequent years, however, its worst impact was at the Isthmus – where there were swamps adjacent to the canal excavation – and at the work sites along the meandering Cataraqui River, where work was proceeding in the swamps and marshes, and the drowned lands flooded by several of the earlier mill dams. In the drowned lands, the men were enveloped in a heavy mist while excavating decayed vegetable matter that gave off a noxious odour reportedly similar to a dead animal in its last stages of decomposition.[69]

In an on-going effort to increase air circulation, Lt. Col. By cut back the forest cover still further to upwards of 300 to 400 feet at the canal work sites, as well as along both sides of the entire canal excavation line at the Isthmus summit level. And more wet lands were drained.[70] At the same time, the height of the dams under construction was raised as high as the river banks would accommodate – without necessitating heavy embanking work – to reduce the amount of excavation work which would be required at the worst of the sickly sites. Costly winter work was also undertaken at the more sickly sites to avoid having to work there during the summer sickly season.

At the Isthmus, a major workcamp was established in the fall of 1829 for the pursuit of winter work. The layout of the canal also was changed to raise the summit level by more than four feet to achieve a corresponding reduction in the depth of the 1/2 mile long canal excavation. It was being carried through an extremely hard granite rock at depths that approached twenty feet in some sections, before the raising of the summit level.

To entice workers to report to such a sickly site, commodious barracks were constructed at the Isthmus for the workers and their families, as well as a cook house, and a Commissariat depot was established to sell provisions of all sorts directly to the workforce at cost. A large hospital was also constructed, provisioned with medicines, and provided with an Ordnance surgeon, Dr. Robinson, to provide medical care and medicines for the canal workers in addition to the military artisans and the engineering establishment at the site.[71]

More generally as the canal construction project evolved, the physical efforts to combat malaria, in conjunction with better provisioning, accommodation, and medical care, greatly reduced the impact of malaria on the workforce, as did the actions of the canal workers themselves. Each year with the onset of the sickly season, anywhere from one-tenth to one-half of the workforce would leave the sickliest work sites out of a dread of the "lake fever and ague".[72] The settlers were able to return to their homes, and the itinerant immigrant canal workers of some means could move on to purchase land elsewhere in Upper Canada or the United States. Those who remained comprised the landless labourers of little means, the military artisans of the two companies of Royal Sappers and Miners, the contractors, and the engineering officers, overseers, and master tradesmen of the canal establishment.

When malaria struck, it did not differentiate amongst the men who remained at work on the canal project. No one was spared as labourers, artificers, overseers, and contractors, as well as the engineering staff, suffered from the 'lake fever and ague', and would suffer repeated bouts of malaria during each successive sickly season.[73] Even Lt. Col. By was struck down with a severe case of malaria following a tour of inspection of the canal work sites in early September 1829. His life was despaired of for several weeks, and he was rendered totally incapacitated for the better part of two months.[74] New immigrants were particularly susceptible to the ravages of malaria.[75] No doubt, the suffering and mortality rate from 'lake fever and ague' was greatest amongst the Irish pauper immigrants who arrived on the Rideau Canal project each summer in a debilitated state after crossing the ocean on poorly-provisioned timber ships.

The efforts made by Lt. Col. By to lessen the impact of the "lake fever and ague" on the Rideau Canal project had a decided effect on the infection and mortality rates. Despite the virulent nature of the malarial strain on the Rideau Canal project, the mortality rate was much lower during the 1830 and 1831 work seasons than in the two previous years. During the 1830 sickly season, 1258 men remained at the work on the Cataraqui section of the canal from the Isthmus to Kingston Mills, inclusive. Overall, the sickness rate was 56% on that section of the canal, and the mortality rate was but 2.15% with 27 men dying. In addition, 13 women and 15 children died from sickness on that section of the canal.[76]

In contrast, almost all of the men who were working on the canal project during the malaria epidemic of the extremely hot summer of 1828 were terribly sick with malaria. Moreover, the mortality rate was much higher – reaching as high as 13% at Kingston Mills – before action could be taken to drain the swamps and marshes and cut back the forest cover to increase the air circulation.[77]

In 1831, malaria did strike hard, and earlier than expected, at the Isthmus. There efforts to drain the adjacent swamps had proved futile; the work site was constantly flooded by the waters

Figure 6. "Royal Sappers & Miners, Uniform & Working Dress, 1825", George B. Campion, Drawing Master, Royal Military Academy, Woolwich, coloured lithograph. (T.W. Connolly, The History of the Corps of Royal Sappers and Miners *(London: Longman, Brown, Green and Longmans, 1855, Volume 2, Plate 13). The 1825 dress uniform comprised a black shako with yellow cords and a white plume, a red jacket with yellow epaulettes, blue trousers with a scarlet stripe, and short Wellington boots. The working dress comprised a dark blue Kilmarnock bonnet with a yellow band and a black chin strap, a red jacket, and grey trousers with a scarlet stripe.*

of Rideau Lake that seeped through fissures in the bedrock. At that work site, the fear of malaria was such that the entire civilian workforce departed when the sickness struck. Only the 51 artisans of the 7th Company of the Royal Sappers and Miners, the commanding officer, Captain Cole, R.E., and the two members of the Commissariat Department, remained at the work site, together with the 27 women and 46 children of the 7th Company and two camp followers. Within two weeks 50.9 % of the men, 40% of the women, and 43.4% of the children were sick. Most were suffering from "the ague"; however, eight of the military artificers were diagnosed as having "remittent typhus".

On the advice of the attending physician, Assistant Surgeon, Dr. William Kelly, Ordnance Medical Service, the men, women, and children of the 7th Company were immediately withdrawn to the Narrows work site on Rideau Lake – five miles distant – where no sickness was reported. There a workcamp was available for occupation. The contractors at that site – Bell, Richardson & Co. – had just finished their contract, and were dismissing their workers. Only a small detachment of Sappers was left at the Isthmus to guard the stores. At the end of the sickly season, the 7th Company returned to work at the Isthmus with no lives having been lost due to sickness.[78]

The number of deaths from malaria on the Rideau Canal project as a whole remains a matter of conjecture. The various reports produced by the Royal Engineers contain only incomplete references to the impact of sickness on the project; and that was intentional. As explained by Lt. Col. By:

> "... in the years 1828 and 1829, the sickness
> extended through the whole line of Canal & the
> mortality was so great, that it was thought prescient
> to make no report on the subject, fearing that if
> the full extent of misery were made public, no one
> would be found willing to work on the Rideau
> Canal."

Only in 1830, when the impact of malaria was confined mostly to the Isthmus and the Cataraqui work sites, was a report prepared that detailed the number of the sick and deceased at each work site on that section of the canal during the sickly season. It was compiled to inform the Ordnance of the heavy costs and delays which were being imposed on the canal construction project by the sickness factor.[79]

Following the completion of the Rideau Canal, a Kingston physician, Dr. Edward Barker, claimed that 500 men had died from sickness at Kingston Mills alone during the construction of the canal.[80] However, that statement is highly questionable given the known number of deaths from malaria at Kingston Mills in 1828 (13 men of a l00 - man workforce), and 1830 (8 men of a 389 - man workforce). In effect, the mortality rate fell from a high of 13% at Kingston Mills in 1828 to 2.05% at Kingston Mills in 1830 amongst the men who remained at work during the sickly season, which undermines the plausibility of Dr. Baker's statement.

Any attempt to ascertain the number of deaths from malaria on the Rideau Canal project as a whole is stymied by fragmentary data and inconsistencies: viz. the exceptionally high mortality rate at some sites during the extremely hot summer of 1828 and again during 1829; the varying numbers of men who remained at the different work sites during each succeeding sickly season; the varying mortality rate from site to site, and a significant decline in the mortality rate over the last two sickly seasons; and the fact that during the 1830 and 1831 work seasons malaria struck principally at the Isthmus and on the Cataraqui section of the canal with the men, women and children on the Rideau section escaping virtually unscathed.

For the artificers of the Royal Sapper and Miners, more precise records were kept. On the Rideau Canal project as a whole, between 1827 and 1832, twenty-one men died from the 162-man combined complements of the 7th and 15th Companies. In sum, five men died of "fever" (a mortality rate of 3%), seven from blasting accidents, four of "apoplexy" (probably heat stroke), three of consumption (tuberculosis), and two by drowning.[81] Yet, these figures are misleading in terms of any estimate of the mortality rate amongst the canal workers as a whole.

Throughout the canal construction period, the 15th Company was employed in Bytown and at the Hog's Back, two of the healthiest work sites on the canal, and the 7th Company was employed at the same stations until its transfer to the Isthmus during the winter of 1829-1830. Hence, only one company of the Royal Sappers and Miners was exposed to infection at a highly sickly site, and only for a period of two summer work seasons, 1830 and 1831. Given that the mortality rate would have been higher amongst the debilitated immigrant labourers who were newly arrived on the canal project, and that the sick who left the project and died elsewhere were not recorded, it is quite possible that upwards of 500 men died from malaria as reported by Dr. Barker. However, the deaths were over the entire course of construction of the Rideau Canal, rather than at one site.

Following the completion of the Rideau Canal in May 1832, when the water was raised behind the high dams, the 'lake fever and ague' was all but eradicated along the waterway and greatly reduced in the interior settlements. Dr. Baker noted – after a round trip from Kingston to Bytown in the late summer of 1834 – that "he did not see or hear of a single case of sickness". Settlement was spreading rapidly along the waterway, and the hamlets of Smith's Falls and Merrick's Mills were now flourishing villages. Moreover, new villages had sprung up at the Isthmus, and at Kemptville on a tributary of the Rideau River, and Bytown and Kingston at either end of the canal were rapidly growing commercial transport centres with populations of 3,000 and 5,000 persons, respectively. Dr. Baker noted further that even the lands along the Cataraqui River, which formerly were "so unhealthy as hardly to be habitable", were now being settled.[82]

Origins, Circumstance, and Acculturation

Where the multi-cultural labour force on the Rideau Canal was concerned, it was the Irish Catholic pauper immigrants who experienced the greatest difficulty in adapting to the demands of living and working in a wilderness environment, and who needed the most support and assistance. They were categorized as 'pauper Irish' owing to their destitute condition upon their arrival in Upper Canada, regardless of whatever their occupation might have been in Ireland. However, the 'pauper Irish' comprised only a component of a much larger group of so-called 'low Irish' – the Gaelic Irish Catholics of southern and western Ireland – who were employed in the construction of the Rideau Canal.

On the Rideau Canal project, a large number of the upwards of 2,700 British immigrants who were employed by the Rideau Canal contractors each summer were Irish Catholics and Irish Protestants of some means. After a period of employment on the canal project they travelled farther inland to settle on the land in Upper Canada or passed into the United States in search of land. In posing no particular problem for the military authorities, they left little record of their presence.[83] In contrast, a smaller component of the Irish Catholic immigrant workforce, the pauper immigrants, are well documented in the historical record because of their destitute condition upon arrival, their poor health, their bellicose response to their suffering, and their need for and receipt of a great deal of aid.[84]

Whether or not the traditional cultural values of the Gaelic Irish Catholics made it particularly difficult for them to adapt to the demands of bush farming in Upper Canada, and to successfully integrate into the frontier settlement culture, is a moot point.[85] However, one thing is clear. The suffering and difficulties experienced by the Irish pauper immigrants in adapting to living and working in a wilderness environment stemmed directly from their previous economic situation in Ireland, their debilitating experience on the ocean crossing, and the all-but-hopeless situation in which they found themselves upon their arrival in Upper Canada.

The pauper Irish who turned up on the Rideau Canal project,

in seeking work and land upon which to settle, had none of the resources which were furnished the earlier British immigrants who settled in the Rideau wilderness to the rear of the waterway. The earlier immigrants were participants in planned emigration and settlement schemes, and had benefited from an extensive support system operated by the Commissariat Department of the British Army. The discharged soldiers, assisted-emigration Scots, and the poor-relief Irish Catholic emigrants who were placed in the Rideau Military Settlement, were much better prepared to settle on the land. They well fed on naval transports or on chartered commercial ships during their ocean voyage to Canada, were provided with a free transport inland to the settlement, were given a free land grant, and each family was given an axe, farming implements and domestic utensils to facilitate their transition onto the land.

Moreover each family had received army food rations during their first year on the land, or longer, and were given seed to grow root crops, and wheat which was ground into flour to supplement their diet of military rations. The Scots emigrants, in particular, were forewarned of the need to bring heavy clothing and of the difficulty of procuring clothing in Upper Canada. As a result, they had brought out hanks of wool yarn, and bolts of cloth for making socks, clothes, and coats for the winter.[86]

In contrast on the Rideau Canal project, the Irish Catholic pauper immigrants arrived empty- handed, with the men dressed in an older style of clothing – knee breeches rather than the trousers worn by other groups – which was poorly suited to the Canadian climate.[87] The economic situation and living conditions of the Irish Catholic emigrants in Ireland and their experiences during the ocean voyage to Canada were also largely different from that of the Irish Protestants (Anglo-Irish Anglicans and Scots-Irish Presbyterians), the Scots immigrants (Catholic Highlanders and Presbyterian Lowlanders), and the English immigrants (Anglicans and dissenters).

In Ireland – after several centuries of English invasions and colonization projects, failed Irish rebellions, and massive land confiscations – the native Gaelic-speaking Roman Catholic population was confined for the most part to the poorer southern and western areas of Ireland, and lived primarily as tenant farmers under the Protestant Anglo-Irish Ascendancy. Under the existing land system, the Irish Catholics tenant farmers leased from Protestant landlords – generally through a Middleman – a farm acreage on which they grew wheat to pay the rent, and had a garden plot for growing food crops for their own sustenance. However, by the late 18th and early 19th centuries, a rapidly increasing population had resulted in the leased farms being continually subdivided until large families were farming as little as five acres, or in extreme cases as little as a half or quarter acre, and living almost exclusively on potatoes which were grown on small garden plots.

With their small farms severely overpopulated, and wheat prices declining in the post-Napoleonic War period, the Irish tenant farmers were caught in a hopeless situation amidst widespread misery and periodic famines. Many were reduced to living in hovels, were poorly nourished and badly clothed, and faced the constant threat of eviction for rent arrears and a resultant starvation for their families. In despair at their situation, secret societies were organized – such as the Whiteboys – that spread terror amongst the landed Protestants in violent protests against evictions. Middlemen were murdered, cattle crippled, sheep maimed, houses burned, pastures turned up, and harvests destroyed, and witnesses intimidated to escape prosecution; all of which resulted in the Irish Catholics developing a reputation for being prone to violence, unruly behaviour, and lawlessness.[88]

The Irish Catholics who emigrated to Canada during the 1820s and 1830s – prior to the Great Famine years from 1845 to 1850 – were mostly tenant farmers who had managed to avoid sinking into abject poverty. They were able to pay for their passage to Canada on a timber ship, or were aided to emigrate by landlords who were anxious to remove them from the land. However, the timber ships that entered Irish ports were not covered by government passenger regulations, and Irish Catholic immigrants with little money sailed on the least seaworthy ships.

On board, they suffered from severe overcrowding in filthy, poorly-ventilated holds, from being malnourished with inadequate and unpalatable food rations, and from the drinking of brackish water. The result was multiple deaths on an ocean voyage that lasted anywhere from six to ten weeks of sailing, and was marked by much suffering from ship fever (typhus) and dysentery. The result was that a good number of the Irish Catholic immigrants arrived in the ports of Quebec and Montreal sick, penniless, and in a throughly debilitated state.

In contrast, the Highland Scots tenant farmers – who were being displaced by the introduction of large-scale sheep farming by their clan chieftains – owned their own cattle, as well as their household goods on their clan lands. When they chose to emigrate, it was in order to secure land to maintain their standard of living. They were able to sell their livestock and household items to pay for their passage on more seaworthy ships, which were better provisioned for the ocean voyage and far less crowded than the timber ships that sailed from the ports of southern and western Ireland. Moreover, the displaced tenants of a clan commonly emigrated together under the tackman (manager of the clan estate), and pooled their resources to engage and provision a ship for their ocean voyage, and were well clothed. Moreover, they brought money with them to purchase land and provisions upon their arrival in Upper Canada.

Among the independent emigrants sailing for Canada, the situation of the lowland Scots Presbyterian weavers, and of the Irish Protestant farmers, farmer-weavers. and tradesmen, was similar to the Highland Scots emigrants. With the postwar depression in the textile trade, and low wheat prices, they were anxious to leave Scotland and Ireland, respectively, to secure land in North America. With property to sell, as well as household items and often livestock, they were able to pay for better accommodations and provisions on board the better outfitted timber ships and general cargo vessels. They arrived in North America in comparatively good health with money in hand to purchase land and provisions during their transition into bush farming. Moreover, they tended to purchase land in areas which had been settled earlier by their kith and kin who rendered them aid in adapting to their new environment on the settlement frontier. Not all of the independent Scots and Irish Protestant emigrants were well off. However, the poorer families were aided to emigrate by emigration societies, and once in Canada were aided further by private emigrant societies that were organized by their fellow countrymen who had proceeded them in settling in Canada.

Comparatively few English farmers and tradesmen emigrated to Canada in the postwar period despite the land clearances for sheep raising and the depressed agricultural economy. In England, the parish poor law relief system and the growing demand for labour by the rapidly expanding industries of the Industrial Revolution, reduced the incentive to emigrate and for private emigration societies and the government to foster emigration. The English farmers, tradesmen, and the half-pay officers who did emigrate unassisted were comparative well off, and had sufficient monies to book passage on good ships, to purchase land and provisions in Upper Canada, and to pay experienced settlers to aid them in erecting a cabin and in settling onto their land.[89]

Despite the paternalistic efforts on the part of Lt. Col. By to provide blankets, clothing, medical care, and employment – and ultimately accommodation and access to hospital facilities – the Irish pauper immigrant labourers suffered a great deal during their first year on the Rideau Canal construction project. Moreover, their suffering was made all the worse by their inability to follow the pattern of previous immigrants and settle on the land, and their particular difficulties in adapting to the demands of their new wilderness environment. Not only were the Irish pauper immigrants in no condition to engaged in bush farming upon their arrival in Canada, but the circumstances in which they found themselves – particularly the land situation – worked against them.

Despite the Rideau and Cataraqui waterways passing through a veritable wilderness for the greater part of their respective courses, immigrants of little means could not settle on the nearby land. All of the surrounding township lands were in private hands, and were either being held for speculative purposes pending the completion of the canal or offered for sale at prices as high as $6.00 (30s.) per acre.   Elsewhere in Upper Canada, the best lands were selling for 7s.6d. to 10s. per acre with bush land going for 5s. per acre.[90] Consequently, any immigrant employed on the Rideau Canal project who wanted to establish a farm would have to penetrate deep into the bush to settle on isolated lots of cheap land in the back concessions which were far removed from the established settlements. That the Irish immigrants were loath – even fearful – to do, and with good reason.[91]

Bush farming in Upper Canada was a demanding and highly hazardous undertaking, totally different from farming cleared land. It presented novel problems for immigrants, and required adaptability, flexibility, the learning of new skills and approaches, and above all a boundless confidence in the face of a seemingly overwhelming task. Immigrants had to be taught how to notch a tree to direct its fall, how to approach the establishing of a bush farm, how to erect a cabin with the assistance of neighbours, what crops to plant, the proper axe to use, and above all they had to quickly learn to use a felling axe expeditiously.

Generally, with the guidance and occasional aid of their more experienced neighbours, most immigrants learned how to wield an axe and the techniques of bush farming – at least well enough to cope with the wilderness in avoiding starvation or a debilitating injury. Bush farming, however, was highly dangerous work in circumstances wherein even experienced axemen occasionally suffered axe wounds or were killed in felling accidents, and where the inept or careless soon were killed or maimed by falling trees and branches or by dull or misapplied axes glancing off tree trunks.

In bush farming, hard work and individual effort were not enough to succeed. Immigrants settling in the bush had to have at least six months provisions to sustain themselves until the first crops – potatoes, Indian corn, and turnips – were harvested.[92] Before proceeding into the bush, it was possible for a poor immigrant to accumulate sufficient capital through wage labour to purchase the provisions required to sustain a family until the first crops could be harvested. Many managed to do so, but it required purposive action and sacrifice.[93]

All of the Irish immigrants suffered terribly during the summers from the intolerable heat at the work sites in the forest clearings, and in winter they experienced a severe cold that was beyond their previous comprehension. In southern Ireland, winters were mild with a January mean of just over 40 degrees Fahrenheit, and summers were moderately warm with a July mean of 60 degrees Fahrenheit.[94] In contrast, at Bytown temperatures could range as low as 22 degrees below zero Fahrenheit for several days on end during the winter, not to mention the annual snow fall which in record years could reach seven feet.[95] And in summer, temperatures in Bytown could soar above 90 degrees Fahrenheit, though usually not for months on end as happened during the extremely hot summer of 1828. The Irish immigrants had no knowledge of, or experience with, the temperature extremes of a North American continental climate, and the Irish pauper immigrants in particular were ill-prepared for what they encountered in labouring on the Rideau Canal project.

The destitute Irish Catholic timber ship immigrants, in coming to Canada from farming cleared land in a mild climate, lacked the resources, skills, and knowhow to engage in bush farming, and lacked the financial resources to purchase land in a settled area where they could receive advice and assistance from neighbours. Among contemporaries, it was noted that the poorer Irish Catholic immigrants were extremely awkward in seeking to master the use of an axe and, to make matters worse, experienced numerous injuries in dropping trees on themselves. As one observer recorded that:

> "When Paddy first commences hewing down trees,
> he often hews them down upon himself, and gets
> maimed or killed; and if he attempts squaring, he
> cuts and abuses his feet in a shocking manner".

On being offered cheap land, a number of Irish families from the Rideau Canal project had penetrated deep into the bush to settle with an axe in hand. Isolated, and deprived of the guidance and aid of experienced neighbours, they commonly failed to establish themselves, emerging from the woods totally defeated and in a starving state, ravaged by mosquitoes.[96] Such experiences, and their poor state of health, no doubt dissuaded later arrivals from among the Irish timber ship immigrants from attempting to settle deep in the bush.[97] The crux of the tragedy was that the Irish Catholic pauper immigrants on the Rideau Canal project represented a new phenomenon in Upper Canada – a landless labour force in a country where there was insufficient wage labour work to keep unskilled labourers employed year round.

On adopting the contract system for constructing the Rideau Canal, the Board of Ordnance had sought to be relieved of the burden of supporting a labour force year-round in a climate where canal construction work could be pursued for only six months of the year.[98] In the then-prevailing laboursettlement situation in Upper Canada, such a system was viable; but the Irish pauper immigrants added a discordant, and totally unexpected element.

Unable to settle on the land, the pauper immigrants were totally dependent on wage labour, and in particular on winter work on the Rideau Canal project to escape from falling into a complete and utter destitution each fall.[99] At the close of a summer work season, the French Canadian labourers and the English, Scots, and Irish Protestant canal workers from the older settled areas and from the Rideau Military Settlement, could return to their homes, as could the Irish Catholic poor-relief settlers from the

Figure 7. "Near Old Sly's, Rideau; August 1830", Lt. Col. James Pattison Cockburn, Royal Artillery, watercolour. A typical French Canadian axeman, dressed in a toque, shirt, trousers, leather leggings, and moccasins. (Library and Archives Canada).

military settlement. The settlers could sustain themselves and their families during the winter months on root crops which were harvested from their land, supplemented through hunting game and ice fishing, and with flour ground from their wheat crop. Some were able to secure employment in the timber trade as ox drivers, teamsters, and axemen, but there was no work for new arrivals who were unskilled with the axe.

Earlier, during the fall of 1826, a number of Irish Catholic immigrants had been recruited in Montreal to work with French Canadian axemen and labourers in clearing and grubbing the newly-selected Entrance Valley, and in working on the construction of the first two spans of the bridge crossing of the Ottawa River. The men were boarded in Wright's Town, a long-settled farming and timber trade community where mills, stores,

and houses stood surrounded by cleared fields. At that time it
was observed that the "low Irish" would pilfer anything that was
left unguarded, and had an annoying tendency to cut branches off
trees left standing in the cleared areas, rather than going off into
the bush for firewood. Otherwise there was no complaint as the
Irish immigrants had performed their work well.[100]

The only potential labour difficulty noted was a strong animosity
evident on the part of the French Canadians towards the Irish
Catholic newcomers. In observing the work underway, the Clerk
of Works, John Mactaggart, was enthusiastic about the French
Canadian and Irish immigrants as potential canal workers: "Give
me plenty of Canadian labourers and Irishmen, but let them work
apart, and wonders may be wrought;...."[101]

Thereafter, the French Canadian labourers had proved equally
good at working in a wilderness environment. They adapted
quickly, kept strong and healthy, and performed their work well
with no complaints; but initially the Irish pauper immigrants
had not. On witnessing the contrasting response of the French
Canadians and the Irish immigrant labourers to the demands
of working and living in a wilderness environment, Mactaggart
concluded that it would have been much more efficacious and
humane had French Canadians been recruited to construct
the canal, and the Irish Catholic immigrants remained in
Ireland. However, gradually the health, strength, behaviour, and
circumstances of the Irish labourers had improved as they began
to receive the benefits of the support system that Lt. Col. By
established.

Elsewhere, the Irish pauper immigrants, who were arriving in
Canada from the timber ships, were not as fortunate. Totally
unprepared for living and working in a frontier settlement
environment within a wilderness setting, unable to settle on
the land, and in poor health upon arrival, it was estimated that
one-tenth of the Irish pauper immigrants perished from disease
following their arrival in Canada, with children dying at three
times the rate of adults. Mactaggart, who had seen at first hand

the wretched living conditions that the Irish Catholic tenant farmers were fleeing in Ireland, considered their plight to be far worse in Upper Canada. The effects of wretched living conditions and poor health were exacerbated by the extremes of the Canadian climate and the demands of living in a totally foreign environment for which they were ill-prepared and ill-adapted.[102]

Provisioning System

From the very beginning of the project, Lt. Col. By instituted a provisioning strategy. He let it be known that "to keep down the imposition of neighbouring stores, the workmen may take pork, flour, rum, gunpowder, and tools out of the King's Magazines, by the price they cost the government".[103] Arrangements also were made for the Commissariat Department to sell barrels of salted pork, flour, and puncheons of rum to contractors in bulk, at cost plus transport from Montreal to Bytown. However, there was no intention to provide cheap subsidized food to the canal workers directly, or through the contractors.

The intent was to use the Commissary provisioning system to keep food prices from soaring, while at the same time keeping prices remunerative enough to encourage the settlers to bring their produce to the work sites, so as to minimize the volume of provisions that the Commissariat would need to ship from Montreal. Keeping food prices moderate was the ultimate goal so as to avoid driving up wages rates, and the cost of constructing the canal, while at the same time precluding the contractors from purchasing cheap food from the Commissariat and engaging in food price speculation on the open market.[104]

At the commencement of construction in 1827 a government bakery was established in Bytown. It was intended to provision the engineering officers, overseers, and military artisans of the canal establishment, but Lt. Col. By soon ordered the bakery to sell bread to the canal workers as well. That was a highly irregular arrangement, and evoked criticism from the Commissariat Department. Nonetheless, Lt. Col. By was determined to provide good quality bread to the canal workers at a fair price after receiving complaints about the weights and measures of the bread which was being purchased by the canal workers from a private bakery in Wright's Town.[105] To serve the canal workers further, the revenue that was received from the renting of lots in Bytown was used to erect a market building, with a weight scale, in Lower Bytown.[106]

As the Rideau project evolved, the provisioning strategy of Lt. Col. By succeeded in keeping food costs from soaring despite the heavy demands of the canal workforce.[107] Moreover, food prices remained high enough to encourage farmers to maximize production on their bush clearings, which brought prosperity to the settlements in the interior, to the merchants of Bytown and to the interior hamlets which were supplying the contractors and workers on the canal project. Several factors were at work.

On the one hand, although the Commissariat sold provisions to contractors at cost plus transport, the transport costs added almost 50% to the price of staples which were brought from Montreal to Bytown. Hence, the local farmers were able to compete in selling their produce, while the availability of Commissariat supplies in the market precluded price gouging. Through such a system, the prices paid by the contractors for provisions were maintained at what was considered to be a cheap or, at the interior work sites, a moderately high level compared to other isolated areas in the interior of the province.[108]

Farmers from the Wright's Town settlement, the St. Lawrence Front, and the interior Rideau Military Settlement townships came to sell produce to the canal contractors, who were also able to purchase flour in bulk from the millers in the several hamlets along the waterway. The food staples of fresh pork, potatoes, and flour, were purchased in that manner, as well as oats and hay for the horses. There was also corn, poultry, eggs and fresh butter readily available for purchase by the canal workers directly.[109] The flour was baked into bread in the work camps, and the dietary staples were further supplemented by peas, beans, tea, sugar and salt which were purchased by the contractors for feeding their workforce. Whisky and tobacco were also readily available for purchase in the contractors' stores, as well as rum.

The stores of the contractors made substantial profits.[110] However, the worst abuses of the truck system – excessively high prices, rotten or adulterated food, short weights, wages paid in beer tickets and script redeemable only at high-priced company stores – were avoided for the most part. The rapaciousness to which contractors were later known to succumb on some large construction projects was largely restrained owing to the close supervision which was exercised by the military.[111]

The only serious difficulty in provisioning the Rideau Canal project was experienced during the winter of 1828-1829. Earlier, the extremely hot summer of 1828 had brought a poor harvest, which was reduced still further when the severe malaria epidemic of the late summer rendered many farmers in the Rideau Military Settlement too sick to harvest their standing crops. As a result, a severe food and forage shortage developed.[112] In the Rideau Military Settlement, the settlers managed to produce only one-half of the wheat which was required to meet their own needs. During the winter of 1828-29 the contractors – in securing provisions for the coming summer work season – were reduced to doubling their normal purchase of Indian corn and coarse grains, in a situation where: "grain of every description [was] not only high in price but almost impossible to be obtained".

On the lower Rideau and lower Cataraqui work sites, the Commissariat Department continued to supply the contractors with food provisions from the Montreal and Kingston depots, respectively, and a crisis was avoided. However, at the work sites in the interior, which depended almost totally on the bush settlers for the bulk of their provisions, a severe provisioning crisis developed.

Previously, some food provisions for the upper Rideau River work sites were imported via Prescott from the United States to meet any shortfalls in the quantity of local produce which was available for consumption, but as of January 1829 the situation deteriorated markedly. Flour and coarse grains were not available for purchase locally at any price. A.C. Stevens, the contractor at Merrick's Mills and Nicholson's Rapids on the upper Rideau River, calculated that he would have to import anywhere from 350 to 400 barrels of flour and 1,000 to 1,200 bushels of coarse grains from the United States to feed his workforce and draught animals during the 1829 work season, until the fall harvest.

In response to that crisis, Lt. Col. By sought to secure a remission of duties on imports, and failing that, permission to pay the cost of the duties out of the contingency account of the Rideau Canal estimate in order to maintain food prices at a reasonable level. Ultimately, permission was apparently received to import provisions duty free. During the 1829 work season, the canal workers were spared the deprivations which were experienced by the settlers in the surrounding districts following on the 1828-1829 winter of scarcity.[113]

At Bytown, a number of steps were taken to keep bread prices from rising out of control. During the first full year of construction, in 1827, the Bytown townsite had been totally transformed from a virtual wilderness to a settlement of over 2,000 inhabitants with numerous houses, several churches, a school, a market place, many stores, a butchery, and four bakeries.[114] To save on costs and to encourage local enterprise in Bytown, Lt. Col. By closed down the newly-erected government bakery. A contract was let – on a competitive bid – to one of the bakers, George Lang, to supply bread at a fixed price to the engineering establishment and military artisans of the Royal Sappers and Miners, with Lang free to sell to the canal workers in the open market together with the three independent bakers.

That situation had changed with the poor harvest of the fall of 1828. In fearing that the four bakers might combine to force up the price of the bread which was being sold to the canal workers, Lt. Col. By arranged for George Lang to take over the government ovens, which were superior to his own. Lang was given a thirty-year lease on the two ovens at a yearly rent of ten percent of the original cost of clearing the lot and building the government bakery. In return, he agreed to provide bread to the canal workers at the same price, and of the same quality, as furnished for the canal establishment under his fixed price contract. With that arrangement, all four bakeries continued to share in provisioning the workforce, but the agreement with Lang served to moderate bread prices in the open market at no cost to the Ordnance. Moreover, ultimately at the conclusion of the lease, the agreement would reimburse the Ordnance threefold for the cost of establishing the government ovens.

The price moderation system worked well initially, but during the 1828-1829 winter of scarcity the three independent bakers began to sell inferior bread at 3d. a quarter loaf more than Lang, who as a government contractor was able to purchase wheat from the Commissariat at cost plus transport from Montreal. In fairness to the other bakers, and to maintain moderate bread prices in Bytown where most of the householders were employed on or dependent on the canal project in one capacity or another, Lt. Col. By sought authorization to sell commissariat provisions to the public at cost plus transport. In that effort, he failed. The Ordnance rejected his proposal on the grounds that:

> "It never could be the intention of the Government
> to transform the King's Magazines into a provision
> store for the convenience of the public,...."[115]

Nonetheless, the agreement with baker Lang – and subsequently wheat imported from the United States – kept bread prices from soaring during the later months of the winter of scarcity, and during the following 1829 summer work season. In the fall 1829 the local harvest was good with wheat, corn, rye, barley, and oats in good supply, as well as pork.

During the following winter of 1829-30, with work continuing in strengthening the Hog's Back dam and in pushing forward rock excavation work at the Isthmus canal cut, provisions were plentiful and prices were maintained at what was considered to be a not unreasonable level.[116] Through the actions of Lt. Col. By, a severe provisioning crisis was successfully overcome with food prices, and hence wages, kept under control.

Wage Rates

Owing to the geographical isolation of the Rideau Canal project and the large number of labourers and artificers required to construct the canal, the keeping of wages at a reasonable level was a serious concern from the commencement of construction. Whether carried on in isolated areas of Upper Canada, the United States or Britain, large construction projects employing thousands of men almost invariably resulted in high cost provisions, miserable working conditions, and severe destitution among unemployed labourers during the winter season. Work seasons were often punctuated with innumerable work stoppages and strikes that pushed wages to exceptionally high levels by local standards, with little real benefit to the workers.[117]

In Upper Canada, a complex situation existed with respect to wage rates. In the towns, the wage rates for labourers were high – ranging from 3s. to 4s. per diem – with the higher rates prevailing in the western part of the province. However, labourers had to secure their own provisions and accommodations on the open market, the work was seasonal, and steady employment was not to be had.[118]

On the Rideau project, labourers were paid from 2s.6d. to 3s.6d. per diem depending on the nature of the work which was undertaken; and somewhat less where the contractors provided room and board on site in bunkhouses.[119] The prospect of steady employment at these rates was sufficient to induce labourers to emigrate from Britain to seek work on the canal, as well as to attract labourers from the Rideau Military Settlement and the St. Lawrence Front settlements, and French Canadian labourers from Lower Canada.[120]

To attract artificers, moderately high wages were paid in keeping with the prevailing provincial rate. The pay was 5s. to 5s.6d. per diem for carpenters, 5s. to 6s.6d. for masons, and 5s. to 6s. for smiths and sawyers.[121] In Bytown, overseers built their own homes and the artificers boarded in private homes. In the interior, the artificers were boarded with settlers in the bush or lived in cabins which were separate from the bunkhouses where the labourers were accommodated. Owing to the large number of artificers required on the project, some difficulty was experienced in replacing the skilled workers who succumbed to malaria.[122]

Canal workers who were employed directly by the military on the Bytown to Hog's Back canal excavation, and at the Hog's Back, were paid regularly each Saturday. Thus, they avoided the indebtedness and destitution to which labourers were often reduced when paid only intermittently at greater intervals on many construction projects.[123] More generally, the workers were customarily paid monthly by the contractors; however, not all of the labourers on the Rideau project were so fortunate. At least one of the contractors, Philemon Wright & Sons, who employed mostly French Canadian labourers, paid his men only after payment was received from the Commissary for the measured work completed, or at the end of the period covered by the service contract signed by a particular group of workers.[124]

Although the high price of land precluded the Irish pauper immigrant labourers from leaving to engage in bush farming, some land did become available at the work sites. It was on the land which surrounded the work sites where Lt. Col. By cleared back the forest cover 250 feet in 1828, and later 300 to 400 feet, to increase air circulation in an effort to combat malaria.[125] The landless Irish immigrant labourers were permitted to take up small plots of land in these clearings for the planting of potatoes around the tree stumps, and soon they erected huts to house their families on site. Visitors to the Rideau Canal project commented to the effect that:

"most of them have their own little cabins to live

in, with a plot of ground to each, enough to grow
potatoes sufficient for their own consumption,
which is a consideration of some importance to
them".[126]

In growing their own potatoes, the Irish canal workers were able
to save on food costs and enjoy their traditional diet at a time
when provisions of all sorts had become readily available on the
Rideau Canal project.

Moreover, winters proved far less daunting for the pauper Irish
immigrant labourers. None of the landless labourers and their
families were to experience the utter deprivation, acute suffering,
and hopelessness of the Irish Catholic immigrant labourers
and their families who had huddled together on the outskirts
of Kingston in the winter of 1827-1828. As the Rideau Canal
project progressed, work was undertaken on the Hog's Back dam
each winter, and as of the winter of 1829-1830 on the canal
excavation at the Isthmus summit level. Work was also continued
year round at the quarry sites in clearing the overburden,
quarrying and rough cutting the large blocks of stones for the
arched keywork masonry dams and the canal locks, and in
transporting the stone blocks on sleds which were pulled by
horses or oxen to the work sites over winter snow roads.[127]

Moreover, on the Rideau Canal project, more and more winter
work was undertaken to make up for the time which was lost
to malaria during the summer work seasons, and to avoid
having to work at the more sickly sites during subsequent
malarial seasons. In effect, winter work provided a solution to
the winter unemployment problem for the landless labourers
through furnishing large numbers of Irish immigrants with
accommodation and provisions on a work site during the winter
months, and with good wages. Hence, they were able to purchase
winter clothing and blankets for themselves and their families, as
well as provisions for their families who were sheltered on or off
the work site.

Figure 8. "Settlement on Long Island on the Rideau River, Upper Canada, 17 Augt. 1830". Lt. Col. James Pattison Cockburn, R.A., watercolour. Primitive cabins, with a peeled tree bark roof covering and no chimney, erected by immigrant canal labourers in utilizing the piles of logs left by axemen in clearing back the forest from the work site to combat the 'fever and ague'. (Royal Ontario Museum).

As of February 1829, a petition was signed by some 635 Irish canal workers who were employed on the lower Rideau section of the canal project. The petitioners expressed their approval for a proposed new assisted-emigration scheme that the British government had in contemplation for introduction in Ireland. The canal workers asked that the benefits of such a program – if, and when established – be extended to their relatives back in Ireland, as well as to themselves and other landless immigrants who were labouring on the Rideau Canal works. Under the proposed scheme, Irish emigrants were to be provided with free passage to British North America, a grant of 100 acres of land for each family and rations for a year to settle on the land, with the cost to be repaid to the British government in annual instalments from the produce of the new farms.

The petitioners attested to the impoverished situation of their relatives back in Ireland, and the need for such a program. It was noted that without government assistance, it was practically impossible for poor immigrants on their own, "without money or friends", to establish themselves on a bush farm. They asserted that: "On the whole we most certainly conclude that the Poor Man's situation is bettered by emigrating to Canada, as our own personal experience has fully convinced us".

What remained unsaid was that these men, and their families, were benefiting from working on a British government canal construction project, and from the paternalistic acts of Lt. Col. John By, the Commanding Royal Engineer. However, as it turned out, no such assisted emigration program was forthcoming from the British government, owing to the heavy flow of unassisted British emigration into Canada at that time.[128]

Each summer, large numbers of British immigrants turned up on the Rideau Canal project seeking work as part of a chain migration in following their relatives to Canada. In the case of the Irish immigrants, that influx was stimulated by letters which were sent home from some of the canal workers who were literate, and by notices that were posted in the towns of Ireland by timber ship owners. The former held out the prospect of immediate employment on the Rideau Canal project at good wages, and the latter enticed potential emigrants with an inflated promise of wages sufficient to purchase a farm in but a short period to time.[129]

On his part, Lt. Col. By did everything possible to encourage the canal workers to save their money for the eventual purchase of land upon leaving the canal project. In August 1829, he proposed that the canal workers be permitted to deposit their savings in the Military Chest at Bytown for safe keeping by the Commissary Department, with the workers to be paid a 4% interest on their money upon withdrawal. However, that proposal was rejected by the Commissary General on the grounds that there were no military regulations in place that would permit it; and that the Commissary was not a savings bank, nor equipped to handle banking transactions.[130]

Where the Irish Catholic pauper immigrant labourers were concerned, Lt. Col. By was particularly anxious about their future welfare. To facilitate their settlement onto the land, and to promote the clearing of the wilderness lands along the canal, he submitted a proposal to the Board of Ordnance. It was that the British Government be approached to purchase the Crown Reserves and the Clergy Reserves in the townships along the canal route; and that once procured they be leased to landless canal workers in 50 acres lots at a low annual rent with the better settlers subsequently to be offered 200 acre lots.[131] In the township surveys, the Clergy Reserve lots accounted for 1/7 of the land, and the Clergy Reserve lots for another 1/7 of the township lands. If the reserve lots were purchased by the British Government, as recommended by Lt. Col. By, it would have made over 28 percent of the land in each township along the Rideau waterway available for settlement by the landless Irish immigrant canal labourers. However, that proposal was not acted upon by either the Colonial Officer or the provincial government of Upper Canada.

Nonetheless, through working on the Rideau Canal project some labourers were able to save up to half their wages, and the wage rates were sufficient to enable the more provident to gain sufficient monies to make a down payment on land in Upper Canada.[132]   However, there were other labourers who became heavily indebted to company stores, despite the best efforts of the military to protect the canal workers from being exploited.[133] Overall, the labourers and artificers who were employed on the Rideau Canal project, and the settlers, merchants, tradesmen and millers who came to reside in the Rideau corridor, benefited greatly from the canal project. In a period of just over six years, the British government expended £822,844 in hard currency on the construction of the Rideau Canal.[134] Not all benefited equally from that expenditure, but the alternative for landless, unemployed immigrant labourers was destitution and distress in the Canadian climate, and the ever present spectre of death from disease or starvation.

Maintaining Order

Through offering steady employment during the summer work season at moderate wages, and year-round employment for many canal workers, plentiful provisions at fair prices, medical care for the sick and injured and financial support for their families, and land on which to erect huts and establish garden plots, Lt. Col. By succeeded in conciliating the Irish Catholic pauper immigrants. After the spring of 1827, strikes and labour unrest were no longer a problem, and the behaviour of the former destitute immigrants was totally transformed. Once in robust health, the Irish labourers proved to be exceptionally good workers with pick, shovel, and wheelbarrow in doing the heavy excavation work.

Non-working hours were spent in drinking at the work sites, or in local taverns such as Mother McGinty's in Corktown where the men imbibed whisky, beer, and Jamaican rum.[135] However, heavy drinking was endemic amongst all of the canal workers who were labouring in the bush amidst swarms of black flies each spring and mosquitoes all summer long. At some work sites, canal workers purchased a gallon of whisky a week, and company stores made substantial profits by obtaining large quantities of whisky from the settlers at 2s. per gallon for resale at 2s.9d. to the canal labourers.[136] Potato whisky was produced in large quantities in all of the newly-established bush settlements, and it was viewed by those who witnessed its illeffects as:

> "... the absolute poison of Upper Canada – the laudanum that sends thousands of settlers to their eternal rest every season. ...this infernal liquid gets hold of and overcomes so many of them.... No hell broth that the witches concocted of yore, can equal it."[137]

Nonetheless, despite the continued heavy consumption of alcohol, the savage brawls and drunken rioting of the Irish Catholic labourers in the spring of 1827 were not repeated. At Bytown, disputes were settled each Saturday afternoon in a boxing ring with bare knuckles for the entertainment of all concerned.[138] Thereafter the Irish Catholic labourers were directly involved in the several labour disturbances that did occur, but they were isolated incidents. None of the disturbances was connected with working conditions, or any supposed ill treatment of the canal workers. Moreover, with but one exception, it was the civil authorities who restored the peace, rather than the military.

On St. Patrick's Day, in March 1828, upwards of 200 Irish labourers from the Hog's Back paraded through Bytown carrying a green flag. Much drunkenness and fighting ensued, which escalated into a fullscale riot in which the Irish canal workers of Bytown fought against the Hog's Back Irish. One man was clubbed to death and a jury subsequently refused to convict the perpetrator, as one witness testified: "They were all Roman Catholics, so there could be no party complaints".

Such behaviour had shocked the new citizens of Bytown who acted immediately to elect a town council and magistracy.

Prominent among the newly-elected officials were members of the Rideau Canal engineering staff and several canal contractors, who were joined by the leading town merchants but newly established in Bytown. Thereafter, only one disturbance of note occurred in Bytown – a donnybrook at the first Bytown fair in July 1829. Fighting broke out following heavy drinking and a betting dispute over the winner of a horse race that ended in a dead heat.[139]

In the interior, disturbances were equally few and quickly settled. One disturbance was over the cutting of trees on private property by an Irish immigrant, Thomas Foley, who had sub-contracted to supply timber to the contractor at the Nicholson's Rapids work site. In September 1829, a constable who attempted to arrest Foley was assaulted and beaten by the Irish canal labourers. Subsequently, when a small sheriff's party returned with a warrant, they were attacked and driven off in a hail of stones. Thereafter, a 60-man body of militia was rushed to the work site from Burritt's Rapids – a Loyalist settlement in the bush along the lower Rideau River – and the ringleaders were arrested.[140]

Another such anomaly occurred in January 1830 at the Hog's Back where several men were violently assaulted in a feud amongst the Irish Catholic workers who were engaged in winter work in strengthening the newly-raised Hog's Back dam. One faction stole some gunpowder and blew up three cabins of the other faction. Thereafter the faction leaders were arrested and escorted to jail in Perth by a guard of soldiers who were sent from Bytown to prevent the culprits from being rescued by their fellows. In that manner, a potentially bloody feud was nipped in the bud, and further violence was avoided – a surprising accomplishment where Irish factionalism and feuds were concerned.[141]

More generally, on the Rideau Canal project, there was a remarkable absence of ethnic and religious conflict in a situation where all of the elements for violent strife were present. Through constant paternalistic efforts to improve the wellbeing of his workforce, Lt. Col. By managed to largely alleviate, if not totally eliminate, most of the causes of violent ethnic and religious strife that would plague many large canal construction projects elsewhere.

There was virtually no conflict between the Irish Catholics and Presbyterian Scots despite early signs of animosity between the two groups in the Rideau Military Settlement.[142] Neither were there any violent clashes between the Irish Catholic immigrant labourers and the French Canadian migrant labourers from Lower Canada.[143] Moreover, there were no reported violent encounters between the Corkmen and Connaughtmen among the Gaelic Irish immigrant labourers; yet those two factions would become notorious for vicious faction fighting on later Canadian canal projects.[144]

 Likewise, despite the presence of large numbers of Irish Ulster Protestants on the Rideau Canal project – the first Orange Lodge in Upper Canada was founded in 1824 at Perth – open strife between Irish Catholic labourers and Irish Protestants was all but nonexistent. There was a major outbreak of fighting at the Isthmus in December 1829 between the Orange and the Green, but it was over securing winter work, not religious differences. It was resolved by the officer in charge hiring both groups – a total of some 400 men – as dayworkers on the canal establishment. They were employed in the winter work, and subsequently as part of an even larger work force which was employed in excavating the Isthmus canal cut during the summer work season.[145] For the landless Irish Catholic labourers, the securing of winter work was critical to their very survival and that of their families; whereas for the Irish Protestants from the military settlement and the older settled areas, winter work presented an opportunity to secure cash for the purchase of extras such as tea and sugar, additional farming implements or domestic utensils, bolts of cloth, and/or a cow.

The general absence of labour unrest, riots, and violent ethnic and religious confrontations on the Rideau Canal project was attributable in part to the scattered nature of the work sites, which kept the labourers of the different ethno-religious groups apart. Moreover, the preference of the labourers themselves for working with their own ethnic group, faction, or coreligionists, resulted as well in potentially antagonistic groups working separately. However, geographic separation was only one factor in maintaining labour peace.[146]

There was an almost total absence of ethnic and religious strife on the Rideau Canal project, even at work sites where it was not possible to keep the different ethno-religious groups physically separate. For the most part, the absence of conflict can be attributable directly to the paternalistic efforts of Lt. Col. By to care for the health and well-being of the canal workers, and the even-handed fairness of the officers of the Corps of Royal Engineers in dealing with the canal workers, regardless of their religion or ethnicity. Such an approach removed potential causes of conflict, and calmed pre-existing ethnic and religious animosities.

It confirmed once again what observers had found surprising several years earlier in viewing the behaviour of the Irish Catholic immigrants who were placed in the Rideau Military Settlement under the poor relief-assisted emigration scheme of the Colonial Office. Where the Irish Catholic pauper immigrants were fairly treated, and "got quit of feelings of hopelessness and despair of ever bettering their condition", they had proved to be the easiest of all the immigrant groups to conciliate.[147]

The general absence of riots and strikes after the spring of 1827 attests to the success of Lt. Col. By in improving the lot of the workers and protecting them from exploitation. On the other hand, any serious discontent would have resulted in riots at the work sites. Had the canal labourers been motivated to riot, the small troop detachment at Bytown would have been incapable of maintaining order at upwards of thirty work sites scattered along an 125 mile long waterway.[148]

As early as the spring of 1830 – if not earlier – with three summer work seasons completed, and the canal project well on its way to completion, it was obvious to observers that Lt. Col. By had succeeded in assembling, provisioning, disciplining, and forging a large multicultural labour force which, in varying degrees of progress over time, had adapted well to the demands of living and working productively in a hostile wilderness environment.[149] On the Rideau Canal project, two serious problems remained intractable – malaria, which recurred each year from mid-August through September, and the difficulty of excavating a hard granite rock that was being encountered on the upper Rideau and Cataraqui sections of the canal.[150] However, the labour unrest that had plagued the canal project at the commencement of construction, had been overcome to the benefit of all concerned.

Conclusion

Labour historians have tended to interpret the living and working conditions on the Rideau Canal project through focussing on the 'poverty, distress, and disease' in evidence at the very commencement of construction.[151] In doing so, they have ignored the fact that these conditions prevailed initially when a large influx of destitute Irish Catholic immigrants – many emaciated and in ill-health – turned up at a wilderness work site before the infrastructure and supply system, which was needed for housing and provisioning a large workforce, could be put in place. What has been further ignored is that Lt. Col. John By, the Commanding Royal Engineer, strove continually – as the Rideau Canal project evolved – to alleviate the suffering of the canal workers and to provide for their basic needs; and that his paternalistic efforts were ultimately successfully in greatly improving the living conditions, health, and welfare of the immigrant canal workers.

Under the contract system of construction, it was the contractors who were responsible for housing and provisioning their workers, and for providing medical care to the ill or injured; yet Lt. Col. By did not hesitate to do whatever he could – far beyond his prescribed duties and responsibilities – to alleviate the suffering of the canal workers and to provide for their physical, material, and moral welfare.

Every effort was made to provide health care for the canal workers and their families, to ensure that provisions were readily available at moderate prices, to provide employment for the debilitated timber ship immigrants to enable them to gain a sustenance, to maintain wages at a moderate level, to eradicate drunkenness and fighting at work sites by restricting access to alcohol during working hours, to make land available for landless immigrant labourers to occupy during the construction of the canal, and lastly, to facilitate the landless labourers in saving their money for the purchase of land for their permanent settlement. Not all of these efforts were fully successful; yet the paternalism of Lt. Col. By did much to alleviate the 'poverty, distress, and disease' that had marked the situation of a good many of the Irish Catholic pauper immigrants and their families upon their arrival on the canal construction project.

The one intractable problem was the scourge of malaria, which struck the Rideau Canal project each summer work season. However, in keeping with the state of the medical knowledge of the day, a sustained effort was made to reduce the suffering from the 'fever and ague' by eliminating the miasma emanating from the swamps and drowned lands along the waterway. Swamps and marshes were drained and the forest cover was cut back to increase air circulation. Costly winter work was undertaken to avoid having to push forward work during the sickly seasons at the worst afflicted sites, and the height of the dams was raised – in so far as was practicable – to reduce the depth of the canal excavations at the sickly sites. These efforts greatly reduced the impact of malaria on the canal workers, and the mortality rate, during the construction of the canal. And ultimately – once the canal waters were fully raised to flood out the swamps and marsh lands – malaria was successful eradicated from the waterway.

Despite the labour challenges which were faced on the Rideau

Canal project, Lt. Col. John By succeeded in assembling, supervising, maintaining and provisioning a robust, multicultural workforce that, at the height of construction each summer, numbered as many as 4,000 men. Although the workforce was scattered at some thirty separate work sites – throughout a 125-mile tract of a heavily-forested wilderness – he managed to achieve and maintain labour peace through his sustained paternalistic effort to improve working conditions and the health of workers on the canal project, while striving to provide provisions at fair market prices and to ensure that the workers received good, but moderate wages.

Through such paternalistic practices Lt. Col. By managed to ease ethnic animosities, and prevented the development of ethno-religious conflicts. On the Rideau Canal project there was a complete absence of the violent clashes that would occur later between the French Canadians and the Irish Catholics in the timber trade on the Ottawa River during the 1830s, and of the vicious faction fighting that raged later between the Irish Catholic Corkmen and Connaughtmen on Canadian canal construction projects during the 1840s.

The 'poverty, distress, and disease' highly in evidence amongst the Irish pauper immigrant canal workers at the commencement of construction was not representative of the labour situation on the entire project through to its completion in May 1832, or of the Irish Catholic labour experience more generally on the Rideau Canal project. Labour historians have erred in seeing the conditions and suffering experienced by the Irish Catholic pauper immigrants in the spring of 1827 at Bytown, and in the fall of 1827 at Kingston, as indicative of what transpired on the Rideau Canal project as a whole. In so doing, they have categorized the labour situation on the canal project as having been similar in nature to what labourers suffered on later Canadian canal construction projects of the 1840s when working conditions were truly abysmal; canal workers terribly exploited; and labour unrest suppressed by military force.[152]

Moreover, Labour historians have neglected to take into account the natural and physical environment through which the Rideau Canal was being constructed. The disease and distress suffered by the canal workers on the canal construction project was attributable largely to their living and working in a wilderness environment amongst malarial swamps. As such, their afflictions were common to everyone – settlers included – living and working in that environment. However, for the canal workers that suffering was alleviated to a significant degree by the actions of Lt. Col. John By.

In contrast, the subsequent canal projects of the 1840s were constructed in a much more hospitable and salubrious environments and were close to established villages, markets, and transportation infrastructures – both road and water. However, on the later canal construction projects it was not the natural and physical environment, but the abysmal working and living conditions and low wages that were imposed by the contractors that bred poverty, distress, disease and unrest amongst the canal workers.

Whether motivated by a sense of noblesse oblige, Christian charity, humanitarianism, or simply self-interest to facilitate the construction of the canal, the paternalistic practices which were introduced by Lt. Col. John By on the Rideau Canal project were far from being an anomaly on canal projects during the opening decades of the 19th Century.[153] In that earlier period, paternalism was widely practised on North American canal construction projects and greatly benefited the canal workers – at least until a canal company ran out of money to pay the contractors, who in turn ceased to pay the workers. Only with the onset of the 1837 depression and the subsequent formation of a large surplus labour pool generated by the massive Irish Catholic emigration during the Great Famine years of the potato blight, 1845-1850, would the labour situation on Canadian canals change dramatically.

At that later juncture, paternalism gave way to a cash nexus governing labour relations on canal projects, and canal workers and their families were reduced to a permanent state of abject poverty, deprivation, disease, and squalor. Unfortunately, it was Irish Catholic immigrant workers – who came to comprise almost the entire labour force on subsequent canal projects – who would suffer severely from that transformation in labour relations. In contrast, earlier on the Rideau Canal project, labour conditions were entirely different, and a robust multi-cultural workforce benefited greatly from the paternalist practices introduced by Lt. Col. John By, the Commanding Royal Engineer.[154]

Generally speaking, historians have failed to appreciate that the Rideau Canal project was a godsend in providing thousands of landless labourers with a steady employment at good wage rates at a time of heavy immigration into Canada, and especially so during a time of depression in the timber trade and of a labour surplus in Lower Canada. The canal construction project created new villages, brought the development of a local market- oriented agriculture through providing a ready market for the produce of farmers during the construction period, made possible the settlement of a hitherto sickly wilderness area, introduced a cash economy in place of a barter economy, and a market-oriented agriculture in place of a subsistence agriculture. Moreover, subsequently the Rideau Canal steamboat waterway – in forming part of an uninterrupted water communication linking Lake Ontario and the ocean ports of Montreal and Quebec – fostered the settlement and development of trade and commerce both in the Rideau corridor and in the Province of Upper Canada more generally.

Endnotes

1. Library and Archives Canada (LAC), MG13, WO44, Vol. 18, reel B-1294, 72, Major General Sir James Carmichael Smyth, R.E., "Memorandum as to the formation of the Rideau Canal between the Ottawa River and Kingston upon Lake Ontario", 14 March 1826. The Board of Ordnance was headed by a Master General, and was responsible for producing gunpowder, guns, and munitions for the army and naval forces of Great Britain, and for constructing

fortifications, as well as transportation facilities when required. In addition, the Ordnance was responsible for the education and command of the Corps of Royal Engineers and the Royal Artillery, for the topographical survey of Great Britain, and for the raising of the artificer companies of the Royal Sappers and Miners, who were placed under the command of officers of the Royal Engineers. In 1823, the Ordnance also took over responsibility for the construction and maintenance of Army barracks.

2. LAC, RG5, A1, Vol. 70, C-4614, pp. D37269 - D37388, Commissioners of Internal Navigation, "Third General Report", 5 February 1825. See also a printed transcript in Ken W. Watson, *Engineered Landscapes, the Rideau Canal's Transformation of a Wilderness Waterway* (Elgin, Ontario: Ken W. Watson, 2006), 116-132.

3. LAC, RG8, Series C, Vol. 42, C-2617, 103, By to Major General Darling, 2 October 1826.

4. Legget, *Rideau Waterway*, 35-39; and Ross, *Ottawa: Past and Present* (Toronto: Musson Book Company Ltd., 1927), 1819.

5. LAC, MG 13, WO 44, Vol. 19, B-1294, 88-89, By to General Mann, 7 July 1827.

6. LAC, RG8, Series C, Vol. 42, C-2617, 103, By to Major General Darling, Military Secretary, 2 October 1826.

7. See, for example, the *Montreal Gazette*, 12 and 19 February 1827, "Government Contract"; and *The Albion, or British Colonial and Foreign Weekly Gazette* (New York), 24 and 31 March 1827, "Rideau Canal", pp. 327 & 335. See also LAC, MG13, WO44, Vol. 19, B-1294, 10-11, By to General Mann, 1 October 1826.

8. Robert W. Passfield, "Ordnance Supply Problems in the Canadas: The Quest for an Improved Military Transport System, 1814-1828", *HSTC Bulletin, Journal of the History of Canadian Science, Technology and Medicine*, Vol. V, No. 3, September 1981, 189190.

9. Eric Jarvis, "Military Land Granting in Upper Canada, following the War of 1812", *Ontario History*, LXVII, No. 3, September 1975, 122-134; Josephine Smith, *Perth-on-Tay: A tale of the Transplanted Highlanders* (Merrickville:

Mortimer Co. Printers, 1987 reprint); and Jean S. McGill, *A Pioneer History of the County of Lanark* (Toronto: T.H. Best, 3rd printing, 1970); and Verna Ross McGiffin, *Pakenham, Ottawa Valley Village, 1823-1860* (Pakenham: Mississippi Publishers, 1963). See also, Wendy Cameron, "Selecting Peter Robinson's Irish Emigrants", *Histoire Sociale/Social History*, Vol. 9, no. 17, May 1976, 24-46; and Lillian F. Gates, *Land Policies of Upper Canada* (Toronto: University of Toronto Press, 1968), 85-97. Of the assisted-emigration Scots who arrived in 1815, it was the Presbyterian Scots who settled in Perth; the Roman Catholic Highlanders chose to settle along the upper St. Lawrence River near their kith and kin in Glengarry County.

10. Smith, *Perth on the Tay,* 255-263; and A Backswoodsman [Dr. William Dunlop], *Statistical Sketches of Upper Canada, For the Use of Emigrants* (London: John Murray, 1832), 67. In the military settlements as of 1826, Bathurst township was producing 4,826 bushels of potatoes, 21,469 bushels of grain, and 11,145 bushels of turnips; and Ramsay township was producing 2/3s of that quantity. The other back townships – Huntley, Goulbourn, Pakenham, Beckwith, and Lanark produced somewhat less than 1/10 of the Bathurst township totals (McGill, *Pioneer History*, 100).

11. Pentland, *Labour and Capital in Canada,* 101-102. Prior to 1817 emigrants paid a flat rate of £10 for each adult and child for passage to New York. After that date, Canadian timber ships carried immigrants to Quebec for £2 or less for each adult, three children being covered by one adult fare. Dunlop confirms that passage to New York on a packet ship, without provisions, cost $40.00, as opposed to less than 40 shillings to Quebec on a timber ship (*Dunlop, Statistical Sketches*, 1832, 91-92).

12. Helen I. Cowan, *British Emigration to British North America, The First Hundred Years* (Toronto: University of Toronto Press, 1961): 38, 49-50 & 82. In 1819 emigration from the British Isles to British North America jumped to 25,000 persons, but that year was an aberration. It has been estimated that 3/4s of the Irish emigrants who left for North America in the postwar decade, 1815-1825, were Protestants and dissenters, and about 1/4 were Catholics; almost all of the Irish emigrants in this period were from Ulster and the adjoining northern counties. However, the Irish Catholics tended to go to Newfoundland, the Maritime provinces, and the United States; whereas the Anglo-Irish Anglicans, who comprised a large number of the Irish Protestant emigrants, preferred to settle in Canada under the British form of government.

See: Cecil J. Houston & William J. Smyth, *Irish Emigration and Canadian Settlement Patterns, Links & Letters* (Toronto: University of Toronto Press, 1990): 31, 46, 71-72.. The Scots-Irish Presbyterians of Ulster settled in the United States, Canada, and the Maritime provinces.

Generally speaking, the Irish Catholic tenant farmers and tradesmen of Ulster were too poor to emigrate to North America, unless aided by a landlord anxious to remove his tenants. In total, the number of Irish immigrants arriving at Quebec several years prior to the commencement of the Rideau Canal project, ranged from 5,580 in 1820, to 4,041 in 1821, to 8,413 in 1823 to 5,168 in 1824; and a very large majority of the Irish immigrants were Protestants. (William Forbes Adams, *Ireland and Irish Emigration to the New World from 1815 to the Famine* (Baltimore: Genealogical Publishing Co. Inc., 1980, 1st printing 1932): 139-145.

13. Pentland, *Labour and Capital*, 101-102, and 115; and Dunlop, *Statistical Sketches*, 6263. Large numbers of Ulster Protestants and Scots immigrants were employed on the Lachine Canal (1821-1824) project at Montreal, but after securing some capital from wage labour for a summer, they moved on to take up land in Upper Canada (Pentland, 103). The Irish immigrants who flocked to canal projects in the Canadas during the 1820s were predominantly Ulster Protestants, but during the 1830s the canal labourers were increasingly Munster and Connaught Catholics. See Bryan D. Palmer, *Working-Class Experience, The Rise and Reconstruction of Canadian Labour, 1800-1980* (Toronto: Butterworth & Co., 1983), 36. Contemporaries did not note any heavy Irish Catholic immigration into Upper Canada until the mid-1820s (Dunlop, *Statistical Studies*, 99-100).

14. Pentland, *Labour and Capital*, 103. During the 1820s Ulster and the adjacent counties in Connaught and Leinster, remained the main centre of Irish emigration, but by the 1830s a significant emigration had developed as well from the ports of the western and southern provinces of Ireland – Connaught; Munster; and Leinster – to the port of Quebec. Protestants continued to predominate during this wave of emigration as well. (Houston & Smyth, *Irish Emigration*, 31-32.) However, it appears that it was during this transition period that large numbers of Irish Catholics first began arriving in Upper Canada, concurrent with the construction of the Rideau Canal. construction project.

15. Dunlop, *Statistical Sketches*, 1832, 63 & 67-68; Pentland, *Labour and*

Capital, 103; Captain Basil Hall, R.N., *Travels in North America in the years 1827 and 1828,* Vol. I (Edinburgh: Cadell and Co.,1829), 298-299; and LAC, MG 24, I 9, 327, Anon. [Dr. A. J. Christie], "To my friend Billy Tyrconnel in the United States". A number of Americans also came to Bytown in the fall of 1826, but they soon left to secure work on American canal projects closer to home (*ibid*). In the early years of the military settlement, men had migrated to the Erie Canal project to secure summer work. See Edward Shortt, ed., *Perth Remembered* (Perth: Mortimer Ltd., 1967), 30-31.

16. Fernand Ouellet, *Lower Canada 1791-1840, Social Change and Nationalism*, transl. Patricia Claxton (Toronto: McClelland and Stewart, 1980), 117-157. See also T. J. A. Le Goff, "The Agricultural Crisis in Lower Canada 1802-12: A Review of a Controversy", *Canadian Historical Review*, Vol. LV, March 1974, 1-31. The Lower Canadian shipbuilding industry, centred on Quebec, was also in recession between 1825 and 1834, throwing many skilled and unskilled workers out of work (Ouellet, 178).

17. David Lee, *Lumber Kings & Shantymen, Logging and Lumbering in the Ottawa Valley* (Toronto: James Lorimer & Co. Ltd, 2006), 15-16 & 2-23;and Arthur R. M. Lower, *Great Britain's Woodyard, British America and the Timber Trade, 1763-1867* (Montreal: McGillQueen's Press, 1973) , 67 & 71-72.

18. Ross, *Ottawa: Past and Present*, 97-99.

19. Wylie, "Poverty, Distress, and Disease", 12. Extant ledgers show that about 75% of the workers on the Wright family's Burritt's Rapids worksite were French Canadians, including both artificers and labourers, and about 2/3's of John Redpath's workers at Jones' Falls likewise (*ibid*). Presumably most of Wright's workforce on the first Dow's Swamp mound raising were French Canadians, as well Jean-Baptiste St. Louis's men working on the second Dow's Swamp mound. At the Hog's Back under the American contractor, Walter Fenelon, most of the labourers appear to have been Irish Catholics. (Ross, *Ottawa: Past and Present*, 109). Pentland (*Labour and Capital*, 105), states that few of the pauper Irish Catholics were craftsmen. They were mostly displaced tenant farmers suited primarily for unskilled labour.

20. Helen I. Cowan, *British Emigration to British North America, The First Hundred Years* (Toronto: University of Toronto Press, 1961): 184; and Captain J.E. Alexander, *Transatlantic Sketches, comprising visits to the Most Interesting Scenes in North and South America and the West Indies with Notes on Negro*

Slavery and Canadian Emigration. Vol. II (London: Richard Bentley, 1833): 187 & 215. Alexander gives a round number of 2,000 immigrant labourers securing work on the Rideau Canal each year; he states that they commonly spent only one year on the canal project before proceeding farther west to settle on the land. If Alexander's figure of 2,000 immigrant labourers finding work on the Rideau Canal each year is accurate, and Cowan's cited figure of 2,700 immigrants finding work on the Rideau Canal in 1829 is representative of most years, then presumably some 700 immigrant artificers must have secured work on the Rideau Canal each year. Such numbers are exclusive of the French Canadian migrant workers, and the settlers of the Rideau Military Settlement and the St. Lawrence Front, who secured work on the canal project during summer work seasons as labourers, and in some cases as artificers for those with a trade.

21. John P. Heisler, *The Canals of Canada* (Ottawa: National Historic Sites Services, 1973): 57.

22. Cowan, *British Emigration*, 289, Appendix B, Table II, "Arrivals at the Port of Quebec from the British Isles, Europe, and the Maritime Colonies, 1829-1859".

23. Pentland, *Labour and Capital*, 101-102; Cecil J. Houston & William J. Smyth, *Irish Emigration and Canadian Settlement, Patterns, Links & Letters* (Toronto: University of Toronto Press, 1990): 23-26 & 71-72; and Captn. J.E. Alexander, *Transatlantic Sketches, comprising Visits to the Most Interesting Scenes in North and South America and the West Indies with Notes on Negro Slavery and Canadian Emigration*, Vol. II (London: Richard Bentley, 1833):213-218.

24. The popular myth that the labourers on the Rideau Canal project were principally Irish Catholics, is totally false. On later Canadian canal projects – during the massive Irish emigration of the Great Potato Famine years from 1845 to 1850, and thereafter – Irish Catholic immigrants monopolize the labour work, but that was not the case on the earlier canal projects. Another myth is that the Irish Protestants in Canada (Upper and Lower Canada) were primarily Scotch-Irish Presbyterians. To the contrary, Houston & Smyth maintain that the Irish Protestants who settled in Canada were predominately Anglicans; and that Canada differs from the United States where the Irish Protestant settlement experience is identified with the Scotch-Irish Presbyterians. The Anglo-Irish Anglicans who settled in Canada were drawn mostly from Ulster and the adjoining northern counties, but also from

Protestant settlements in Munster and south Leinster; all of which were the most economically advanced agricultural and commercial centres of Ireland. (Houston & Smyth, *Irish Emigration and Canadian Settlement*, 8). However, oddly enough Houston & Smyth examine the Irish immigration experience in Canada simply in terms of an Irish Protestant and Irish Catholic dichotomy, and make no effort to distinguish Anglo-Irish Anglican areas of settlement from Scotch-Irish Presbyterian areas of settlement. Where the Rideau Canal project is concerned, presumably Anglo-Irish Anglicans immigrants comprised a significant component of the Irish Protestant labourers, but to date no record has been found that specifically mentions Anglican labourers.

25. Mactaggart, *Three Years in Canada: An Account of the Actual State of the Country in 1826-7-8 comprehending its resources, productions, improvements, and Capabilities and including Sketches of the State of Society, Advice to Emigrants, etc.* (London: Henry Colburn, 1829), Vol. I, 159-162; and LAC, RG8, Series C, Vol. 42, C-2617, 103, By to Major General Darling, Military Secretary, 2 October 1826.

26. LAC, RG 8, Series C, Vol. 43, C-2617, 65-66, C.I. Forbes, Deputy Commissary General, Montreal, to Peter Turquand, Commissary General, Quebec, 30 January 1827. As early as March 1827, some 2,774 lbs of flour, 6,600 lbs of salt pork, and 47 barrels of rum were forwarded to Wright's Town for the Rideau Canal project,(*ibid*, vol. 45, C-2618, 201, "Statement of provisions furnished the Royal Engineer Department by the Commissariat Department", 7 June 1828.

27. LAC, MG 13, WO 55, Vol. 863, B-2809, 70, By to Respective Officers, Quebec, 1 November 1826; and PAC, MG24, I9, Vol. 21, 5582 "Extract from *The Examiner*, Perth", 26 November 1830.

28. LAC, RG8, Series C, Vol. 43, C-2618, 181-182, By to Colonel Durnford, 4 May 1827; and MG13, WO44, Vol. 19, B-1294, 96. By to Sir P. Maitland, 15 May 1827.

29. LAC, MG24, I9, Hill Collection, vol. 2, Christie Correspondence, 376, Dr. A. J. Christie to Lt. Col. By, 31 February 1827, and 329, John Mactaggart to Dr. Christie, 2 February 1827. See also vol. 6, Christie Miscellaneous, 1982, Voucher: 15 June 1827, and Contract: 21 September 1826. The "Monthly returns of disease and casualties" are in volume 6 for May through December 1827, inclusive. No statement has been found of the medicines administered.

30. LAC, RG 8, Series C, Vol. 43, C-2618, 181-182, By to Colonel Durnford, 4 May 1827; MG 13, WO 44, Vol. 19, B-1294, 96, By to Sir P. Maitland, 15 May 1827; and Ross, *Ottawa: Past and Present*, 95-97.

31. *The Gleaner*, (Niagara), 17 March 1827, "Rideau Canal"; RG 8, Series C, Vol. 43, C-2618, 212-213, Major General Darling, 12 April 1827; Mactaggart, *Three Years in Canada*, Vol. I, 160; and McGill, *Pioneer History*, 77-78.

32. LAC, RG 8, Series C, Vol. 43, C-2618, 212-213, By to Major General Darling, 12 April 1827. Lt. Col. By wanted the Commissariat to send the blankets up on the first steamboat of the spring, scheduled to leave Lachine on April 23rd; but the blankets apparently were not sent that early. In the spring of 1827, Dr. A.J. Christie saw little evidence of anything being done to ameliorate the suffering of the Irish immigrant workers (MG 24, I 9, 318, "To my friend Billy Tyrconnel in the United States", n.d. [spring 1827].)

33. LAC, RG 8, Series C, Vol. 43, C-2618, 212-213, By to Major General Darling, 12 April 1827; and RG8, Series C, Vol. 43, C-2618, 211, "Progress Report of the Works carried on by the Royal Engineer Department between 21 September 1826 and 21 January 1827", Lt. Col. By, January 1827; and MG 24, A12, Section 3, A-534, Dalhousie Muniments, n.p., Lt. H. Pooley to Lord Dalhousie, 10 June 1827.

34. Ross, *Ottawa: Past and Present*, pp. 96-97; LAC, RG8, Series C, Vol. 43, C-2618, 212-213, By to Major General Darling, 12 April 1827; and Brault, *Ottawa: Old and New*, 58.

35. Mactaggart, *Three Years in Canada*, Vol. II, 243-244, and 251; LAC, RG 5, A1, Upper Canada Sundries, Vol. 84, C-6863, 45755, Andrew Wilson, Bytown, to Major George Hillier, 18 May 1827; and MG 24, I 9, 317, [Dr. A.J. Christie], "To my friend Billy Tyrconnel in the United States", n.d. [spring of 1827]. The quote is from Christie. The crude hovels erected by the Irish Catholic pauper immigrants were typical of the "tilts" and "dug-outs" found in impoverished areas of Ireland at that time. See John J. Mannion, *Irish Settlements in Eastern Canada: A Study of Cultural Transfer and Adaptation* (Toronto: University of Toronto Press, 1974), 143-144.

36. LAC, RG 5, Vol. 83, C-6863, 45220-45224, Captain Andrew Wilson to Major General Hillier, 4 April 1827; and Vol. 184, 45755-45758, Wilson to Hillier, 18 May 1827. Owing to the high wages rates and scarcity of labour

in Upper Canada, new immigrants often developed an inflated view of the worth of their labour, demanding exorbitant wages (Russell, "Wage Labour Rates", 65). In many ways, the bellicose, drunken and lawless behaviour of the Irish Catholic immigrant labourers in the spring of 1827 was the same as that of Irish navvies under desperate working and living conditions on English and Scottish railway construction projects. See Terry Coleman, *The Railway Navvies, A History of the Men who made the railways* (London: Penguin Books, 1981), 23, 28, 30, 93, 104-106, 120 & 141.

37. LAC, RG8, Series C, vol. 43, C-2618, 212-213, By to Major General Darling, 12 April 1827.

38. LAC, RG 8, Series C, Vol. 43, C-2618, 212-214, By to Major General Darling, 12 April 1827; MG 24, A 12, Section 3, A-534, n.p., Pooley to Lord Dalhousie, 10 June 1827; and Brault, *Ottawa: Old and New*, 49. Two companies of Royal Sappers and Miners, totalling 162 men, eventually served on the Rideau Canal project. In November 1826, Lt.Col. By had planned to station a Sergeant and 12 men at Bytown to guard the stores and military chest (LAC, RG8, Series C, Vol. 43, C-2618, pp. 13-14, By to Col. Durnford, 22 November 1826). In view of the spring disturbances, that detachment was increased to 30 men (*ibid*, Vol. 44, 138, By to General Mann, 22 October 1827).

39. LAC, RG 5, Al, Vol. 89, C-6865, 49204, By to General Mann, 10 June 1828. As late as April 1831, an attempt to set up a tavern beside the Entrance Valley work site was thwarted by a sergeant's guard sent by Lt. Col. By (Brault, *Ottawa: Old and New*, 82).

40. LAC, MG24, I9, Vol. 2, 330, Dr. Christie to Sir [Lt. Col. By], 12 February 1827.

41. LAC, MG 24, I 9, Vol. 2, 375, Dr. A.J. Christie to Lt. Col. By, 17 October 1827, "Returns of the Diseases and casualties", and 376, Christie to By, 31 October 1827; MG 13, WO 44, Vol. 15, B-217, 18, By to General Mann, 8 September 1828; and Mactaggart, *Three Years in Canada*, vol. II, 20. See also MG24, I9, vol. 6, 1987-1994, "Returns of the Diseases and casualties", for 1 May to 30 September, and 2017-2023, for October 1827, and 2024-2025, for November 1827. Dr. Christie also treated a number of cases of ophthalmia, as well as a few cases of a wide variety of other diseases.

42. LAC, RG 8, Series C, Vol. 44, C-2618, 137-138, By to General Mann, 22 October l827; and *ibid*, Vol. 45, 34, Captain Bolton, "An Account of monies expended on the Rideau Canal between lst November 1827 and the 22nd January l828", 23 January l828. The smaller barracks hospital was converted to house the Royal Sappers and Miners who had lived under canvas during the summer of l827 (*ibid*, 7677, By to General Mann, 19 March l828). One of the two-and-a half storey civilian barracks erected on Rideau Street, was later converted into a hotel, the Rideau Hotel. See Nick & Helma Mika, *Bytown, The Early Days of Ottawa* (Belleville, ON: Mika Publishing, 1982), 150.

43. LAC, MG24, I9, vol. 6, 1997-2004, Monthly return of the Diseases and casualties for July 1827. Surprisingly, there were only seven deaths due to accidents amongst the labourers during the May-December 1827 period. These involved: drowning (2), cave ins (2), blasting accidents (2), and a quarry accident (1).

44. LAC, RG 8, A 1, Vol. 45, C-2618, 30, By to General Mann, 23 January l828. After Walter Fenelon gave up his contract at the Hog's Back, additional buildings were constructed by Lt. Col. By to house the two companies of Royal Sappers and Miners sent to the Hogs Back, and Fenelon's buildings were purchased to house the civilian artisans and Irish Catholic labourers already employed at the site. The artificers and labourers were hired on the canal establishment as dayworkers to carry on the work (LAC, MG 13, WO 44, Vol.18, B-1294, 344, Document K, [14 January l831].

45. Only one Irish immigrant is recorded as having absconded from Bytown in the spring of 1829 without working to pay for the provisions given his large family during the winter months. See LAC, WO44, vol. 27, B-1300, 389, "Statement of Supplies of Provisions", n.d [c. June 1829].

46. Mactaggart, *Three Years in Canada*, Vol. II, 244; and LAC, MG l3, WO 44, B-217, Vol. l5, 1718, By to General Mann, 8 September l828, and 29-30, By to General Mann, l9 January l829. Many labourers were loath to enter hospitals. They were seen as places where the sick and injured went to die, either from their disease or injury, or from infections contacted at the hospital.

47. LAC, RG 5, A l, Vol. 86, C-6864, 46930-46931, R.W. Tunney to Major General Hillier, 24 October l827; and 46958, Rev. Alexander Macdonnel, Glengarry, to Major General Hillier, 26 October l827. Wage labour in cities, where large numbers of landless Irish Catholic immigrants also sought

work, was but a further guarantee of destitution and distress in the Canadian climate. See Judith Fingard, "The Winter's Tale: The Seasonal Contours of Pre-Industrial Poverty in British North America, 1815-1860", *Canadian Historical Association, Historical Papers*, 1974, 65-94.

48. LAC, MG 13, WO 44, Vol. 15, B-217, 35, By to Col. Durnford, 7 August 1829, and 29-30, By to General Mann, 19 January 1829, 35, By to Col. Durnford, 7 August 1829. The quote is from the August letter. The Irish immigrant labourers seeking work on Canadian canals were not the brawny navvies of popular myth upon their initial arrival. On the Welland Canal in the 1840s Irish labourers, weakened by near starvation, staggered under the weight of their shovels on first commencing work (Bleasdale,"Class Conflict on the Canals of Upper Canada in the 1840s", *Labour/Le Travailleur*, Vol. 7, Spring 1981,14).

49. LAC, MG 13, WO 44, B-217, Vol. 15, 36-37, Office of the Ordnance, "Regulations for making Medical Stoppages for Foremen, Artificers and Labourers, of the Civil Department at Foreign Stations", 17 April 1826; and LAC, MG 13, WO 44, Vol. 15, B-217, 3132, "Memorandum on the remuneration to be granted Mr. Tuthill for his attendance of the Sick Labourers employed on the Rideau Canal", December 1828, and 35-36, Extract of letter, By to Colonel Durnford, 7 August 1829.

50. LAC, MG 13, WO 44, Vol 15, B-217, 22-23, John Webb, Director General, Ordnance Medical Department, to Richard Byham, Secretary to the Board of Ordnance, 6 December 1828, and Board of Ordnance marginalia, dated 8 December 1828; and 33-34, Webb to Richard Byham, 30 November 1829, marginalia dated 7 December 1829. See also WO55, Vol. 867, B-2812, 17, Office of Ordnance, R. Byham to Commanding Royal Engineer Canada, 26 March 1830.

51. LAC, MG13, WO55, vol. 865, B-2811, 209, By to Colonel Durnford, Commanding Royal Engineer for Canada, 1 April 1828.

52. LAC, MG 13, WO 44, Vol. 15, B-217, 18, By to General Mann, 8 September 1828. Presumably the canal workers and their wives, and the adult residents of Bytown were vaccinated as well, or perhaps the infected children were simply isolated and the other children vaccinated as a precaution. The engineering officers and military artisans and their families would have been vaccinated already as that was the practice in the British military at that time.

53. John J. Heagarty, *Four Centuries of Medical History in Canada, and a Sketch of the Medical History of Newfoundland*, Vol. I (Toronto: Macmillan Company, 1928), 84-87 & 95.

54. LAC, RG8, Series C, Vol. 45, C-2618, 213-214, By to Sir James Kempt, 26 June 1828.

55. LAC, MG13, WO44, reel B-217, vol. 15, 17, Lt. Col. By to General Mann, 8 September 1828.

56. *Montreal Herald*, Vol. XVII, no. 91, 13 September 1828, reprint of article "Upper Canada, Niagara", 28 August 1828; and Douglas Library, Queen's University, Kingston, Rev. William Bell Diaries, Vol. 6, Entries for 1828: August, p. 38, September, 51 & 57; and October 1828, 59-60.

57. Mactaggart, *Three Years in Canada*, vol. I, 52-58; and LAC, MG 24, H12, John Burrows, Sketch Book, n.d., 129-130, 136, 142 & 148.

58. LAC, MG13, WO44, vol. 15, reel B-217, 25-26, Captain Henry Savage, R.E., to Lt. Col. By, 6 September 1828. Among the dead were John Sheriff, the Chaffey's Mills contractor, and Samuel Clowes Sr., the contractor for the Jack's Rifts, Billidore's Rifts, and Lower Brewer's Mill work sites. Both men died in September 1828. (*Montreal Gazette*, 2 October 1828.)

59. LAC, WO44, vol. 15, B-217, 17-18, By to General Mann, 8 September 1828. Dr. Tuthill was assigned to the Rideau Canal project as of 30 April 1827 to provide medical care, and medicines, for the canal military establishment. Dr. Christie continued to tend to the canal workers under his arrangement with Lt. Col. By.

60. Rev. William Bell Diaries, vol. 4, 179, entry for June 1826, and vol. 5, 55, entry for March 1827.

61. Mactaggart, *Three Years in Canada*, vol. I, 18; and Wylie, "Poverty, Distress and Disease", 14.

62. LAC, MG13, WO44, vol. 15, B-217, 17-18, By to General Mann, 8 September 1828, and 27, William Tuthill, Assistant Surgeon, to By, 8 September 1828.

63. Mactaggart, *Three Years in Canada*, vol. I, 18; and Bell Diaries, vol. 5, 80-81, entry for May 1827.

64. Mactaggart, *Three Years in Canada*, vol. I, 17. The strain of malaria on the Rideau Canal and its environs was much more severe than the 'lake fever and ague' previously encountered in the swamps and marshes of Upper Canada. However, a similarly virulent strain of malaria had been encountered earlier by the British Army on Walcheren Island in the Scheldt Estuary of the Lowlands. In July 1809 a British expeditionary force of 40,000 men landed on the island, and in August the soldiers were ravaged by a severe fever. Over 4,000 men died – a mortality rate of 10 % – and over 11,500 were removed to hospital before the expeditionary force was withdrawn in 1810. See J.W. Fortescue, *A History of the British Army*, Vol. VII, (London: Macmillan, 1912), 91. Whether that particularly virulent strain of malaria was transported to Upper Canada in the post-1810 period is unknown. Some historians claim that the high morality rate amongst the British troops in the marshes of Walcheren Island was due to a combination of malaria, typhus, and typhoid.

65. LAC, MG13, WO44, reel B-1294, vol. 18, 215-248, By to Colonel Durnford, Document K [14 January 1831]. This summary report records what was done at each work site and the costs incurred.

66. Thomas John Graham, M.D., *Modern Domestic Medicine: or A Popular Treatise illustrating the Character, Symptoms, Causes, Distribution, and Correct Treatment of all Diseases incident to the Human Frame* (3rd. ed., London: Published by Author, 1827), "Ague", 214.

67. In the period 1880-1899 malaria parasites were observed in human blood, several species of malaria parasites were identified and named, and ultimately it was discovered that the disease was transmitted by the bite of the female anopheles mosquito. ("Malaria", Centers for Disease Control and Prevention). See also Ken Watson, "Malaria on the Rideau" (http://www.rideau-info.com/canal/history/locks/malaria.html).

68. Bell Diaries, vol. 6, 59-60, entry for October 1828.

69. Mactaggart, *Three Years in Canada*, Vol. II, 17; and Edward John Barker, M.D. *Observations on the Rideau Canal* (Kingston, Upper Canada: Kingston Whig Office, 1834), 18-19.

70. LAC, MG13, WO44, Vol. 18, B-1294, 216-248, By to Colonel Durnford, Document K [14 January 1831].

71. LAC, MG13, WO44, Vol. 18, B-1294, 167-168, By to General Mann, 15 March 1830. A mortuary was also constructed in recognition of the deadly impact of malaria each sickly season.

72. LAC, MG13, WO44, Vol. 18, B-1294, 482, By to Colonel Durnford, 14 January 1831.

73. Mactaggart, *Three Years in Canada*, Vol. II, 244; and Captain Basil Hall, R.N., *Travels in North America in the years 1827 and 1828* (Edinburgh: Cadell & Co.,, 1829), Vol. I, 296; and LAC, RG8, Series C, Vol. 51, B-1294, 32, By to Colonel Durnford, Document K, [14 January 1831].

74. LAC, MG13, WO44, Vol. 19, B-1294, 47, By to General Mann, 31 December 1831, in reporting on the state of his health.

75. Mactaggart, *Three Years in Canada*, vol. I, 18; and Captain Basil Hall, R.N., *Travels in North America* , Vol. I, 1829, 296.

76. LAC, MG13, WO44, Vol. 18, B-1294, 482, Lt. Col. Boteler to Lt. Col. John By, "General Return Shewing the extent of the Sickness which has prevailed lately at the Several Works of the District under the charge of Lt. Col. Boteler from Kingston Mills to the Narrows, Rideau Lake", 15 September 1830. Ultimately the overall death rate may have been somewhat higher as 89 men who had recovered from the sickness, were reported as having suffered a relapse. The highest mortality rates from sickness that year were at the Isthmus where 14 men of a 273 man workforce died (5.13%), and at Kingston Mills where 8 men of a 389 man workforce died (2.05%). At the Narrows and Chaffeys no deaths were reported. Generally speaking the infection rate remained high at all sites reported – except for the Narrows on Rideau Lake – and ranged from 42.5% at Lower Brewers, to 85.7% at the Isthmus, and a high of 100% at Chaffey's Mills. However, the severity of the sickness was much less than in previous years and, with the exception of the Isthmus and Kingston Mills, no more than one or two deaths was recorded at any one of the other work sites.

77. LAC, MG13, WO44, Vol. 15, B-217, 25-26, Captain Henry Savage, R.E., to Lt. Col. By, 6 September1828.

78. LAC, MG13, WO55, vol. 868, B-2813, 188, Captain Cole to Lt. Col. Boteler, Isthmus, 22 July 1831; 189-190, William Kelly, Assistant Surgeon, to Captain Cole, Isthmus, 22 July 1831; 191, Lt. Col. Boteler to By, Jones Falls, 28 July 1831; and 187-188, By to R. Byham, Secretary, Board of Ordnance, 18 September 1831. Dr. Kelly was the successor at the Isthmus hospital to Dr. Robinson who had drowned in a boating accident on Rideau Lake.

79. LAC, MG13, WO44, vol. 18, B-1294, 481, By to Colonel Durnford, 24 January 1831, and 482, Lt. Col. Boteler to By, "General Return shewing the extent of the sickness", 15 September 1830.

80. Barker, *Observations on the Rideau Canal,* 15.

81. WO25, Vol. 2972, "Registry of Deceased Soldiers, Corps of Royal Sappers and Miners", as cited by Way, *Common Labor*, 160, footnote #74. No doubt the high mortality rate from blasting was due to the 7th Company being employed in the heavy granite rock excavation work at the Isthmus in 1830-1831.

82. Barker, *Observations on the Rideau Canal,* 46 & 60.

83. Using census data from 1851 and 1871, Donald Akenson concludes that the vast majority of Irish immigrants settled on the land in the pre-Great Famine emigration years, and suggests that they did relatively well compared to other immigrants. In sum, he has challenged the prevailing American stereotype view of Irish Catholic immigrants as urban dwellers, culturally adverse to the solitary North American farming life. Akenson also has posited that the Irish immigrants who settled on the land in Ontario were "much quicker, more technologically adaptive, more economically alert, and much less circumscribed by putative cultural limits inherited from the Old Country than is usually believed". Donald Akenson, *The Irish in Ontario: A Study in Rural History* (Montreal/Kingston: McGill/Queens, 1984), 345-353. (See also Donald H. Akenson, *Being Had, Historians, Evidence, and the Irish in North America* (Port Credit, Ontario: P.D. Meany Publishers, 1985.)

Houston and Smyth have pointed out as well that the Irish Catholic immigrant settlement experience in post-War of 1812 Canada differed in time and character from the Irish immigration experience in the United States; and that the Canadian experience does not fit the American stereotype of the Irish Catholic immigrants as lower-class, unruly and heavy drinking, urban slum dwellers who were unable to make the transition into farming. They point out that the Irish Catholics who emigrated to Canada in the pre-Famine years were from Ulster and the adjoining northern counties, which were areas of anglicized commercial agriculture and domestic textile production wherein the farmers and tradesmen enjoyed a modest economic status. To which one might add they presumably spoke English, and were accustomed to working and living in a commercial economy which enjoyed trade links with Canada.

According to Houston and Smyth, the American stereotype of Irish Catholic immigrants was formed during the Great Famine years (1845-1850) when the "hordes fleeing the Great Famine" to the United States were almost all Catholics from the southern counties. (Houston & Smyth, *Irish Emigration*, 5, 36, 39 & 71.) In effect, the Irish emigrants who went to the United States during the Famine years were from the impoverished Gaelic-speaking areas of Ireland, where a primitive subsistence agriculture was practised with families growing wheat for the landlord to pay for their farm lease, and potatoes on garden plots for their subsistence. It was these Irish Catholic immigrants who were ill-prepared and ill-adapted for settling on the land when they arrived in the United States during the 1840s, and who gave rise to the American stereotype of the Irish Catholic immigrants. This particular immigrant group was the product of a destitute, demoralized and oppressed people; and those who managed to flee to the United States during the Potato Famine often arrived sick, malnourished, and penniless, which rendered them incapable of settling on the land regardless of any imputed cultural limitations.

84. For example, John Pennyfeather the contractor for the Entrance Valley excavation was an Irish Catholic, and a prominent citizen of Bytown during the canal construction period; yet little is known of him. Although the vast majority of Irish Catholic immigrants settled peacefully on the land – as Akenson has convincingly argued – there was also a significant number who arrived in Canada totally destitute and who gravitated to the cities and canal projects seeking wage labour. These so-called "pauper Irish" were incapable of settling on the land, and their oft-times violent and irresponsible behaviour attracted a good deal of attention in overshadowing, if not totally obscuring, the transition of the majority of Irish Catholic immigrants into farming on the Upper Canada frontier. It was the behaviour of that smaller segment of pauper Irish under severe economic distress, destitution, and dislocation, that gave rise to the stereotypes that succeeding generations have applied to the Irish Catholic immigration and settlement experience as a whole in wrongly

applying American stereotypes to the Canadian experience.

85. Despite the assertions of Donald Akenson, one cannot say that cultural factors were insignificant in the Irish immigrant settlement experience in Ontario. John Mactaggart (*Three Years in Canada*, Vol. II, 25) observed a complacent attitude and lack of initiative amongst the Irish Catholic poor-relief settlers in the Rideau Military Settlement. They cleared only enough land for their subsistence and were not motivated to do more to better their condition, which was in startling contrast to the other British immigrant groups in the settlement. Similar observations were made elsewhere about the complacency and fatalism of the Irish Catholic tenant farmers. (See Kerby A. Miller, *Emigrants and Exiles, Ireland and the Irish Exodus to North America* (New York/Oxford: Oxford University Press, 1985, 107-117). Miller attributes the perceived fatalism and complacency of the Irish Catholic tenant farmers to the survival of a pre-modern mentality, and to an impoverished peasant culture rather than to religious values *per se*. He holds that the pre-modern mentality was rooted in the ancient Gaelic culture, but nonetheless was supported by Roman Catholicism with its emphasis on tradition and its rejection of the individualistic capitalist values of the modern liberal world. A contemporary French observer attributed the fatalism and lack of initiative of the Irish Catholic tenant farmers to seven centuries of exploitation by rapacious Protestant landlords, and the hopelessness bred into the tenant farmers over generations of being reduced to privation, and to a hand-to-mouth existence, with no hope of ever bettering themselves. (Beaumont, *Ireland*, 191-196).

The adaptation of immigrants from various cultures to the demands of North American bush farming is a complex subject that has been little studied. One excellent study focuses on three Irish Catholic settlement areas: the Avalon Peninsula in Newfoundland (1810-1835); the Miramichi in New Brunswick (1815-1835); and the later poor-relief Irish Catholic emigrants settled by Peter Robinson in the Peterborough settlement of Upper Canada (1825). In a material culture study focussing on the transfer of tools, technology, and settlement patterns, John Mannion, concludes that the Irish Catholics who settled in the ethnically-mixed, commercial agriculture settlement at Peterborough soon discarded their traditional material culture; whereas the Irish Catholics who settled in the Avalon Peninsula, in a more isolated, subsistence economy area, retained their traditional material culture to a large extent during the pioneer era, and were very slow to clear the land. See John T. Mannion, *Irish Settlements in Eastern Canada: A study of Cultural Transfer and Adaptation* (Toronto: University of Toronto Press, 1974).

86. McGill, *Pioneer History*, 67-69 & 77.

87. Mactaggart, *Three Years in Canada*, Vol. II, 244.

88. Gustave de Beaumont, *Ireland, Social, Political and Religious*, ed. & translated by W.C. Taylor (Cambridge: Harvard University Press, 2006, 1st ed. in French, 1839), 5-159; and Cowan, *British Emigration,* 34-37. Under penal laws imposed by the Protestant Ascendancy in the 17th and 18th centuries, the only employments open to Irish Catholics were as tenant farmers on short-term leases, as farm labourers, or as journeymen in the trades, in a throughly repressive system that precluded the native Irish from ever bettering their social status or economic situation in Ireland. (Beaumont, *Ireland*, 56-71). Under the Gaelic system of land inheritance, each male child was entitled to an equal share of their father's property.

89. Cowan, *British Emigration*, 18-17, 34-39, 47-52, 65-82, 146-153 & 209; and Pentland, *Labour and Capital*, 99-108. In Ulster, the farms were not sub-divided as there was a primogeniture system of land inheritance. The younger sons sought employment in either the army, the linen industry, the trades, or they emigrated to obtain land. On the settlement experience of the Scots, see: Lucille H. Campey, *The Scottish Pioneers of Upper Canada, 1784-1855, Glengarry and Beyond* (Toronto: National Heritage Books, 2005).

90. LAC, MG l3, WO 44, Vol. 18, B-1294, 161, By to General Mann, 15 October l830. The Canada Land Company demanded $6.00 per acre. The company was founded by John Galt in l826, and bought up some 1,200,000 acres of Crown land in Upper Canada to sell to immigrants. In the back townships surrounding the military settlements – Bathurst, Beckwith, Burgess, Dalhousie, Darling, Drummond, Horton, Lanark, Montague, and Pakenham – the Company bought the scattered lots of l00 and 200 acres that had yet to be settled (McGill, *Pioneer History*, 110). On land prices see also Henry, *The Emigrants' Guide*, 332. In Upper Canada, the dollar circulated at 5 shillings (*ibid*, 25). In the contemporary British currency, there were 20 shillings (20s.) to one pound (£1), and 12 pence (12d.) to one shilling (1s.).

91. LAC, MG13, WO 44, Vol. 19, B-1294, 64, By to R.J. Routh, 10 July l830. The fear that Colonel By noted amongst the Irish immigrants was not all that uncommon. Many immigrants were terrified at the prospect of coping

with the demands of the bush environment (Norman R. Ball, "The Technology of Settlement and Land Clearing in Upper Canada prior to 1840", Ph.D. Thesis, University of Toronto Institute for the History and Philosophy of Science and Technology, 1979, 81).

92. On the demands and dangers of bush farming, and the crops raised, see Ball, "The Technology of Settlement", 80-219 & 255-259. Ouellet (*Lower Canada, 1791-1840*, 140-141) states that a poor immigrant could manage to settle on the land without initial capital, if his farm were near a market. However, that is highly questionable as even Indian corn (maize) took 12 to 16 weeks to yield a crop. On bush farming see also, "Bush Life" in Glen J. Lockwood, *Beckwith, Irish and Scottish Identities in a Canadian Community 1816-1991* (Carleton Place, Ontario: By Author, 1991), 76-95.

93. Ouellet, *Lower Canada, 1791-1840*, 141. To acquire capital for settlement, immigrants commonly took employment in Lower Canada before proceeding inland. To facilitate that process, the King's Shipyard hired labourers only for a month at 2s.6d. per day. During the 1820's, many immigrants also worked grubbing cleared land in the Eastern Townships for a summer. Experienced axemen were paid $12 to $14 per month with room and board; and immigrants grubbing the land were paid $7 to $10 per month with room and board (*ibid*). Even if given free grants of land, it was all but impossible to settle in the backwoods without some capital (Ruth Bleasdale, "Class Conflict on the Canals", 10).

94. Mannion, *Irish Settlements*, 31.

95. Bell Diaries, vol. 6, 176, February 1830 entry.

96. Mactaggart, *Three Years in Canada*, Vol. II, 242-243. The number of felling and axe injuries was particularly high among new immigrants on first entering the bush. Even allowing for an anti-Irish bias on the part of some observers, it appears that the Irish Catholic immigrants were noted for suffering an inordinate number of axe injuries. (See Ball, "The Technology of Settlement", 134). The quote is from Dunlop (*Statistical Sketches*, 8).

97. Mactaggart, *Three Years in Canada*, Vol. II, 250-254. As Irish emigration to British North America soared to 30,574 in 1830, 58,067 in 1831, and 66,339 in 1832, some Irish Catholic immigrants who turned up on the Rideau Canal project were in even more impoverished circumstances. In the summer

of l830, Irish pauper immigrants were arriving on the Rideau Canal project "in a starving state, asking for land" (LAC, MG 13, WO 44, Vol. 19, B-1294, 65, By to R.J. Routh, 10 July l830).

98. LAC, MG 13, WO 44, Vol. l8, B-1294, 72, Smyth, "Memorandum", 14 March l826, and 10, By to General Mann, l October l826 and Board of Ordnance marginalia, dated 5 January l827.

99. Mactaggart, *Three Years in Canada*, Vol. II, 242-243. For immigrants the possession of some capital was necessary to enable them to purchase supplies to survive in the bush until they learned to use an axe proficiently, and cleared some land and planted their first crop. However, a critical element in settling on the land was gaining a knowledge of bush farming. Here the native born sons of Loyalists and American immigrants from the frontier settlements of the United States, had a critical advantage in venturing into the Canadian bush. As described by a traveller, an American settler would take a location ticket, locate his land, clear upwards of eight acres and plant corn (maize) seeds around the stumps through employing his axe to open the ground, which he then closed up with his foot. He would then go off to secure employment to secure some capital – in presumably working as a farm labourer in older settled areas, as an axeman clearing land for others, or on a canal project. He would return in the fall to harvest his corn crop, and with the help of neighbours would erect a log cabin built entirely of wood with wooden hinges and door lock, and oiled paper over the window openings. Once the cabin was erected he would bring in his wife, and some supplies – several barrels of salted pork, and perhaps some flour, and would proceed to clear more land. Soon he would have a farm clearing with several animals – usually pigs, some poultry, a cow, a few cattle and/or an ox. (Alexander, *Transatlantic Sketches*, vol. II, 220). In sum, for those knowledgeable about bush farming, and able to live off the land, little capital was required to establish a bush farm, but that was not the case with British immigrants.

100. LAC, RG 8, Series C, Vol. 43, C-26l8, l3-l4, By to Colonel Durnford, 22 November l826. Pentland (*Labour and Capital*, 108) states that pilfering was an old Irish custom. More correctly, that proclivity was a characteristic of pre-modern communal societies where goods were used in common, as needed, in the absence of the strict sense of private property and property rights that is more characteristic of individualistic 'modern peoples'.

101. Mactaggart, *Three Years in Canada*, Vol. I, 329. Mactaggart cites an

anonymous letter published in the *Kingston Chronicle*, 3 November 1826. On the Wright's Town settlement see Ross, *Ottawa:Past and Present*, 12-20, and Bruce S. Elliott, "The famous Township of Hull: Image and Aspirations of a Pioneer Quebec Community", *Histoire Sociale/Social History*, Vol. 12, No. 24, November 1979, 339-367.

102. Mactaggart, *Three Years in Canada*, Vol. II, 244-245 & 248-251. Mactaggart condemned the sending of Irish pauper emigrants to North America as a cruel hoax. He observed that only one in fifty of such impoverished people were capable of making the transition from wage labourers to bush farmers. Hence emigration condemned most of them to terrible suffering, deprivation, sickness and death. Instead, he proposed that the British government provide employment in Ireland by improving the Shannon River as a river navigation.

103. Letter of Lt. Col. John By printed in the *Kingston Chronicle*, 6 April 1827.

104. LAC, RG 8, Series C, Vol. 43, C 2617, 65-66, C.I. Forbes, Deputy Commissary General, Montreal, to Peter Turquand, Commissary General, Quebec, 30 January 1827; and RG 8, Series C, Vol. 47, C2619, 45-47, By to Col. Durnford, 5 January 1829.

105. LAC, MG 13, WO 44, Vol. 19, B-1294, Lt. Pooley, General Outline of Works performed, 15 December 1827; RG 8, Series C, Vol. 47, C2619, 1138-138a, By to Respective Officers, His Majesty's Ordnance, Quebec, 26 January 1829, and Vol. 48, 221-222, By to Respective Officers, Quebec, 29 April 1827. See also RG 5, A 1, Vol. 84, C-6863, 457-458, A. Wilson to Major General Hillier, 18 May 1827. Initially, bread was purchased from Wright's Town; the government bakery was the first erected in Bytown.

106. Mika, *Bytown, The Early Days of Ottawa*, 1982, 102.

107. LAC, RG 8, Series C, Vol. 47, C-2619, 45-47, By to Colonel Durnford, 5 January 1829.

108. Williams, *A Speech*, 22; Henry, *The Emigrant's Guide*, 60; Dunlop, *Statistical Sketches*, 67-68; and *Brockville Recorder*, Vol X, 11 May 1830, A.J.C. (Dr. Christie), "Memoranda taken during a tour through the line of the Rideau Canal from Kingston to Bytown, in February 1830". Prices varied from

one area to another along the canal, and owing to the different currencies and systems of packaging, it is difficult to assess prices. In Bytown, fresh pork sold for $5 to $6 per hundred (1/2 barrel), beef at $5, mutton at 3 shillings a quarter, and poultry of all kinds was very plentiful and cheap (Henry, p. 60). At the Isthmus, a Perth merchant supplied pork for $4 a barrel, flour at $8 a barrel, bread at 10d. per quarter loaf, and rum at 3s.6d .(Provincial Archives of Ontario, Baird Papers, Reel 1, George Buchanan, Perth Mills, to N.H. Baird, 18 July l832). At Jones' Falls, Hog Pork sold for about £3.5 per barrel, prime pork for £3 per barrel, potatoes for ls.3d., flour for £1.10s. per barrel, and oats at 1s.9d to 1s.11d.(AJC "Memoranda").

109. PAO, Baird Papers, Reel 1, Buchanan to Baird, 18 July 1832; Dunlop, *Statistical Sketches*, 6263; and Henry, *The Emigrant's Guide*, 60. See also AJC "Memoranda", *Brockville Recorder*, May 1830; and Glen J. Lockwood, *Beckwith*, 117-118. The Rideau Military Settlement farmers delivered their produce to the interior Rideau Canal worksites along three road systems: the Brockville Road from Perth to the Rideau Lake; on a bush road from Franktown on the Richmond Road to Matiland's Rapids (Kilmarnock) from where provisions were transported upstream as far as Smith's Falls and downstream as far as Burritts' Rapids; and on the Richmond Road to the Bytown market, from where supplies were moved inland , by the contractors, to the Hog's Back, Black Rapids, and Long Island worksites.

110. Wylie, "Poverty, Distress and Disease", 15, 19 & 20.

111. On the abuses of the traditional truck system, see Bleasdale, "Class Conflict on the Canals of Upper Canada in the l840s", 16-18 & 26-27. Having supplied provisions to the contractors at cost plus transport to keep the workers healthy and wages from escalating, Lt. Col. By would not have stood for contractors charging excessively high prices or engaging in the more nefarious practices of the truck system.

112. Bell Diaries, Vol. 6, Entries for l828: August, 38; September, 57; and October, 59-60; *Montreal Herald*, Vol. XVII, No. 91, 13 September 1828, "Upper Canada"; and *Bathurst Independent Examiner*, Vol. II, No. 31, 15 January l830, "Wanted".

113. LAC, RG 8, Series C, Vol. 47, C-2619, 77, A. C. Stevens & Co., to By, 6 January 1829; RG 8, Series C, Vol. 47, C-2619, 76, By to Colonel Durnford, 10 January 1829, and 78-79, Colonel Durnford to Colonel Cooper,

Military Secretary to the Commander-in Chief, 20 January 1829.

114. *Farmers' Journal and Welland Canal Intelligencer*, St. Catharines, 9 January 1828, "Bytown City". Many of the early tradesmen and merchants who settled in Bytown in 1827 and 1828 are named in William Lett, *Recollections of Bytown and its Old Inhabitants* (Ottawa: Citizen Printing and Publishing Company, 1874), reprinted as *Lett's Bytown* (Ottawa: Bytown Museum, 1979).

115. LAC, RG8, Series C, Vol. 47, C-2619, 45-46, By to Colonel Durnford, 5 January 1829, 138-138a, By to Respective Officers, H.M. Ordnance, Quebec, 26 January 1829, and 50. R.J. Routh, Deputy Commissary General, Memorandum, 15 January 1829. The quote is from the Routh Memorandum.

116. *Bathurst Independent Examiner*, Vol. II, No. 31, 15 January 1830, "Wanted"; and *Brockville Recorder*, Vol. X, No. 19, 11 May 1830, A.J.C. (Dr. Christie), "Memoranda taken during a tour through the line of the Rideau Canal, from Kingston to Bytown, in Feb. 1830".

117. See Ruth Bleasdale, "Class Conflict on the Canals of Upper Canada in the 1840s", *Labour/Le Travilleur*, Spring 1981, 15-17 and 27; and Coleman, *The Railway Navvies*.

118. John McGregor, *British America,* vol. I (Edinburgh: W. Blackwood, 1832), 483; and Dunlop, *Statistical Sketches*, 1832, 63-112. Russell ("Wage Labour Rates in Upper Canada, 1818-1840", 70) states wage rates for day labourers averaged 2s.6d. to 3s. per diem ca. 1820-23, but included lodging and board; and that by 1830 wages ranged higher still, from 3s. to 6s. per day. See also, George Henry, *Canada as it is: comprising details relating to the domestic policy, commerce, and agriculture of the upper and lower provinces, comprising matters of general information and interest, especially intended for the use of settler and emigrants* (New York: W. Stodart, 1832), and especially page 60, wherein Henry states that canal workers in Bytown were paid 3s. a day.

119. Edward Frome, Lt, R.E. "Account of the Causes which led to the Construction of the Rideau Canal, connecting the Waters of Lake Ontario and the Ottawa", in Great Britain, Corps of Royal Engineers, *Papers on Subjects Connected with the Duties of the Corps of Royal Engineers* (London: John Weale, 2nd ed., 1844), Vol. I, 98. Wylie ("Poverty, Distress and Disease", 10) states that Philemon Wright paid his French Canadian labourers 1s.3d. to 1s.10d. per diem with room and board provided. In Lower Canada the

King's Shipyard paid 2s.6d. per diem (Ouellet, *Lower Canada*,141), which was probably a top wage rate. Both Pentland (*Labour and Capital*, ll6 &190) and Wylie, ("Poverty, Distress and Disease", 9-10, citing Pentland), stress poor working conditions and low wages prevailed on the Rideau Canal project. This, however, was not the case. Even the lower wages paid by Philemon Wright were not unreasonably low when the cost of accommodation and provisions provided by the contractor are taken into account. In l820, skilled labourers – axemen – working in the bush near York were allowed 1s.6d. a day for rations in addition to their wages (Russell, "Wage Labour Rates in Upper Canada, l8l8-l840", 70).

120. Williams, *A Speech*, 30; Henry, *The Emigrant's Guide*, ix and x; Dunlop, *Statistical Sketches*, 63; and Ross, *Ottawa: Past and Present*, 97-99.

121. Frome, "Account of the Causes", 98. Stonecutters made as much as 6s. to 7s. a day on measured piecework (*ibid*). On the wages of artisans, see McGregor, *British America*, Vol. I, p. 482; and Peter A. Russel, "Wage Labour Rates in Upper Canada, l8l8-l840", *Histoire socialeSocial History*, XVI, no.31, May l983, 6l-80. According to Russell's statistics (74-75) the Rideau Canal rates for carpenters, masons, and smiths were slightly below the mean of the range of provincial rates, but wage rates were generally lower in eastern Upper Canada.

122. LAC, RG 8, Series C, Vol. 45, C-26l8, 75-76, By to R. Byham, l9 March l828, and Vol. 5l, C-2620, 233, By to D. Jonas, l December l830.

123. *Lett's Bytown*, 99. The Scots immigrants from Perth who worked on the Oswego Canal in New York state in l823-24 were well aware of how canal workers could be exploited by some contractors. They went for months without pay on that American canal project, and had no recourse to the courts when cheated of their full wages. Ultimately they had to settle for only 1/4 to 1/3 of what was owed them simply to get their arrears of pay and to return to their bush farms in the Rideau interior for the fall harvest ("A Settler's Story", in Shortt, ed., *Perth Remembered*, 30-31).

124. LAC, MG 24, D8, Vol. 33, 14814, P. Wright and Sons to Colonel By, 16 December l828. The Wrights were following the labour system that they employed in the timber trade. Shanty men in the timber trade signed service contracts for either a full work season, or several months of work. They were provided with a pair of boots, room and board, and credit at the company

store for the purchase of tobacco and whiskey while cutting timber during the winter months. Those who signed on for the entire winter work season were not paid until after the spring timber drive, when the squared timber was sold.

125. LAC, MG13, WO44, Vol. 18, B-1294, 215-248, By to Colonel Durnford, Document K, [14 January 1831], various references.

126. Henry, *The Emigrant's Guide*, 60. See also, Bell Diaries, Vol. 7, 79, Entry for August 1830. An historian who has compared the names of the canal workers on the 1829 petition with the names on the Nepean Township Census of 1852, confirms that a significant number of the Irish canal workers who signed the petition were squatters or lessees on the canal lands cleared and purchased by Lt. Col. By – the so-called Ordnance Lands – around Dow's Lake and along the canal to the Hog's Back. They remained settled there two decades after the completion of the canal. See Bruce S. Elliott, *The McCabe List, Early Irish in the Ottawa Valley* (Toronto: The Ontario Genealogical Society, 2002), 4.

127. LAC. MG 13, WO 44, Vol. 19, B-1294, 69-70, By to General Mann, 15 March 1830: and *U.E. Loyalist*, (York), 24 February 1827, "Rideau Canal".

128. Elliott, *The McCabe List*. The petition of 5 February 1829 is reprinted on page 6. According to Elliott, most of the signees were Irish Protestants and Irish Catholics from the more anglicized areas of Ireland – principally Ulster in the north; and Leinster (particularly Tipperary) in the south. Only a few of the petitioners were Irish Catholic from the south and west – the poorer, Gaelic-speaking, pre-modern areas of Ireland. It stands to reason that few of the illiterate Gaelic-speaking Irish labourers on the Rideau Canal project would have signed a petition; although a few men did affix their 'X'.

129. C.W. Williams, *A Speech on the Improvement of the Shannon, Being in Continuation of the Debate in the House of Commons, 12 May 1835, Giving a Comparative View of the Navigation of the Rideau Canal, in Canada and the River Shannon, in Ireland with Observations on the value of a connection by steam packets, with British America* (London: J. Bain, I. Haymarket, 1835), 30 & 53.

130. LAC, RG8, Series C, Vol. 49, C-2619, 92, By to Lt. Col. Couper, Military Secretary to the Commander of the Forces, 20 August 1829; and 94-95, R. J. Routh, Commissary General, Quebec, "Memorandum", 24 August

1829. During this year a money vault was constructed in the Commissariat Building at the Entrance Valley to house the military chest. It is not known whether it was also intended to be used to safeguard the canal workers savings. See RG8, Series C, vol. 50, C-2619, 82, By to Respective Officers, 13 February 1830.

131. LAC, MG13, WO44, Vol. 19, B-1294, 64-65, – to R.J. Routh, Commissariat Department, 10 July 1830; and vol. 18, 161-162, By to General Mann, Board of Ordnance, 15 March 1830. Earlier Lt. Col. By had arranged for a guide to settle a party of 30 poor Irish families on cheap land in the bush over ten miles from the canal works, but "starvation drove them from their lots". He then realized the necessity of placing the poor Irish on land close to the canal works so they could sustain themselves with wage labour while settling onto the land. (LAC, RG5, A1, C-6867, Vol. 93, 52099, By to A.C. Buchanan, 28 March 1829.)

132. Glenn J. Lockwood, "Irish Immigrants and the 'Critical Years' in Eastern Ontario: The Case of Montague Township, 1821-1881", 158 and 163-164 in Donald H. Akenson, ed., *Canadian Papers in Rural History*, Vol. IV (Gananoque, Ontario: Langdale Press, 1984); and Dunlop, *Statistical Sketches*, 67-68. Lockwood attests that at the conclusion of the Rideau Canal project at least a few Irish labourers had as much as £20 to £30 saved to make a down payment on land, and others who wanted to settle on the land were able to lease and ultimately buy land from the Canada Land Company or lease land on Clergy Reserves . Still others squatted on land owned by absentees, paying a modest rent for poor land.

133. Wylie, "Poverty, Disease and Distress", 15. Labourers who engaged in improvident behaviour had no prospect of settling on the land, and condemned themselves to poverty and want given the existing labour situation in Upper Canada.

134. LAC, MG13, WO44, Vol. 15, B-217, 197, Seth Thomas, Clerk of Ordnance Office, AStatement of the Receipts and Expenditures of the Ordnance Department on account of the Rideau Canal to 30 June 1833", 29 January 1834. That sum included the construction of four blockhouses, and the monies expended on land purchases, and was the greatest expenditure on any defence project in the British Empire to that date.

135. Brault, *Ottawa: Old and New*, 63, quoting Thomas McKay concerning his Irish labourers; and *Lett's Bytown*, 3 & 8182. At the Entrance Valley, two-thirds of the 300-man work force of Thomas Mckay, the masonry contractor, were Irish Catholics. In 1828, at nine years of age, William Lett settled in Bytown with his family and witnessed at first hand the events that he describes in his book. According to Lett, Mother McGinty's Tavern had whitewashed walls, and was a place where the labourers sang and danced and received good measure and a fair credit on their drinking tabs. An Irishmen, Michael Burke, also established a brewery near Corktown about that time.

136. Wylie, "Poverty, Distress and Disease", 15 & 20.

137. Mactaggart, *Three Years in Canada*, Vol. I, 198. Ironically, Mactaggart himself was dismissed during the summer of 1828 for being inebriated and insubordinate while on duty.

138. *Lett's Bytown*, 84-85 & 99.

139. Lett's Bytown, 86-87, "The Fair of 1829"; and Ross, *Ottawa: Past and Present*, 109110. In the new town government, John Mactaggart, the Clerk of Works, was Treasurer; the Entrance Valley masonry contractor Thomas McKay was a Bailiff; and the Overseers Thomas Burrowes and John Burrows were Councillors, as were Robert Drummond, who was constructing several spans of the Chaudière bridges crossing, and Alexander McMartin, a subcontractor at the Hog's Back.

140. *Bathurst Independent Examiner*, (Perth), 11 September 1829, "Daring Outrage". The ringleaders were Pat O'Brien, Thomas Casey, Harry Lee, and James Carry who were jailed in Perth. Foley escaped before the militia arrived. Clearly as of 1829 there were Irish Catholics immigrants who had become skilled with the axe, and who had the financial resources to post securities in sub-contracting for the delivery of timber to a canal contractor.

141. *Bathurst Independent Examiner*, (Perth), 22 January 1830, "Daring Outrage". For the violence on later canal projects see, for example, Bleasdale,"Class Conflict on the Canals of Upper Canada in the 1840s", 21-23. During the summer of 1842, the Welland Canal project resembled a war zone as two factions of Irish Catholic labourers – the Corkmen and Connaughtmen – engaged in open warfare for weeks on end with heavily armed parties of 200 to 300 men attacking each other in fierce bloody skirmishes that resulted in

severe beatings and several deaths. On faction fighting amongst Irish Catholic labourers on canal projects, and their pathological behaviour, see Peter Way, *Common Labor, Workers and the Digging of North American Canals, 1780-1860* (Baltimore: John Hopkins University Press, 1997), 165-167, 193-199 & 246-247.

142. At an earlier date, animosity between the Scots settlers and Irish Catholic immigrants in the military settlements had resulted in at least one clash – the Ballygiblin Riots at Stegman's Mill in the Rideau interior, 23 April 1824 – which resulted in one man being killed, and several wounded (McGill, *A Pioneer History*, 94-96.) On railway construction projects in Scotland during the 1840s, open warfare raged between the Scots and Irish Catholic navvies, which resulted in the army being called in to suppress bloody riots (Coleman, *The Railway Navvies*, 93-104).

143. The lack of any violent conflict between Irish Catholic and French Canadian labourers on the Rideau Canal project is in stark contrast to the situation later in the timber trade on the Ottawa River during the 1830s. See Michael S. Cross, "The Shiners' War: Social Violence in the Ottawa Valley in the 1830s", *Canadian Historical Review*, Vol. LIV, No. 1, March 1973, 126.

144. Bleasdale, "Class Conflict on the Canals", 9-39.

145. LAC, MG13, WO44, Vol. 18, B-1294, 166, By to General Mann, 15 March 1830; and *Bathurst Independent Examiner* (Perth), 1 January 1830.

146. Mactaggart, *Three Years in Canada*, Vol. I, 329; and Bleasdale, "Class Conflict on the Canals of Upper Canada in the 1840s", 21, fn. 60, & 37-39. Bleasdale points out that workers preferred to labour with members of their own faction or ethnic group. In an effort to prevent violent conflicts, the contractors on the Welland Canal in the 1840s acted accordingly in deploying their immigrant workers on the job site, but that policy alone did not prevent bloody battles between the Corkmen and Connaughtmen.

147. Dunlop, *Statistical Sketches*, 74 & 99. The Board of Works of Canada in 1842 had a similar experience in employing Irish Catholic canal labourers. Under government employ, when wages were paid in cash rather than store pay and shanties were erected to shelter the men, the Irish labourers were wellbehaved. After contractors took over, and began exploiting the workers, violence flared in a series of bitter strikes (Pentland, *Labour and Capital*,

237, fn. 50). More generally, in 1851 the English railway contractor Samuel Morton Peto stated his experience with Irish Catholic labourers: "But give him legitimate occupation, and remuneration for his services, show him you appreciate those services, and you may be sure you put an end to all agitation" (Coleman, *The Railway Navvies*, 70).

148. In attempting to account for the absence of strikes and bloody riots on the Rideau Canal project after the spring of 1827, Labour historians have attached a great deal of significance to a statement of Lt. Col. By to the effect that the Royal Sappers and Miners were "most usefully employed; their presence on the ground enables me to check the disorderly conduct of the Labourers" (LAC, RG5, Al, Upper Canada Sundries, By to General Mann, 10 June 1828). From this premise, both Pentland (*Labour and Capital*, 190) and Wylie ("Poverty, Distress and Disease", 28-29) deduce that troops were used to suppress the workers. The presence of a troop detachment in Bytown, and of Royal Sappers and Miners at Bytown and the Hog's Back, and after 1829 at the Isthmus, no doubt had some influence on the workers' behaviour, but in no way does it account for the relative lack of labour strife on the Rideau Canal as a whole.

149. *Brockville Recorder*, Vol. X, No. 20, "Rideau Canal", 18 May 1830; and Henry, *The Emigrant's Guide*, 60. Lt. Col. By was by no means the first to win over unruly workers through paternalistic practices. At the St. Maurice Iron Works in Lower Canada the proprietor, Matthew Bell, successfully used the same approach in dealing with unruly French immigrant ironworkers.(Palmer, *WorkingClass Experience*, 14).

150. LAC, MG13, WO44, Vol. 19, B-1294, 46-47, By to General Mann, 31 December 1829, and Vol. 20, B-1296, 528-531, By to Colonel Durnford, 30 December 1829.

151. A recent publication, Katherine M.J. McKenna, ed., *Labourers on the Rideau Canal 1826-1832: From Work Site to World Heritage Site* (Ottawa: Borealis Press, 2008), includes a reprint of the Wylie article on "Poverty, Distress and Disease", as well as a paper by McKenna on "Working Life at the Isthmus, Rideau Canal, 1827-1831". The McKenna paper continues the earlier focus of the Wylie paper on the afflictions suffered by the canal workers. Neither paper recognizes, in any substantive way, the efforts made by the Commanding Royal Engineer, Lt. Col. John By, to alleviate the afflictions suffered by the workers in so far as was humanly possible.

152. During the post-1837 depression years, with canal construction at a standstill in the United States, hundreds of Irish Catholic immigrant canal workers emigrated to Canada to secure work on Canadian canal construction projects which were financed by a £1.5 million loan and interest guarantee given to Canada by the British government in 1841. Contractors bid low to secure work, and took advantage of a huge surplus of Irish immigrant labour – augmented by a great influx of Irish Catholic immigrants entering North America during the great Irish Potato Blight famine, 1845-1850 – to drive down wages. In such circumstances, the canal workers suffered from abysmal living and working conditions. They were responsible for their own accommodation; were hired by the day, when and if needed; and received low pay at irregular intervals. Moreover, often their pay was in truck (script) redeemable only in purchasing high-priced provisions and goods from a company store. The workcamps were marked by disease, destitution and squalor, drunkenness, brawling, and extremely violent clashes between two Gaelic Irish Catholic factions – the Corkmen and the Connaughtmen – with the militia employed to break strikes and maintain order. See Bleasdale, "Class Conflict on the Canals", 9-39; and Way, *Common Labor*, 194-199. These appalling living and working conditions, and Irish faction fighting, prevailed during the construction of the Beauharnois Canal (1842-1845), the Second Welland Canal (1842-1850), and the Second Lachine Canal (1843-1848).

153. These several different possible motives for the paternalism practised by Lt. Col. By, are suggested simply for the consideration of the reader. For the author, it is clear that the paternalism practised by Lt. Col. John By was a product of his character, cultural values, and world view, which were rooted in Anglican Toryism – or what today would be called 'High Toryism'.

154. On the transformation from what has been called the "contractor paternalism" era of canal construction to the cash nexus period, see Way, *Common Labor*, 3-7, 9, 35-37, 68, & 265-274. From a Marxist perspective, Way interprets the 1840s as a transformation period marked by the breakdown of an hierarchical agrarian social order and the emergence of a market-driven, impersonal, industrial capitalism. However, rather than experiencing the loss of skill and control of production that artisans suffered, the loss of canal labourers was in their material conditions which resulted in the development of a class consciousness and class conflict.

Part Two

Lt. Col. John By, Commanding Royal Engineer, Rideau Canal

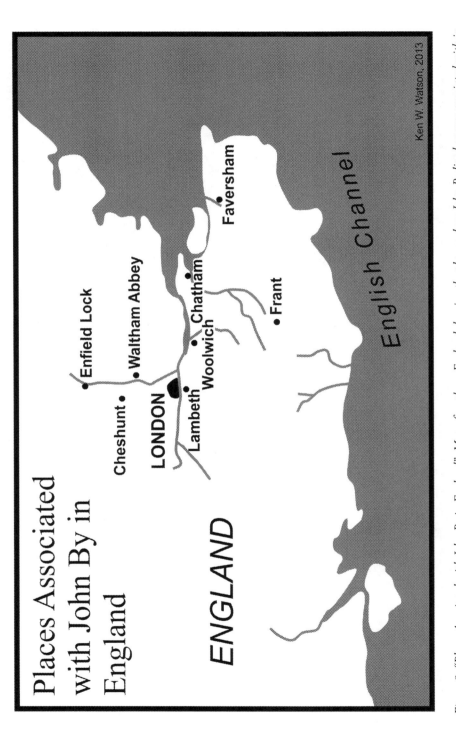

Figure 9. "Places Associated with John By in England". Map of southern England showing the places where John By lived or was associated with in a professional capacity, during his youth, cadet years, and as an officer in the Corps of Royal Engineers. (Ken W. Watson, 2013).

Ken W. Watson, 2013

Places Associated with John By in England

ENGLAND

Cheshunt •

• Enfield Lock

• Waltham Abbey

LONDON

Lambeth •

Woolwich

• Chatham

• Frant

• Faversham

English Channel

Lt. Col. John By, Commanding Royal Engineer, Rideau Canal

Introduction

On March 14, 1826, Lt. Col. John By, an officer on the inactive list of the Corps of Royal Engineers, was notified of his appointment to superintend the construction of the Rideau Canal in Canada. Included in the communication from the Board of Ordnance was a copy of a memorandum setting forth how the projected Rideau Canal project was to be undertaken and orders to report to the Ordnance office at the Tower of London, on March 17th at noon, to meet with General Gother Mann, the Inspector General of Fortifications.[1]

Upon his appointment as Commanding Royal Engineer, Rideau Canal, Lt. Col. John By was living the life of a country gentleman on a large estate, Shernfold Park, in the Village of Frant in East Sussex, about 35 miles south of London. He was living with his wife, Esther By, their two young daughters, Esther March By and Harriet Martha By, and their household staff, and had a number of tenants on his outlying farms. Over the previous five years, since his placement on the inactive list by the Board of Ordnance, he had devoted his energies to enlarging and improving the Shernfold Park Estate through purchasing adjoining farmlands and introducing advanced agricultural practices, which were based on his reading in the latest scientific agricultural literature.[2]

For Lt. Col. By, his return to duty involved a major sacrifice in his standard of living, his comforts of life as a country squire and a major disruption for his young family; yet he had a good reason for doing so. His earlier service with the Corps of Royal Engineers had been exemplary, and he was well respected within the Corps as a highly competent engineer. However, after twenty years of past service to his King and Country, his name was not associated with any outstanding engineering work. The Rideau Canal assignment presented an opportunity to design and construct a major engineering work of critical value for the defence of the Province of Upper Canada and of public benefit for the economic development of a province of the British Empire. It was a project that he was well qualified to superintend based on his engineering capabilities and experience, and for which he was well suited by his character, cultural values, and worldview, where the welfare and well-being of a large labour force was concerned.

Biographical Sketch: the Early Years

John By was born in 1783 into a prominent family of high public office holders of some means. His father, George By, and his father before him, held the position as Chief Searcher in the Customs House for the port of London – by far the busiest port in all of England – and in that position received a commission on the import duties levied on cargoes entering the port. During his boyhood, John By lived in the By family household in Lambeth, Kent, in a semi-rural area on the right bank of the Thames River, across from the metropolis of London. His boyhood home was a substantial house on the prestigious Bishop's Walk road which led from the river at Westminster Bridge to the Palace of the Archbishop of Canterbury, which was nearby.

His father was also a member of the Watermans' and Lightermans' Guild, the members of which were responsible for transporting goods across the Thames River, as well as for lightening the cargoes of the larger sailing ships which passed up river to the City of London, and for loading large sailing ships carrying goods for export. Such a membership suggests that the By family had an ownership interest in a shipping company. The By family was clearly a family of some standing and influence in holding a lucrative Crown patronage appointment, which was passed down through several generations from father to eldest son.

The By family were members of the St. Mary's-at-Lambeth (Anglican) Church, and as a boy, John By would have received an excellent education at a Grammar School. As of the mid-18th Century, the education offered at grammar schools varied greatly from a strictly classical education to a mixed classical and modern curriculum. However, by the late 18th Century the grammar schools were teaching mathematics, geography, English grammar, moral and natural philosophy, and modern languages (French and German), as well as English history, rhetoric, logic, and ethics, in addition to the traditional grammar school curriculum of Greek, Latin, and the Classics.[3]

At the young age of thirteen – with his elder brother George Jr. in line to join the Customs Office and eventually succeed his father as Chief Searcher – the By family determined on a career for John By as a military engineer. At that time, Army officers could purchase their commissions, but entry into the Corps of Royal Engineers was through graduation from the Royal Military Academy at Woolwich. Most of the cadets at the military academy were the sons of high ranking military officers; many of whom were from the landed gentry. Entry into the Royal Military Academy was dependent on a recommendation from the Master General of the Board of Ordnance and the passing of an entrance examination. Candidates were required to have a knowledge of mathematics, proficiency in English composition, and a knowledge of Latin and French, and were encouraged to have some proficiency in drawing.

Moreover, the Corps was the preserve of 'gentlemen' and every effort was made to keep it so. Even the pay of the engineering officers was kept low in order to ensure that the candidates who were attracted to the military engineering life would be 'gentlemen' of some independent means. Military engineers were expected to be able to maintain themselves as an officer and a gentleman, and not be dependent on their military pay to maintain a household. It was a testament to the influence, financial worth, and good-character standing of the By family, and the academic achievements of young John By, that he was able to achieve entry into the Royal Military Academy as a "Gentleman Cadet", despite the lack of any family military connection.[4]

The Royal Military Academy was located in the village of Woolwich in Kent, just south of London. At Woolwich, cadets were taught the practical and theoretical knowledge which was required by artillery and engineering officers. This included such diverse subjects as the constructing of gun and mortar batteries, the erection of fortifications and buildings, surveying and levelling, gunnery, the mechanics of moving and raising great weights, sapping and mining, and the making of fascines, as well as drawing, drafting, trigonometry, geometry, arithmetic, French, and military architecture. The drawing and drafting courses included Indian Ink landscapes, Large coloured landscapes (watercolours), Naturally coloured landscapes, Embellishments of landscapes for military purposes, Perspective in drawing buildings and fortifications, and the Practice and Theory of Perspective. After completing the prescribed course of study, a cadet would join the Ordnance Survey in Wales for six months of practice in surveying and levelling, before receiving his commission.

After receiving their commission and gaining several years of practical experience in the field, officers of the Corps of Royal Engineers were expected to be competent in all branches of military engineering. They were expected to be capable of superintending military works projects, framing cost estimates and preparing plans for the construction of fortifications, military roads and bridges, barracks buildings, drainage systems, irrigation canals, wharves, storehouses, and military hospitals.

At the age of sixteen, John By graduated from the Royal Military Academy as part of a class of five officer cadets. He received his commission on August 1, 1799, as a Second Lieutenant in the Royal Artillery. Five months later, on December 20th, he transferred to the Royal Engineers, which was the customary procedure for entering that Corps.[5]

While in the Royal Engineers, he served in England (1800-1802), in Lower Canada (1802- 1811), in the Peninsular War (February -August 1811), and again in England (1812-1821). In April 1821, he was placed on the inactive list. His return to active service in March 1826 was occasioned by his appointment to superintend the construction of the Rideau Canal in Upper Canada. During his earlier engineering career, he rose steadily through the ranks: First Lieutenant, April 1801; Second Captain, March 1805; Captain, June 1809; Brevet Major, June 1811, and Major in the fall of 1814. While on the inactive list, he was promoted to the rank of Lieutenant Colonel in December 1824.[6]

During his first posting at Plymouth in England, he was on the staff of the Royal Engineers commanding the Sixth Company of Royal Sappers and Miners, who were engaged in constructing fortifications for the defence of the harbour. While on that posting, young John By entered into matrimony. On November 12, 1801, he married Elizabeth Johnson Baines the eldest daughter of Captain Cuthbert Baines, R.N., who owned extensive lands around Penzance in Cornwall. Second Lieutenant John By was only 18 years old, and his bride 21 years of age.[7]

Soon after his marriage, Lieutenant By was posted to Lower Canada. Upon returning to England, almost a decade later, the young couple lived for a time with his elder brother, George By, who had inherited the family home at Lambeth. Then Captain By was posted to the Duke of Wellington's command in Portugal where, while serving in a siege operation, he became ill and was invalided back to England. Four months later, having recovered his health, Brevet Major By was appointed Commanding Royal Engineer for the Royal Gunpowder Mills. He and Elizabeth established a home at Waltham Abbey, about 15 miles northeast of London where the gunpowder mills were located.

The next year – presumably upon inheriting monies from the By family estate – the John By household moved to Rendlesham Lodge, a large house with extensive grounds, in nearby Waltham Cross. While living there, they attended St. Mary-the-Virgin

Figure 10. "Lt. Col. John By", n.d. Photograph of a portrait by "C.K" (Royal Engineers' Museum, Chatham, England).

(Anglican) Church in the nearby market town of Cheshunt. In December 1814, Elizabeth By died after a short illness; she was childless.

Four years later, on 14 March 1818, Major By – then 35 years of age – married a 20- year old heiress and ward of chancery, Esther March, who was the daughter of the late John March of Harley Street, Cavendish Square, London. Prior to his death, March was a wealthy printer to the Bank of England with large financial holdings and property in Clapham, Surrey. Esther was well-connected as well with the landed gentry. Her deceased mother was the eldest daughter of John Raymond Barker, the Lord of the manor of Fairford Park in Gloucestershire, where the Barker family had large land holdings and occupied prominent positions in the Church, the local judiciary, and the parish government.[8]

Although Major By was a gentleman of some independent means

prior to his marriage to Esther March, and in command of the Royal Gunpowder Mills, he was not then a significant land owner or a member of the landed gentry. The purchase of a large landed estate was beyond his means.

During the first two years of their marriage, the newly-weds leased a substantial house on Great Cumberland Place in a highly-fashionable suburb of London (now Marylebone), not far from Harley Street where Esther March had resided in her early childhood. At Great Cumberland Place, a daughter, Esther March By, was born in early 1819.[9] However, as a result of his second marriage, it was not long before John By attained the life of a country gentleman, for which he was ideally suited by his education and cultural values.

According to the marriage settlement of 10 March 1818 the inheritance of Esther March, which comprised £10,000 of bank stock and £34,000 of government consols, was to be held in trust by three trustees "for the absolute use of Esther March, in case of her surviving her intended husband, John By". In the interim, Esther was to receive the income from the annual interest on the investments. In addition, the trustees were to raise another £20,000 from the sale of property from the March estate to purchase lands, which were to be owned outright by Esther in fee simple.

Thereafter, in January 1820, the trustees purchased an estate, Shernfold Park, in the Village of Frant, Sussex, for £17,607 in fulfilment of the terms of the marriage settlemen and the John By household took up residence there.[10] While resident at Shernfold Park, the By family attended St. Alban's (Anglican) Church in Frant, and were active in the parish. Soon after their arrival, Major By was appointed "Surveyor for Frant Green Division", with responsibility as a land owner for the repair and maintenance of the county roads. He also served on a five-member parish committee, comprising "noblemen and gentlemen", which was responsible for securing the construction of a new church to replace the old St. Alban's Church.

Why an estate was purchased over 50 miles to the south-east of the Royal Gunpowder Works at Waltham Abbey, remains unclear. It may be that Major By was contemplating retirement. After twenty years of service with the Corps of Royal Engineers, retirement to the life of a country gentleman would have held a strong appeal. The Shernfold Park was a place to establish his family, and to devote his retirement years to managing and enlarging the new family estate. While resident at Shernfold Park, a second daughter, Harriet Martha By, was born in 1821, and in August of that year Major John By was placed on the inactive list. Nonetheless, the Board of Ordnance remained aware of his past service and capabilities, and in December 1824 Major By was promoted to the rank of Lieutenant Colonel while on the inactive list.[11]

Upon his recall and appointment in March 1826 to superintend the Rideau Canal project, Lt. Col. John By already had experience in canal construction work and possessed an exemplary record in superintending engineering works. During his earlier tour of duty in Lower Canada in 1802-1810, then Captain By had superintended the reconstruction and enlargement of the Cascades Canal (1805-1806), which was a 1500-foot long batteaux canal with a three-foot navigable depth. It had a single 20' x 120' lock of stone masonry, with narrower 13' wide gates, and was capable of passing six batteaux in a single lockage. The Cascades Canal by-passed the rapids of the same name, and was one of a series of rapids in the St. Lawrence River above Montreal.[12]

John By was also on the engineering staff at Quebec during the period when the officers of the Corps of Royal Engineers constructed three Martello towers on the Plains of Abraham to strengthen the defences of Quebec. More generally, he had gained a familiarity with heavy construction work at Quebec during a period when a number of powder magazines, storehouses, barracks and dockyard defence works, were constructed under the supervision of his superior officers of the Corps of Royal Engineers.[13] When off duty, he showed a commendable initiative in working with a draftsman-surveyor, Jean-Baptiste Duberger, to build an elaborately detailed scale model of the town of Quebec and its new defences.[14]

Thereafter, when serving in Portugal under the Duke of Wellington's command, Captain By took part in the first siege (6 May 1811-10 June 1811) of the Spanish fort at Badajoz, which had been captured earlier by the French. After being invalided home, he recovered his health and, in January 1812, was appointed Commanding Royal Engineer of the Royal Gunpowder Mills at Waltham Abbey and Faversham, with responsibility for the musket manufacturing establishment at the Tower of London and the storehouses at Purfleet on the Thames River.[15]

While in command of the Royal Gunpowder Mills, Captain By was responsible for designing new industrial buildings and gunpowder manufacturing machinery. He built two gunpowder mills at Waltham Abbey, and designed and erected an innovative hydraulic gunpowder press in consultation with Joseph Bramah (1748-1814), the inventor of the hydraulic ram press. The new hydraulic gunpowder press incorporated a mechanical system for removing the 'press cake' of gunpowder. This innovation eliminated the highly-dangerous hand-removal process which was previously used and enabled the workers to shelter behind a protective wall while performing the dangerous work of removing the cake from the press. Two of the new hydraulic presses were able to do the work of twelve of the conventional screw presses which were previously employed. In addition to his engineering work at Waltham Abbey, he also designed and constructed a new Brimstone (sulphur) Storehouse and a Saltpetre Refinery at Faversham, and designed a more efficient charcoal press that greatly reduced the dangerous dust which was generated in crushing charcoal.

During the same period, Captain By had gained a good deal of experience in managing a building construction project, in designing hydraulic machinery and in laying out a manufacturing complex complete with worker housing. One of his major undertakings was the carrying out of a Board of Ordnance directive to establish a musket manufactory near Waltham Abbey by relocating and integrating the existing barrel forges and manufactory from Lewisham, Kent, and the musket assembly plant from the Tower of London. In that endeavour, he worked closely with John Rennie (1761-1821) – one of the pre-eminent civil engineers of the age – in the selection of the water-power site at Enfield Lock for the new manufactory, and in the designing of the water wheels and gearing for the new hydraulic-power system.

In addition Captain By modernized the manufacturing process through purchasing lathes of the latest design for turning musket barrels in the new factory, thereby greatly reducing the amount of grinding, filing and polishing which was required in the older manufacturing process. He also prepared the plans for the layout and construction of the industrial buildings of the new manufacturing complex. He superintended its construction, as well as designed the row-house cottages to house the workforce: the Superintendent, two foremen, 35 welders, 18 rough borers, 12 smooth borers, 12 grinders, 30 filers, and 20 women and children, who were employed at the works.[16]

During his earlier career, John By had shown a keen interest in the design of engineering structures. In 1811 he designed a wooden arched truss bridge on what he considered to be a revolutionary principle, and in March 1816 he constructed a scale model of an 1,000 foot span bridge, with an 100' rise, which illustrated his novel arched truss. The scale model was presented to the Master General and Board of Ordnance, and placed on display at the Institution of Royal Engineers at Chatham.[17] He was also among the earliest designers and builders of cast iron bridges. In 1816, it was reported that several cast iron bridges had recently been constructed by British engineers; and that "a portable iron bridge was being constructed under the immediate direction of Major By, of the Corps of Royal Engineers. Moreover, the principle of the portable iron bridge was being "highly spoken of" and a scale model was on display at the War Office in Pall Mall.[18]

Following his placement on the inactive list in August 1821 –
during a general postwar reduction of the military establishment
– Major By continued to show a keen interest in civil engineering
work, particularly bridge and canal construction. He maintained
a close friendship with John Rennie until the latter's death in
1821 and corresponded with several leading Montreal merchants
whom the Province of Lower Canada had appointed as Canal
Commissioners to oversee the construction of the Lachine Canal
(1821-1825) at Montreal.[19]

Over the span of his engineering career prior to his appointment
to construct the Rideau Canal, Lt. Col. By had a surprisingly
wide and varied experience in heavy construction work and
appears to have excelled at every task assigned to his charge. This
was particularly in evidence at an early date when, following
the completion of the Cascades Canal, his superior officer at
Quebec expressed a high regard for the "great judgment and
ability" apparent in his conduct of the work. It was a judgement
which was apparently shared by Colonel Gother Mann, the
Commanding Royal Engineer for Canada at that time.[20]

It was Lt. General Gother Mann, in his later capacity as Inspector
General of Fortifications at the Board of Ordnance, who
appointed Captain John By to the position of Commanding
Engineer of the Royal Gunpowder Mills; and it was General
Mann who turned to Lt. Col. By in March 1826 when directed
by the Board of Ordnance to "select a competent Officer of
Engineers" to superintend the construction of the projected
Rideau Canal.[21] It was the most demanding of the several
major military canal and fortifications projects that the Board of
Ordnance had in contemplation for construction in Canada, and
General Mann did not hesitate to call on his former subordinate.
Only four days after General Mann received the Rideau Canal
project directive, orders were issued to Lt. Col. By to report for
duty at the Ordnance in London.[22]

While at the Ordnance offices in London, Lt. Col. By was

directed to peruse the documents that embodied his preliminary instructions for constructing the Rideau Canal and to raise any points of concern. Otherwise, he was ordered to hold himself in readiness to proceed to Canada as soon as the Colonial Office responded with its comments on the preliminary instructions which set forth the route to be followed by the Rideau Canal, the contract system to be employed for its construction, the scale of canal to be constructed, and the manner in which the canal was to be financed by the British government.[23]

On April 18th, a communication was received from the Colonial Office informing the Board of Ordnance, that Lord Bathurst, the Secretary for War and the Colonies, was in agreement with the preliminary instructions prepared by the Board of Ordnance for constructing the planned Rideau Canal.[24] Once the Colonial Office gave its support to the canal construction project, Lt. Col. By was ordered to Canada. His final instructions, and authorization to commence work on the Rideau Canal construction project, would follow. The Master General of the Ordnance, the Duke of Wellington, was in Russia on the British government diplomatic mission and the Board of Ordnance wanted to secure a final approval from the Master General, as well as a vote of funds by parliament – on the Colonial Estimates – before it would authorize construction to commence..[25]

On April 21st, just three days after receipt of the Colonial Office missive approving his preliminary instructions, Lt. Col. By embarked for Canada on the barque *Endeavour*, with his wife Esther. They were accompanied by their two young daughters – Esther, who was seven years old, and Harriet, who was five years old – and several servants. The By party arrived in Quebec on May 30th, and two days later Lt. Col. By met with Colonel Durnford, the Commanding Royal Engineer for Canada, and the Respective Officers of the Ordnance at Quebec. He informed them of his orders, and consulted reports on several reconnaissance surveys undertaken earlier by the Royal Engineers of the projected Rideau Canal route. He then proceeded to Montreal to set up a temporary headquarters, where he was soon joined by Captain Daniel Bolton, R.E., and John Mactaggart, a civilian Clerk of Works, both of whom were sent out from England by the Ordnance.

While awaiting his final orders to commence the construction of the canal, Lt. Col. By gathered information on the cost of building materials and labour in Canada, inspected the Lachine Canal, interviewed potential contractors and hired several civilian overseers for his canal establishment. He was also able to secure a copy of a survey report of the proposed Rideau Canal route, that had been prepared a year earlier by a Canadian land surveyor, Samuel Clowes.[26]

On 4 September 1826, a package arrived at Lt. Col. By's temporary headquarters in Montreal from the Board of Ordnance. It contained the final instructions for the undertaking of the Rideau Canal construction project and approval for an immediate commencement of construction. After a careful perusal of his Instructions, Lt. Col. By and his new engineering staff departed from Montreal by canoe and were accompanied by several Montreal contractors who were anxious to secure work on the Rideau Canal project. On September 21st the party arrived at Wright's Town, a timber trade and farming settlement located on the Lower Canada side of the Ottawa River. The town was situated just upstream and across the river from the Rideau Falls, where the Rideau River fell 30 feet over a high rocky bluff into the Ottawa River.[27]

Once on site, Lt. Col. By immediately set to work in examining the rocky right bank of the Ottawa River, both upstream and downstream of the Rideau Falls, and selected a narrow gorge in the river bank at Sleigh Bay as the entrance for the canal. He then engaged men to work in clearing and grubbing the newly-selected entrance valley, and in erecting support buildings and a dock. In addition, contracts were let on the spot for the construction of the first two spans of a projected seven span bridge of communication, which was intended to link Wright's Town to the Entrance Valley across a series of islands in the

Ottawa River. Preparations were also made for the undertaking of a winter survey and the levelling of the first section of the canal.

Having perused the survey report of Samuel Clowes, Lt. Col. By planned to avoid the shallow rapids of the lower Rideau River by routing the first section of the canal overland for five miles from the Entrance Valley to the Rideau River at a deep stillwater above the Hog's Back Rapids. With several support buildings constructed, and arrangements made for the undertaking of the winter survey, he returned to his winter quarters in Montreal to await the completion of the winter survey. Once completed, he intended to prepare plans and estimates to enable contracts to be let early in the spring of 1827 for the construction of the first section of the canal.[28]

Character, Cultural Values, and Worldview

Lt. Col. By was determined to get the canal construction work underway as quickly as possible; yet from the very beginning of construction, he was also committed to doing whatever could be done to promote the welfare and well-being of the canal workers. Hence, with the commencement of construction in the spring of 1827, he acted to ensure that the canal workers would be well provisioned at reasonable prices, were provided with health care when needed, were paid a reasonable wage and were provided with tools and clothing that could be purchased at cost.[29] It took some time to set up his base workcamp and to establish the needed infrastructure and support system, but he managed to do so as soon as it could be done. Likewise, he did everything possible to reduce the suffering from 'fever and age' – malaria – in keeping with the medical knowledge of the day.

The paternalism that he practiced during the construction of the Rideau Canal was a product of his character, cultural values, and worldview, which were formed by the Anglican Tory culture in which he was raised. Anglican toryism embodied the religious, social, and moral values, instilled by the clerics of the Established Church of England (through their teachings from the Scriptures, church traditions, and the Book of Common Prayer), and concepts adopted from classical political philosophy as interpreted by Anglican divines and clerics within a Christian belief and teleological framework. Moreover, the character, cultural values, and worldview of young John By were reinforced through being raised in a family of public servants, through his attendance at the Royal Military Academy, and his position as an officer and gentleman in the Corps of Royal Engineers.

His Anglican Tory beliefs entailed not only a sense of duty and responsibility to God, King and Country, and support for the established National Church, but a sense of responsibility pertaining to one's position in the natural social order. Each order had its particular function to perform for the benefit, and proper functioning, of the whole of society. Moreover, those in superior positions of authority were under a moral obligation to maintain harmony among the various social orders, to promote the common good of all members of society, to exercise a Christian charity towards 'the deserving poor", and to strive to maintain peace and order through providing good government.[30]

Glimpses of the character and deportment of the Commanding Royal Engineer, Rideau Canal, can be found in the writings of William Lett, a contemporary. As a youth residing in Bytown during the canal construction period, young William Lett had occasion to see and form an opinion of Lt. Col. By, the town's founder and most prominent citizen. Years later, Lett published a long poem on life in Bytown and the men of Bytown who worked on the Rideau Canal project. His poetic description of Lt. Col. By ran as follows:

> "The portly Colonel I behold
> Plainly as in the days of old,
> conjured before me at this hour
> By memory's undying power;
> Seated upon his great black steed
> Of stately form and noble breed.
> A man who knew not how to flinch –

> A British soldier every inch.
> Courteous alike to low and high
> A gentleman was Colonel By!"[31]

In another of his writings, William Lett described Lt. Col. By in the following terms:

> "Colonel By was what a physiognomist would call 'a man with a presence'. He was about five feet nine or ten inches tall, stoutly built, almost corpulent, and quite military looking. His hair was dark, complexion rather florid, and altogether he was rather jovial and good natured in looks. He was a man of great energy and determination, ... and was always alive to the encouragement of any project calculated to advance and aggrandize the little town called after him."[32]

At 43 years of age – upon his appointment to superintend the construction of the Rideau Canal – Lt. Col. By fully undertook that he was undertaking an arduous task of organizing and overseeing a large work force in the wilds of Upper Canada, under the most trying of conditions imaginable. From his earlier service in Canada, he knew that the construction of a 125-mile long canal through the interior of Upper Canada, would entail difficult engineering challenges, physical hardship and the risk of sickness from debilitating swamp fevers. Nonetheless, he accepted the challenge out of a sense of duty and a professional responsibility to the Corps, and as well, no doubt, from a desire to distinguish himself as an engineer in the service of his King and Country through constructing an outstanding public work.

Ultimately, Lt. Col. By paid a heavy price for constructing the Rideau Canal through sacrificing his health, and in having his competence and character publically questioned for supposedly indulging in exorbitant expenditures and expending unauthorized sums of monies on the canal project.[33]

In so far, as Lt. Col. By sought anything from his public service in constructing the Rideau Canal, it was not a monetary reward. What he requested from the Board of Ordnance was that he:

> "Be honoured with some public distinction as will show that my character as a soldier is without stain, and that I have not lost the confidence or good opinion of my Government".

In sum, what he sought was some mark of distinction from the King (King William IV) to publically attest that his reputation as an officer and a gentleman was above reproach, and to serve as an acknowledgment of his public service in constructing an outstanding engineering work.[34] As such, he was a product of a traditional political culture – Anglican Toryism – which embodied religious, social, economic, moral, and political values far removed from the Lockean-liberal political culture of the contemporary bourgeoisie with their belief in individual rights, enlightened self-interest, laissez-faire government, and the pursuit of personal happiness and wealth.[35]

Endnotes

1. LAC, WO 55, vol. 863, reel B-2809, 209-210, Lt. Col. Ellicombe, R.E., Pall Mall, to Lt. Col. By, 14 March 1826.

2. The Bytown Museum in Ottawa, has in its possession a number of volumes from the former Shernfold Park Estate library bearing the inscription: "John By, Major Royal Engineers, 13th July 1819". Among the books are: Francis Clater, *Every Man his own Cattle Doctor, or a Practical Treatise of the Diseases of Horned Cattle* (4th ed., London 1814); George Culley, *Observations of Live Stock containing Hints for Choosing and Improving the Best Breeds* (4th ed., London, 1807); Sir Humphrey Davy, *Elements of Agricultural Chemistry, or a Course of Lectures for the Board of Agriculture* (2nd. Ed, London, 1814); John Morley of Blickling, *Cheap and Profitable Manure and Compost: Plan and Easy Directions for Preparing, and Method of Using Excellent Compost for Manuring Arable, Meadow & Pasture Lands in General, in the cheapest manner, from which Greater Production of Grain &c will be obtained than any Other Manure of Equal*

Expence (3ʳᵈ. Ed, Norwich, 1812); and Society of Practical Gardeners, *Rural Recreations; or, The Gardener's Instructor: Exhibiting in a clear and perspicuous Manner, All the Operations Necessary in the Kitchen, flower, and Fruit Garden, &c. &c. for Every Month in the Year: with a Treatise on the Management of Bees &c. To which is subjoined a Complete catalogue of Useful and Ornamental Trees, Shrubs & Plants, with Their Varieties, and Parts Used for Medicinal and Culinary Purposes.* (London, 1806). As cited by Robert Legget, *John By*, 18-19.

3. Robert Legget, *John By Builder of the Rideau Canal, Founder of Ottawa* (Ottawa: Historical Society of Ottawa, 1982): 4-5, 17-18; and Mark E. Andrews, P. Eng. *For King and Country, Lieutenant-Colonel John By, R.E., Indefatigable Civil-Military Engineer* (The Heritage Merrickville Foundation: Merrickville, Ontario, 1998): 17, 21, 26-30 & 92. In his own research work, the author has focussed on the engineering, technological, and financial aspects of the Rideau Canal project, and the labour situation, as revealed in the War Office records and Colonial Office records pertaining to the canal construction project. Unfortunately, there are no By family papers in existence. As a result this biographical sketch draws heavily on secondary sources that set out only the main developments in John By's life from which, however, inferences can be drawn concerning the political culture in which he was raised and lived prior to the construction of the Rideau Canal.

When Lt. Col. By died in February 1836, his widow erected a commemorative plaque with the Coat of Arms of the ancient Bye family, but it is not known whether the John By family was actually in a direct line of descent from that noble family. During his lifetime John By did not claim a noble lineage. (*ibid*, 31). The comment on the curriculum of a late 18ᵗʰ century grammar school was worked up through an Internet search of several postings on "English Grammar Schools".

4. Legget, *John By*, 6-8; and Andrews, *For King and Country*, 31, 36-37 & 39. At that time, John Rennie, C.E., was a consultant to the Customs Service. Mark Andrews speculates that Rennie may have known the By family and encouraged young John By to pursue an engineering career. (*ibid*, 28). If so, it was most likely the By family that would have insisted on a professional military engineering career, rather than have young John serve as an apprentice to a civil engineer.

5. Hamnet P. Hill, "Lieutenant Colonel John By, A Biography," *The Engineering Journal*, XIV, No. 8, August 1931, 452. See also Great Britain,

Corps of Royal Engineers, *Aide Mémoire to the Military Sciences*, vol. I, 413, "Engineering, Military," August 1846; and Marianne McLean, "The Education of the Royal Engineers" (Parks Canada: Research Bulletin No. 23, July 1975), 3-4. This summary of the engineering officers' education at the Royal Military Academy is based on the cited sources, but is taken almost verbatim from an earlier work of the author's: viz. Robert W. Passfield, *Building the Rideau Canal: A Pictorial History*, 38 & 170.

6. Robert F. Legget, "By, John", *Dictionary of Canadian Biography Online*, Vol. VII.

7. Legget, *John By*, 8. Captain Cuthbert Baines, R.N. was a half-pay naval officer, who at the turn of the century was well-connected with large land holdings in Cornwall. In 1774 he had married Lydia Veale of Trevaylor House, Gulval Parish, Penzance, Cornwall, who was the eldest daughter of a rich and influential Anglican family that owned the Manor of Alverton at Penzance. Soon thereafter, Captain Baines attained a part ownership of the manor lands and effects. The manor was granted to the Veale family by Queen Elizabeth I, and originally comprised 60 acres of woodlands and 300 acres of pasture lands. (Internet genealogical searches.)

From his marriage to Elizabeth Johnson Baines, Second Lieutenant By does not appear to have received any substantial marriage settlement. Her mother, the widow of Captain Baines lived until 1828 and upon her death, according to Captain Baines' will, the house in Penzance was to be sold, and the family estate divided amongst their five children. At that time, Elizabeth – John By's first wife – was already deceased. Apparently her 1/5 share of her father's estate, including the proceeds of the manor house sale, was about £5,000. However, owing to Lt. Col. By's absence in Upper Canada during the construction of the Rideau Canal, and the recalcitrance of the Baines' family executor, John By did not receive his first wife's inheritance until sometime after his return to England. (The National Archives, East Sussex Record Office, online archival documents and archival administrative history.)

8. Legget, *John By*, 14-17; Andrews, *For King and Country*, 61, 67, & 76-78; and Personal Communication, Chris Hobson, Fairford History Society, to author, 9 March 2013. Following the death of their father, the March sisters – Esther and Martha – lived in Cheshunt with the family of Oliver Cromwell, one of the trustees of their late father's estate, and attended the parish church of St. Mary-the-Virgin. It was presumably at Church that the widower Major

By made the acquaintance of the young heiress, Esther March. Subsequently, they were married in that Church.

9. Andrews, *For Kings and Country*, 77-79 & 89; and Legget, *John By*, 17. John March had died in 1804, at which time his property and financial investments were placed in trust with three executors for his two young daughters, Esther and Martha. Upon the death of Martha in November 1817, Esther March became the sole heir of John March.

The extent of John By's personal worth during his marriage to Esther By, is not known. His father was long since deceased, and upon the death of his mother he would have received monies from his father's estate. However, he had two brothers to share in the estate: George, his elder brother, who inherited the family home on Bishop's Walk in Lambeth and succeeded their father as Chief Searcher in the London Custom's House; and a younger brother, Henry, who was a customs broker.

10. The marriage settlement agreement, and the final resolution of the estate of Esther By after her death in 1838, is set forth in: "Ashburnham v. Ashburnham", *The Law Times and Journal of Property from October 1849 to March 1850*, Vol. XIV (London: Office of The Law Times, 1850), 367-368.

11. Legget, *John By*, 17-19; and Andrews, *For King and Country*, 89-92. While at Shernfold Park before his departure to superintend the construction of the Rideau Canal, and later after his return to England, Lt. Col. By continued to expand his personal land holdings through purchasing outlying farms. When his personal property was ultimately sold long after his death, his estate comprised 385 acres of farmlands and buildings, £3,407.10.1 in investments, and a house on Aldersgate Street in London, as well as land in Bytown, and 20 shares of stock in the Commercial Bank of the Midland District of Upper Canada. The Shernfold Park Estate, the £10,000 in bank stock, and the £34,000 in government consols belonging to his wife, Esther By, were inherited by their two daughters according to her will.

12. Andrews, *For King and Country*, 45-53. Earlier the Corps of Royal Engineers constructed four short military canals (1779-1783) on the St. Lawrence River to enable batteaux to ascend a series of rapids between Lake St. Louis and Lake St. Francis: the Faucille Rapids Canal, Trou du Moulin Canal, Split Rock Canal, and Coteau du Lac Canal. At the turn of the 19th century, the Royal Engineers enlarged the Split Rock and Coteau du Lac batteaux

canals to pass Durham boats. The Faucille Rapids and Trou du Moulin canals were replaced in 1804-1805 by a single enlarged canal, the Cascades Canal, constructed under the supervision of Captain John By. See John Heisler, *The Canals of Canada* (Ottawa: National Historic Sites Service, 1973):17-20.

13. The last heavy construction work carried out by the military at Quebec previous to the 1808-1812 period, consisted of the construction of a temporary citadel complex of earth works and wooden palisade construction during the years 1780-1781 (Glenn A. Steppler, "Quebec, The Gibraltar of North America?", Parks Canada: Manuscript Report Number 224, 1976, pp. 44-45 and 70-74). Eventually four Martello towers were constructed on the Plains of Abraham, but the construction of the fourth tower postdated Captain By's service in Canada. See Ivan J. Saunders, *A History of Martello Towers in the defence of British North American, 1796-1871* (Ottawa: Canadian Historic Sites, Occasional Papers in Archaeology and History, 1976), 29-32.

14. Bernard Pothier, *The Quebec Model* (Ottawa: Canadian War Museum Paper No. 9, 1978). The Quebec model is exceptionally large, 18 feet x 18 feet, with streets and buildings of the upper and lower town, the docks, and the defensive works reproduced in detail to scale. A controversy has developed over the years as to the respective roles of Captain By and a draftsman-surveyor Jean-Baptiste Duberger in the building of the model. Pothier attributes the original idea of building a model to Major-General Gother Mann, but it was clearly Captain By's initiative that led to the model being undertaken. Duberger promised to work with Captain By on the project, both working on their own time and at their own expense when not on duty. (See *ibid*, 67, reprint of letter, signed John B. Duberger, Royal Military Surveyor and Draftsman, to Major-General Gother Mann, February 16, 1807; and *ibid*, 69, reprint of a letter, Captain John By to General Morse, Inspector General of Fortifications, Board of Ordnance, 7 February 7, 1811).

15. Edward F. Bush, *Builders of Rideau Canal, 1816-1832* (Smith Falls: Friends of the Rideau CD Book, 2009), 4; and Hamnet P. Hill, "The Construction of the Rideau Canal, 1826-1832", *Ontario Historical Society Papers and Records*, 1925, 118. Captain By was not present at the second, successful siege of Badajoz (March 16, 1812 - April 6, 1812). For a description of the type of engineering work and equipment required in conducting a major siege operation, see Great Britain, Corps. of Royal Engineers, *Aide Mémoire to the Military Sciences*, Vol. I, May 1845, "Attack of Fortresses," pp. 68-99; and Vol. II, January 1850, "Mining," pp. 347-405; Vol. III, December 1851,

"Sap", pp.393-425, and "Siege and Engineer Equipment", 423-427.

16. Andrews, *For King and Country*, 69-75 & 79-87, including illustrations. In LAC, MG13, WO 44, vol. 679, there is a "Plan for a hydrochemical Press for Gunpowder", signed by Captain John By, as well as references to a "Plan for a salt-peter refinery," and a "Plan for a brimstone storehouse."

17. LAC, MG24, A12, Dalhousie Muniments, Section 3, A534, n.p., Lt. Col. By to General Mann, 19 October 1828; and *ibid*, Lt. Col. By to Lord Dalhousie, 7 December 1828; and LAC, MG 24, I9, Hill Collection, vol. 21, miscellaneous material 1812-1832, 5384-5385. See also Andrews, *For King and Country*, p. 88. Thereafter on the Rideau Canal project Lt. Col. By constructed the Great Kettle span of the Chaudière Bridges crossing in keeping with his arch truss design (*op. cit.*, By to Mann, 19 October 1828). In response to an expression of interest by Lord Talbot (2nd Earl Talbot) in the truss design, Lt. Col. By had a drawing prepared, as well as a 1/4" to l'-0" scale model made of the 212 foot arched truss Great Kettle span. It was forwarded to General Mann at the Board of Ordnance for Lord Talbot's perusal, and eventual presentation to the Duke of Wellington (*op. cit.*, By to Dalhousie, 7 December 1828).

18. Charles James, *Universal Military Dictionary*, 4th ed., 1816), 63.

19. LAC, RG 11, Series 1, vol. I, reel 4243, 7, Lachine Canal Commissioners, "Committee Report", to Mr. Auldjo, 31 July 1819.

20. LAC, RG 8, Series C, vol. 38, C-2616, 69, Captain R.H. Bruyeres, Commanding Royal Engineer, Quebec, to Lt. Col. Green, Military Secretary to Lt. General Hunter, 16 January 1805; and LAC, MG13, WO 55, vol. 857, reel B-2805, 473, Captain R.H. Bruyeres, Commanding R.E., Quebec, to Captain Rowley, R.E., 1 August 1805.

21. LAC, MG 13, WO 44, vol. 18, B-1294, 65, W. Griffin, Office of Ordnance to General Mann, 10 March 1826.

22. LAC, WO 55, vol. 863, B-2809, 209, Lt. Col. Ellicombe, R.E., Pall Mall, to Lt. Col. By, 14 March 1826.

23. LAC, MG 13, WO44, vol. 18, reel B-1294, 74, Smyth, "Rideau Canal Memorandum", 14 March 1826, and addendum, n.d., signed General Mann.

24. LAC, MG13, WO44, vol. 18, B-1294, 78-79, J. Morton, Colonial Office, Downing Street, to William Griffin, 18 April 1826.

25. LAC, MG13, WO44, B-1294, vol. 18, 144-145, Rideau Canal Memorandum, prepared by the Board of Ordnance for the Master General, the Duke of Wellington, 26 May 1826. The absence of the Duke of Wellington in Russia from February through early May 1826 accounts for the inordinate delay in getting Lt. Col. By's instructions finalized and sent to Quebec for forwarding to him in Montreal. Wellington's diplomatic mission was completed with the signing of the Anglo-Russian Protocol of 4 April 1826, which committed England to work with Russia to establish Greece as an autonomous tributary state of the Ottoman Empire, and to secure the withdraw of Turkish troops from Greece. The Porte had to either accept the protocol guidelines for a compromise settlement of the Turko-Greek war, or face a war with Russia.

26. LAC, MG13, WO44, vol. 18, B-1294, 7, Lt. Col. By to General Mann, 1 October 1826, and WO55, vol. 863,   B-2809, pp. 212-213, George Rennie to General Mann, 21 April 1826, and Mg13, WO55, B-2809, 258, By to General Mann, Inspector General of Fortifications, 1 September 1826. John Mactaggart was highly recommended to the Ordnance by George Rennie, an English civil engineer, and one of the sons of the late John Rennie (1761-1821) with whom Lt. Col. By had worked earlier at Enfield Lock.

27. LAC, MG13, WO44, vol. 18, B-1294, 9-10, Lt. Col. By to General Mann, 1 October 1826; and LAC, RG8, Series C, vol. 43, reel C-2617, pp. 12-14, Lt. Col. By to Col. Durnford, 22 November 1826. Wellington approved the preliminary instructions given to Lt. Col. By, but with one exception. The Board of Ordnance had established the Rideau Canal project as an independent command with Lt. Col. By reporting directly to the Inspector General of Fortifications in London. To the contrary, Wellington insisted that the regular chain of command be followed. Lt. Col. By was ordered to report through the Commanding Royal Engineer for Canada, and was to keep the Commander-in-Chief for Canada informed of his progress as well. However, Wellington made it clear that the superior officers were not to interfere with the canal project under Lt. Col. By's command. Their role was to keep abreast of developments and to report any concerns.

28. LAC, MG13, WO55, vol. 863, B-2809, 69-70, Lt. Col. By to Gentlemen [Respective Officers], Montreal, 1 November 1826.

29. LAC, RG8, Series C, vol. 42, C-2617, 103, By to Major General Darling, Military Secretary to the Commander-in-Chief, Lord Dalhousie, 2 October 1826; and Mactaggart, *Three Years in Canada*, vol. I, 159-162. See also Part One herein.

30. The traditional Anglican Tory political philosophy in its social, political, and economic worldview, comprised a synthesis of Christian beliefs and concepts taken from the ancient Greek philosophers. Foremost among whom was Plato with respect to human reason, the Form of "the Good', and the ethical state, and his metaphysical system which was surprisingly similar to Christianity, and Aristotle with respect to rule by law, the concept of an organic constitution, and constitutional government. Among the major Christian figures in that evolving intellectual process of integration that ultimately produced Anglican Toryism, were St. Augustine (*City of God*, written 413-427 A.D.) and Thomas Aquinas (*Summa theologica*, written 1264-1274 A.D.) working within a universal (Roman Catholic) Church context, and the Anglican divine, Richard Hooker (*The Laws of Ecclesiastical Polity*, written 1594-1597 A.D.), working within a national State-Church context. See George H. Sabine, *A History of Political Theory*, 3rd. ed., (London: George G. Harrap & Co. Ltd., 1963), on Richard Hooker 437-442, 453, and on Richard Hooker and John Locke, 523-526, 529, 533, 535 & 609.

31. W.P. Lett, *Recollections of Old Bytown* (Ottawa: Ottawa Historical Society, 1979 reprint), edited with an introduction by Edwin Welch. When first published by Lett in 1874, the original title was: *Recollections of Bytown and Its Old Inhabitants*. Lett was born in August 1819 while his father, Captain Andrews Lett, was serving with 26th Regiment in Upper Canada. In 1820 the family settled on land in Huntley Township within the Rideau Military Settlement.

32. Edwin Welch, ed., *Lett's Bytown* (Ottawa: Ottawa Historical Society, Bytown Series No. 3 , 1979), as quoted by Legget, *John By*, 40.

33. For the charges ultimately leveled against Lt. Col. By in England by a Select Committee of Parliament and the Treasury Lords, and a refutation of the same, see Robert W. Passfield, "Engineering the Defence of the Canadas: Lt. Col. John By and the Rideau Canal" (Ottawa: Parks Canada, Manuscript Report Number 425, 1980):109-111, 214-216 & 259. A published summary can be found in Robert W. Passfield, *Building the Rideau Canal*, 33-35.

34. LAC, MG13, WO44, vol. 16, B-217, 19, By to Major-General Pilkington, Inspector General of Fortifications, 22 July 1833.

35. For the political philosophy of John Locke, see Sabine, *A History of Political Theory*, 255, 433, 518, 523-540, 546-547, & 598. Sabine sets forth Locke's philosophy concerning empiricism, property, natural law, the separation of church and state, the compact theory of society and government, self-evident individual rights, enlightened self-interest, and human reason. More generally, Sabine comments on the political influence and secularizing impact of Locke's political philosophy on 18th Century Europe. Lockean-liberal political and social values, were writ large in the Declaration of Independence of the new United States of America (July 1776).

Part Three

Military Paternalism
and the
Rideau Military Settlement

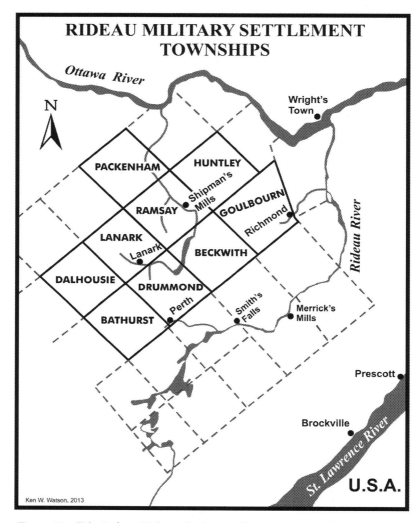

Figure 11. "The Rideau Military Settlement Townships". The three townships – Bathurst, Drummond, and Beckwith – of the Rideau Military Settlement survey are shown, as well as the adjoining township surveys, before military access roads were opened into the interior. (Ken W. Watson, 2013).

Military Paternalism
and the
Rideau Military Settlement

Introduction

Following the termination of the War of 1812, the British government was determined to strengthen the British character, and loyalty, of the Province of Upper Canada, as well as strengthen its defences. To facilitate those objectives, a Military Settling Department was established immediately after the war to settle discharged soldiers at strategic locations in the province; efforts were made to preclude further American immigration into Upper Canada; and an assisted-emigration program was established in Britain to encourage British emigrants to settle in Canada rather than go to the United States. One of the strategic areas selected for priority settlement by discharged soldiers was in the interior wilderness of the Province to the rear of the Rideau River.[1]

The settling of discharged soldiers into a heavily-forested wilderness presented major logistical challenges for the military authorities, which increased substantially when large groups of Scots and Irish Catholic immigrants, who were brought out to Canada under assisted-emigration programmes of the Colonial Office, were located in the newly-established Rideau Military Settlement. In providing support for the soldier-settlers and assisted-emigration settlers, the military authorities went far beyond their prescribed duties and took steps to ensure that the settlers were well equipped and well provisioned until they became self-sufficient. In sum, the entire Rideau Military Settlement experience provides a good example of the practice of paternalism by officers of the British Army.

Strengthening the British Character of Upper Canada

During the War of 1812 Lord Bathurst, the Secretary of State for War and the Colonies, became alarmed at the large number of American settlers in Upper Canada who were disaffected, and who refused to turn out with the militia to defend the province against American invading armies. In response to that situation, in October 1813 Lord Bathurst proposed that the militia be strengthened by providing government assistance to Scots tenant farmers willing to emigrate immediately to Upper Canada. Before the War, large numbers of Highland Scots had emigrated to the United States, and even more were anxious to emigrate, awaiting only the end of the war to do so.

What Bathurst had in mind was to offer land grants and a free ocean passage to the Highland Scots who wished to emigrate. The intention was to direct prospective emigrants to Canada where they would form "a valuable class of settlers" and strengthen the loyal population of the province. The immediate concern was whether the British Army in Canada – during wartime – would be able to spare sufficient provisions to sustain a large number of immigrant families until they were settled on the land. To find out, Lord Bathurst sent his proposal to Lt. General Sir George Prevost, the Commander-in-Chief/Governor-in-Chief for the British North America, who forwarded the communication to Lt. General Sir Gordon Drummond, the Commander of the Forces in Upper Canada, for comment.[2]

In reply, Lt. General Drummond declared his support for the British government proposal to encourage emigration from Scotland to Upper Canada. It would help address a serious wartime manpower crisis in "a country already too much inhabited by Aliens from the United States, very many of whom are avowedly disaffected to the British Government, and as many more of doubtful principles". Drummond agreed that the proposed emigration scheme would greatly strengthen the ranks of the militia, and despite an existing scarcity of provisions, he recommended that the proposed programme be implemented by the government early in the spring of 1814. However, he cautioned that it would not be sufficient to simply provide free passage and a land grant for each family, and provisions in the short term. The immigrant families would require assistance and provisioning for some time after they were settled on the land. Thus, Drummond advised that:

"A large supply of Provisions of all kinds should accompany them, besides felling axes, and other requisite Implements, which cannot be procured in the Country, together with a suitable proportion of Scarlet Militia Clothing, Shoes &c complete. The lands to be granted to these people, must inevitably be of those at present unsettled...." [3]

Plans were prepared in November 1813 to secure the naval transport vessels that would be required to convey a projected 4,000 Scots emigrants to Canada in the following spring. However, that effort was postponed when the Allied Powers forced the abdication of Napoleon in April 1814, and brought an end – at least temporarily – to the war in Europe. At that juncture, Royal Navy transports were needed to convey British troops to North America to prosecute the war with the United States. With heavy British troop reinforcements arriving in Canada during the summer of 1814, there was no pressing need to immediately strengthen the militia of the upper province. Subsequently, in December 1814, the signing of the Treaty of Utrecht brought the War of 1812 to a close in North America on the basis of the *status quo ante bellum*. In such circumstances, the implementation of the assisted emigration plan was delayed.

Yet another reason for the delay was the emergence of a strong political opposition to an assisted-emigration programme. In parliament, the Tory government of Lord Liverpool came under attack for seeking to encourage emigration from Britain. In response, the government denied that the new programme was intended to encourage emigration. To the contrary, it was explained that the proposed programme was intended simply to encourage Britons, who were about to emigrate, to chose Canada as their destination rather than the United States. The aim was to bring about an increase in the loyal population of the Canadian provinces.[4] Despite some parliamentary opposition, the Tory government remained committed to strengthening the British character and loyalty of Upper Canada through an assisted-emigration programme, and was planning as well to the settling discharge soldiers in the Canadian provinces.

During the War of 1812, the men of the British Army regiments serving in Canada were promised a grant of 100 acres of land, and officers 200 acres, or more depending on their rank, if they wished to be discharged in Canada at the end of the war. At the same time, a similar promise of a free land grant was made to the men of the fencible regiments which had been raised in Canada. Hence, at the conclusion of the war, the Colonial Office ordered steps to be taken to provide land for the British troops who wished to receive their discharge in Canada, and for the fencible regiments which were to be disbanded in Canada.

Almost immediately, differences emerged among the Colonial Office, the military, and the local provincial government over where to place the discharged soldiers. Initially, the military wanted to settle the soldiers on the provincial Crown Reserves, which comprised one-seventh of the surveyed land in each township of Upper Canada. However, the provincial government of Upper Canada opposed that proposal. It wanted to keep the Crown Reserve lands for granting to the sons of Loyalists, who were entitled to land grants for the loyal service of their fathers during the American Revolution, and for granting to the men of the loyal militia units who had fought against the Americans during the war of 1812.[5] At the Colonial Office, Lord Bathurst initially suggested that the discharged soldier, and the projected Scots emigrant families of his proposed assisted-emigration scheme, be placed in an unsettled area of Lower Canada, along the 45 parallel border with the United States to prevent an infiltration of American settlers.[6]

In response to the proposal of Lord Bathurst, Major-General,

Sir Frederick Robinson, the provisional Lt. Governor of Upper Canada, advocated the keeping of a wilderness buffer along the border with the United States. Where the land grants for military service were concerned, he recommended that the discharged soldiers be settled on contiguous lots, by regiment, in military settlements; and that the military settlements be located at strategic positions on existing, or projected, military transport routes in the interior of the Canadian provinces.

Where Upper Canada was concerned, the areas that Robinson designated for the establishment of military settlements were: on the Rideau River; on the Trent River; and in the Lake Simcoe area to the rear of York – the provincial capital – on the military transport route from Lake Ontario via Lake Simcoe to Georgian Bay on the upper lakes. Major-General Robinson further recommended that a priority be given to establishing the proposed Rideau military settlement.[7] Following the receipt of Robinson's recommendations, Lord Bathurst instructed the Lt. Governor of Upper Canada, Sir Francis Gore, upon his return to Upper Canada from England, to secure lands for the settlement of the discharged soldiers on the Rideau River.[8]

Implementing a Military Settlements Strategy

The decision to place the discharged soldiers in an interior settlement was based strictly on military considerations. In particular, it was an outgrowth of the knowledge that had been gained by the British military during the war of the vulnerability of the frontier settlements to being overrun and plundered by American marauders in wartime. Many of the loyal militia men from the Niagara region, and from the settlements along the shores of Lake Erie and Lake Ontario, had suffered heavy losses during the war through having their farms and mill properties burned, their livestock slaughtered, and their property looted, during incursions by American marauder guided by renegade American settlers who led the marauders to the homes and properties of the loyal militia officers and the old Tory Loyalist families. Rather than settling the discharged soldiers on border lands, Major-General Robinson wanted them settled in compact military settlements, in the interior of the province, for the security of their families and property in any future war with the United States. Robinson also favoured settling the prospective Scots immigrants on the Crown Reserves.

While the men were away fighting with the militia in defence of the frontiers of the province, their families would be safe from harm in the interior. Moreover, the interior military settlements would foster the development of settlement along the interior military supply lines, of which the Rideau River was by far the most strategically important.[9]

During the War of 1812, the greatest difficulty that the British Army had faced in defending Upper Canada had been the operation of the St. Lawrence River transport system. The St. Lawrence River was the sole transport artery by which guns, supplies, equipment, and provisions could be moved inland from the ocean port of Montreal to supply the British troops in Upper Canada. The province was sparsely settled and – in being dependent on subsistence agriculture – was unable to equip, or fully provision an army. As a result, the British army divisions in Upper Canada were totally dependent on a extremely slow, costly, and inadequate supply system stretching from the ocean port of Montreal inland on the St. Lawrence River and beyond on the Great Lakes.

The movement of convoys of batteaux inland on the St. Lawrence River was impeded by numerous rapids and a strong river current. It took anywhere from eleven to fourteen days for the heavily-laden batteaux to be worked upriver on the 120-mile voyage from Lachine, at the head of the Island of Montreal, to Kingston on Lake Ontario. The river navigation placed heavy manpower demands on the Army in transhipping cargoes at the portages; and that burden had increased immeasurably in 1813 when naval transport requirements were added. For the last two years of the war, the Royal Navy was engaged in a shipbuilding race with the United States Navy for naval supremacy on the Great Lakes.

Moreover, the St. Lawrence River lay exposed for much of its length along the border of Canada with the United States, and its defence was a critical undertaking in wartime.

In the fall of 1814, the British military authorities had begun to fear that the Americans were planning to concentrate their forces during the coming 1815 campaign season to cut the St. Lawrence River supply route. If the Americans were to succeed in doing so, it was evident that British troops and the Canadian fencible regiments would have to be withdrawn from Upper Canada, the Upper Canadian militia disbanded, and the province abandoned to the Americans, unless an alternative supply line could be opened. Hence, explorations were undertaken during the winter of 1814-1815 to determine whether a batteaux navigation could be constructed through the interior of Upper Canada – along the Rideau and Cataraqui rivers – to enable troops, guns, equipment and supplies to be forwarded inland in wartime from Montreal to Kingston, independent of the highly vulnerable upper St. Lawrence River. The ending of the war did not end that effort.[10]

In the immediate postwar period, the construction of a secure military waterway through the interior of Upper Canada was regarded as the *sine qua non* for the defence of the Province of Upper Canada in any future war with the United States. As of October 1815, Lord Bathurst ordered that steps be taken by the Commander-in-Chief to secure detailed surveys, and a plan and cost estimate for constructing the proposed Rideau batteaux navigation. Efforts were also undertaken by the Colonial Office to secure a financial contribution from the provincial government of Upper Canada. At that time, the Treasury Lords were insisting that the province contribute half the cost of construction on the grounds that the military waterway would serve a commercial, as well as military purpose, for the economic benefit of the province.[11]

Once a decision was made to give a priority to settling discharge soldiers in a military settlement on the Rideau River, the first step was to secure the land. Most of the land along the Rideau River was in a wilderness state, but it had been granted to Loyalists and their descendants or was in the hands of land speculators. However, that was not the case with the lands deep in the bush to the northwest of the Rideau River, which belonged to the "Chippawa and Mississaguay Nations". Lt. Governor Gore immediately despatched a provincial agent to secure approval from the Natives for the establishment of a settlement on their lands, pending the conclusion of a treaty to purchase the lands. He also ordered a survey to be made of the lands for three new townships, which he named Bathurst, Drummond, and Beckwith. In all, a range of land comprising 300,000 acres was secured for the founding of a military settlement, and placed under the administration of Sir Sydney Beckwith, the Quarter-Master General of the British forces. In arranging for the transfer of the lands, Lt. Governor Gore requested that any of the acquired land in excess of what was required for the settlement of the discharged soldiers, be turned over to the provincial government for satisfying the land claims of the descendants of the Loyalists.[12]

To locate the soldier-settlers on their land grant, and provide support during their initial settlement period, a Military Settling Department was established under the command of the Commander of the Forces for the Canadas, Lt. General Sir Gordon Drummond, and placed under the direction of Sir Sydney Beckwith, Quarter-Master General. Commencing in the fall of 1815, Canadian land surveyors were employed to survey the new townships to the rear of the Rideau River. Thereafter, new townsites were laid out at Perth (1816), on the Pike River (renamed the Tay) tributary of the Rideau River; at Richmond (1818) on the Jock River tributary of the Rideau River; and to the rear of Perth at Lanark (1820), on the Clyde River on an adjacent watershed.

To provide access for the settlers to the lots of the newly-surveyed back townships, the military employed axemen to cut bush roads through the heavily-forested interior. During the winter of 1815-1816, a 42-mile long road (the Brockville Road) was opened from the St. Lawrence Front at Brockville inland to Perth. The road ran inland to Rideau Lake, where a ferry was established to connect with the last six-mile section of the road from the lake to Perth. Later, during the fall of 1818, a second military road (the Richmond Road) was cut twenty-one miles through the bush from the foot of the Chaudière Falls on the Ottawa River to the Richmond townsite. Two years later, a fourteen mile long road was cut from Perth to the new Lanark survey and, thereafter, the Richmond Road was extended thirty miles through the interior from Richmond to Perth.

A commissariat depot was established at each townsite, and a Superintendent, Deputy Superintend, and Clerk, were appointed by the Commissariat Department to oversee the distribution of tools, implements, and rations, to be issued to the soldier-settlers during the initial settlement phase until the land could be cleared and crops planted and harvested. A military Surgeon was also assigned to the Perth Military Settlement. Although the initial survey was made for the settlement of discharged solders, from the very beginning of settlement local exigencies necessitated the placing of British immigrants in the Rideau Military Settlement, and the expansion of the military support system.

The military settlement was counted on to serve as nuclei for the development of farming communities in the townships of the Rideau interior to overcome several serious impediments to what was initially envisaged as the construction and operation of the 125-mile long batteaux navigation through a veritable wilderness. Once established, the farming communities were expected to be able to provide the labourers, tradesmen, and draught animals which would be required for the construction of the projected Rideau batteaux navigation, as well as food and fodder. The military settlement would also provide a workforce for operating the military transport system, and a trained militia for its future defence. It was hoped that the increasing trade of the Rideau Military Settlement would eventually encourage the provincial government to undertake, or at least contribute substantially to, the construction of a proper canal through the Rideau interior.[13]

The Assisted-Emigration Scots

In the immediate postwar period, while the Military Settling Department was engaged in the surveying the new townships to be settled with discharged soldiers, the Colonial office in London proceeded to implement the proposed assisted-emigration programme.[14]

In Scotland, the introduction of sheep farming in the Highlands in the 1790s had led to the eviction of tenant farmers and the destruction of clan estates that were based on cattle raising and communal farming. Whole townships and islands were cleared as clan lairds evicted their tenants to obtain large open acreages for sheep grazing to profit from the high demand for wool in the cities. Fearing for their future, tenant farmers sought to emigrate to North America to secure land of their own. Prior to the War of 1812, tenant farmers on several large estates had sold their cattle and possessions to emigrate. They banded together under the direction of the estate tackman to charter a ship, and emigrated to the United States or the British North American provinces where they settled as a clan community with their family, kith and kin.

The vast majority of tenant farmers lacked the financial resources required to emigrate and settle in North America. Hence, with the coming of peace in 1815 the Colonial Office was besieged with petitions from the Highlanders who were seeking assistance to emigrate.[15] Lord Bathurst responded. In February 1815, a Proclamation was published in Edinburgh, and circulated throughout Scotland, that promised government assistance to enable prospective emigrants to settle in the British provinces of North America. Families interested in emigrating were offered conveyance to North America on naval transports, a free grant of 100 acres of land for each family, rations from government stores for their support for the first six months, and axes, ploughs, and other farming implements were to be supplied by government at prime cost. Moreover, prospective emigrants were assured that they would be settled as a community on lands contiguous to one another; that a lot would be provided for a church; and that the

Colonial Department would provide support for a clergyman and teacher. Subsequently the salaries were set at £100 and £ 50 per annum for a clergyman and teacher, respectively, for the period of the programme.

The aim of the emigration programme was to attract emigrants of means and initiative, who would be capable of successfully settling in the heavily-forested environment of North America. To that end, a deposit was required from each family: £16 for each male over 16 years of age; and two guineas (£2/2s) for a wife, with children conveyed free of charge. The total deposit was to be returned after two years of settlement, as an incentive to ensure that the families would stay on the land. Prospective emigrants also had to provide a testimonial, signed by a Justice of the Peace, a clergyman, or an elder of the parish, attesting to their good character, as well as furnish information as to their profession, their marital status – married or widower – and the number and ages of their children.[16]

The Proclamation brought a flood of applicants from tenant farmers. The Colonial Office was prepared to provide transport to North America for 2,000 emigrants, with bedding and rations provided en route, but that number was not reached. The £16 deposit per adult male was well beyond the means of most tenant farmers desiring to emigrate, and severely limited the number who were able to take advantage of the assisted-emigration programme.[17]

Ultimately 699 emigrants – inclusive of women and children – from Perthshire in Scotland, managed to pay the deposits which were demanded. Half of the families were from the Presbyterian Lowland parishes and the other half from the Gaelic-speaking Highland parishes of Perthshire. During the spring and early summer of 1815, they gathered at the embarkation ports of Glasgow and Greenock on the Clyde River in the western Lowlands. The prospective emigrants were provided with daily rations while awaiting the Royal Navy transports. After some further delay, three naval transport vessels sailed from the Clyde

River estuary for Canada in mid-July, and a fourth transport in early August 1815. Although confined in cramped quarters, the Scots emigrants were well fed during the voyage with beef, and pork, dried pease, oatmeal, bread, and rum; and a naval Surgeon was attached to each ship to care for their medical needs during the voyage to Canada. Moreover, the Scots emigrants were able to bring some tools, furniture, and even a few firearms with them.[18]

Upon arrival at Quebec in September, the Scots immigrants and their baggage were taken in hand by the Commissariat Department of the British Army, which paid for their transport by steamboat up river to Montreal and for the 8 ½ mile cartage of their baggage overland to Lachine. The military batteaux establishment was then employed to transport them inland on the upper St. Lawrence River where they were dispersed along the St. Lawrence Front for the winter. A few families with a pregnant woman requiring confinement or with sick children, were provided with accommodation in Montreal. Eight single men of the group were taken on to Kingston where they were employed for the winter by the Engineering Establishment at the fort. Otherwise the Army Commissariat Department provided shelter and provisions for the winter.

Over half of the families were accommodated in three vacant military barracks at Cornwall, and the rest in smaller barracks at Brockville and a blockhouse on the Raison River in Glengarry County. Several families were lodged in neighbouring homes, and in Fort Wellington at Prescott. The wartime barracks along the St. Lawrence Front were repaired, windows replaced, beds and stoves installed; and each barracks was equipped with cooking utensils and provided with firewood for the winter. In addition, in December 1815 the Army Commissariat issued 400 pairs of serge pants, and 400 waistcoats, to the Scots emigrants temporarily accommodated on the St. Lawrence Front during the winter months.[19]

The Rideau Military Settlement

During the winter of 1815-1816 preparations went forward for the establishment of a military settlement for discharged soldiers in the Rideau interior. The 300,000 acres of land identified by Lt. Governor Gore, to the rear of the Rideau River, were purchased from the Chippewa and Mississauga Nations by the Provincial Government, and the Commissariat Department selected a site for a supply depot and townsite on the Pike River. A Superintendent, Deputy Superintendent, and Stores Clerk were appointed by the Quarter-Master General to administer the planned new military settlement, as part of the Military Settling Department establishment on site. An Upper Canadian land surveyor, Reuben Sherwood, was engaged to direct surveys for laying out the lots in the three new townships – Bathurst, Drummond, and Beckwith – as well as a townsite survey in Drummond Township.

At the newly-surveyed townsite, a depot building, 60 feet x 20 feet, was constructed for the storage and distribution of the farm implements, domestic utensils, and military rations. At this time, the access road was opened through the bush from Brockville to Rideau Lake, and beyond from the mouth of the Pike River to the new townsite survey. A ferry was established for crossing Rideau Lake. As of March 1816, thirty loads of provisions and supplies were moved by sleigh over the snow on the newly-opened Brockville Road to the new commissariat depot in readiness for the arrival of the first soldier-settlers.[20]

Initially, only discharged soldiers were to be settled in the Rideau Military Settlement. The intention of Lt. General Drummond – the newly-appointed Commander-in-Chief /Governor-in-Chief of the British North American provinces – was to settle the assisted-emigration Scots in Glengarry County, next to the earlier Highland Scots settlers, and to avoid placing new immigrants in the Rideau wilderness. The established settlers were counted on to provide assistance in settling the new arrivals on the land. To that end, the Crown Reserves in Glengarry County were opened for settlement during the winter of 1815-1816; a supply depot was established for the distribution of rations to the £10 deposit Scots immigrants; and the remaining vacant lands were surveyed for settlement in the adjacent counties of Stormont and Dundas.

When the land available for settlement in the Glengarry area proved insufficient to accommodate all of the families of the assisted-emigration group, Lt. General Drummond gave a preference to placing the Gaelic-speaking Highland families near their kith and kin in Glengarry County. Ultimately, 362 of the Gaelic-speaking Scots immigrants were granted land in the Glengarry settlement. The rest of the party were offered land in the Rideau Military Settlement townships which had yet to be settled by any of planned soldier-settlers. Almost immediately the Presbyterian families of the assisted-emigration Scots objected to being located in the Rideau wilderness far from existing settlements and water transport. They forwarded a petition to the Lt. Governor of Upper Canada requesting land on Lake Ontario in the Bay of Quinte area. The petition request was denied. In the spring, the remaining 337 members of the immigrant party were given location tickets in the Rideau Military Settlement survey.[21]

The Perth Settlement

In April 1816, the first of the Presbyterian Scots arrived at the surveyed townsite in the Rideau wilderness on foot, followed by wagons transporting their baggage. The wagons were provided by the Commissariat Department, and each family head was provided with an axe and a backpack. Once at the survey, the first arrivals were provided with a guide and permitted to choose their locations, with the later arrivals receiving the less desirable lots. Subsequently all of the families were settled on contiguous 100 acre lots near the military depot townsite on what became known as the "Scotch Line". During the summer they lived in tents provided by the Commissariat, or occupied crude huts, while commencing the clearing of their land.

The Commissariat Depot issued each family with cooking utensils (a skillet and a camp kettle), a blanket for each family member, carpentry tools (an adze, hand-saw, drawing knife, shell auger drill, and two gimlets), a metal door lock and two hinges, and farming implements (a scythe and snath, two hoes, and a hay fork). In addition, each group of four families was provided with, and expected to share, a cross-cut saw and a whip-saw (two-handed saws for cutting across the grain and for ripping with the grain, respectively), as well as a grindstone for sharpening their tools. The Commissariat Depot also provided each family with potato seeds and three bushels of Fall Wheat for planting as soon as a plot of land could be cleared. In addition, all of the members of each family were to be issued army rations on the 24th of each month at the depot, for a period of six months following their location on the land.[22]

This initial group of settlers in the Rideau Military Settlement was comprised mostly of tenant farmers, but included a substantial number of artificers from a variety of trades, as well as a number of young labourers who were family members. It consisted largely of Presbyterians from the lowlands of Perthshire, but included some Baptists and Congregationalists, as well as a few families of Catholic Highlanders from Inverness-shire.[23] Among the tradesmen were three weavers, a dyer-clothier, a shoemaker, two stone masons, a millwright, a whitesmith (tinsmith), and a ship's carpenter. Not long after the arrival of the Scots immigrants, the new townsite was given the name, Perth, and the Pike River was re-named the Tay River.[24]

In June 1816, the assisted-emigration Scots were joined by the first of the discharged soldiers to settle in the Rideau interior. These soldier-settlers comprised a number of the officers and men of the Glengarry Light Infantry Regiment of Fencibles, which was disbanded at Kingston in June 1816, and soldiers of the Canadian Fencibles Regiment, which was disbanded at Montreal in May 1816. In addition, there were soldiers of the DeWatteville Regiment, who had requested their discharge in Canada before the regiment returned to Britain. The Glengarry and Canadian

Fencibles were settled compactly in Bathurst and Drummond townships near Perth. The De Watteville Regiment soldiers were settled in Burgess Township, after the concession lots which had been surveyed for their grants in Bathurst Township were found to be too wet and unsuitable for settlement.

Both the Glengarry Regiment and the Canadian Fencibles comprised men from the Canadian provinces who had been recruited from amongst the Loyalist families and the pre-war British immigrant settlers. Although the Glengarry Regiment had been recruited in Glengarry County, only sixteen of the veterans who settled in the Rideau Military Settlement were Highlanders. The remaining 24 veterans of the regiment who settled in the military settlement comprised Lowland Scots, Irish Protestants, and Englishmen. The Canadian Fencibles were raised in Lower Canada, but the regiment was comprised primarily of men from among the same English-speaking groups with but a few French Canadians members. In contrast, the De Watteville Regiment was a Swiss mercenary regiment serving with the British Army. It was commanded by Swiss officers, but only a fifth of the soldiers were Swiss. For the most part, the regiment comprised Germans, Italians, Poles, Hungarians and Russians, as well as a few Greeks and a small number of Frenchmen; all of whom had been prisoners of war who agreed to serve with the British Army in North America. The De Watteville Regiment had been sent to Canada in April 1813 for service during the War of 1812.

The soldier-settlers were provided with an axe, farming implements and carpentry tools, domestic utensils, blankets, potato seeds and several bushels of wheat from the Commissariat Depot, in keeping with what had been provided to the assisted-emigration Scots who were located in the Rideau Military Settlement earlier in the spring. Only two distinctions were made. The discharged soldiers were entitled to receive twelve month's military rations for each family member; whereas the assisted Scots immigrants were to receive only a six month's supply of military rations from the date of their location on the land. In addition, the military settlers were granted land

according to their rank: 1200 acres to a Lt. Colonel; 1000 acres
to a Major; 800 acres to a Captain; 500 acres to a Subaltern,
300 acres to a Sergeant-Major or Quartermaster Sergeant; 200
acres to a Sergeant; and 100 acres to a Private; whereas the Scots
immigrants received an 100 acre lot.[25]

On their first arrival on the land, a great difficulty was
experienced by the new settlers in attempting to clear the forest
cover. The axes forwarded from England by the Colonial Office
proved of little use as the heads of the English axes were too
narrow and too long, and of an insufficient weight for felling
trees. They were suited only for splitting firewood. Moreover, the
English axes were manufactured differently than the American
felling axe, and did not stand up to heavy use. (They were prone
to break at the eye of the axe head where the handle was inserted.)
Unable to use the English axes supplied by the Commissary
Department, the first settlers had to purchase American felling
axes from merchants on the St. Lawrence Front. That situation
was remedied in the fall of 1817 when the Quartermaster
General ordered 200 felling axes to be produced at Quebec,
on the American pattern, for distribution in the Perth Military
Settlement. Ultimately, several different types of axes were
distributed to the settlers in the military settlement: a felling axe;
a broad axe; a squaring axe; and a pickaxe.[26]

During their transition unto the land, the Military Settling
Department did everything possible to facilitate and support the
soldier-settlers and Scots immigrants until their first crops could
be harvested. Nonetheless, the first year of settlement in the
Rideau wilderness was one of misery for the new settlers, both
from their situation and inclement weather. Upon their arrival
in an alien wilderness environment, British immigrant settlers
commonly experienced a feeling of helplessness when faced with
the daunting task of clearing a dense forest growth of trees. Some
of the hardwoods (white and red oak) ranged upwards of 50' to
100' in height, and could range anywhere from six inches to four
feet in trunk diameter, and some of the softwoods (white pine)
were upwards of 100' to 150' in height, and anywhere from two

to four feet in their trunk diameter.

The first step in opening a farm clearing in the forest was to clean out the underbrush and saplings, which were piled in one area. Then the trees were cut down, the branches cut off, and the tree trunks cut into twelve-foot lengths for rolling to one edge of the clearing where they were burned with the underbrush and branches. Three-foot high stumps were left in the ground for years – while crops were planted around the stumps with a hoe – until the stumps rotted sufficiently to be readily pulled out with a chain and yoke of oxen. The clearing of the forest to establish a bush farm involved a great deal of hard physical labour, as well as a constant danger of serious injury from a glancing axe blow or a falling tree. Land clearing in a dense forest also imposed a psychological burden. New immigrants were prone to experiencing a feeling of gloom from living in isolation in a dark, impenetrable forest where the tree canopy shut out the sun and the wind.[27]

In addition to the physical hardship and emotional strain suffered by immigrant settlers upon entering onto their lots in the bush, the new settlers in the Rideau Military settlement experienced an ever greater fear and uncertainty. It was engendered by severe weather fluctuations and unprecedentedly cold temperatures in the new settlement during their first summer on the land.

During the spring and summer of 1816, an unusually heavy cloud cover played havoc with normal weather patterns in Upper and Lower Canada, and along the eastern seaboard of the United States, as far south as New York. The clouds reflected solar radiation from the sun, and enabled dry arctic air to move southward in a series of severe cold waves that struck in the late spring and repeatedly over the course of the entire summer. The cold waves brought rapid, and dramatic temperature variations, killing frosts, and several summer snowfalls.[28]

When the first settlers arrived at the Rideau Military Settlement survey in April and May 1816, the weather was abnormally cold and the coming of spring was delayed throughout the Canadian provinces. Thereafter freezing temperatures and a severe frost were experienced every month over the course of the spring and summer: principally on May 2nd, from May 12th to 19th, on May 30th, from June 6th to 10th, on June 28th-29th, from July 6th to 9th, on August 13th-14th, August 20th-21st, and August 28th-29th. The first fall frost occurred in mid-September, followed by the onset of an early and abnormally cold winter.

What was worse, the misery of the new settlers was further increased during the summer of 1816 by heavy rains and intermittent high winds, as well as the great fluctuations in temperature. The freezing temperatures of mid-May gave rise to several days with temperatures as high as 95 degrees Fahrenheit from June 2nd to June 5th, followed on June 6th by a heavy snowfall that blanketed both Upper and Lower Canada with snow to a depth of 1½", with a depth of a foot of snow recorded in some areas. Then, in the period June 22nd through June 24th , the Perth settlement was struck by a second heat wave.[29]

As early as the mid-summer, there was a fear of famine everywhere in Upper and Lower Canada. Corn failed to ripen, the fruit in apple orchards withered and died, and all of the vegetable crops – potatoes, cucumbers, beans, and turnips – were killed off. With the destruction of the cereal crops (wheat, rye, and oats), the mills were unable to produce flour for making bread, and with the loss of the barley and hay crops, no forage was available for feeding the cattle. With no bread, vegetables, or fruit to eat, settlers in the older areas of settlement managed to live by hunting (deer, porcupines, ground hogs, and squirrels), trapping (pigeons and wild turkeys) and fishing in the lakes and rivers. Farmers in the older areas of settlement had to slaughter their cattle and pigs to avoid their dying of starvation. Such a meagre diet of game and fish was supplement by the settlers through eating ground nuts (walnuts, hickory nuts, butternuts, and beechnuts), boiling the young buds of trees and wild plants in a stew; and harvesting whatever grain they could from the dead plants to boil and make a gruel.[30]   In the towns of the older settled areas, food was available for purchase, but was scarce and high priced.

Faced with the spectre of famine in the Canadian provinces, as early as 9 July 1816, the newly-appointed Governor-in-Chief/ Commander-in-Chief of British North America, Lt. General Sir John Sherbrooke, issued a Proclamation that prohibited the export from Lower Canada of "wheat, wheat flour, biscuit, Beets, Pease, Barley and Grains of all kinds used in the making of Bread", except for the supplying of the fisheries of Labrador. In addition to forbidding merchants to export food already in storage, Sherbrooke issued a second proclamation in the fall of 1816 that enabled "grain, flour, livestock, and provisions of every kind" to be imported from the United States for a period of six weeks duty free.[31]

In the Rideau Military Settlement, the "summerless summer" reduced the new arrivals to a total dependence on their military rations for survival. The freezing temperatures during the summer killed the newly-grown potato plants, and what little wheat the new settlers were able to sow. Faced with a potentially disastrous situation, in October 1816 both the officers of the Commissariat Department, and the Lt. Governor of Upper Canada, recommended that the military provisioning be continued for the soldier-settlers and the assisted-emigration Scots beyond their respective periods of entitlement until June 1817, with a proviso that a further indulgence might well be absolutely necessary beyond that date.

A fall tour of the settlement by the Lt. Governor of Upper Canada revealed that none of the settlers were in a position to provide food for themselves during the coming winter, and many were suffering from the cold in living under canvas or in crude huts. Lt. Governor Gore lamented that shelters had not been provided for them. He informed the Commander-in-Chief that although the settlers were exerting themselves to clear the land for planting, there was no way for them to purchase provisions in a wilderness, even if they had the money to do so, which they did not. Only the British Government, through the military, could supply the settlers, and it was critical to do so for "if provisions are withheld, certain starvation will ensue."[32]

Although the earlier termination of the War of 1812 had relieved the Commissariat Department of the heavy expense, and the all but overwhelming transport difficulties which were experienced in moving troops, heavy ordnance, munitions, equipment and provisions inland on the St. Lawrence River navigation for the defence of Upper Canada, the establishment and provisioning of the Rideau Military Settlement placed a continuing heavy burden on the manpower and resources of the Department. The farming implements, utensils, and some of the provisions for the Perth depot were carried by horse-drawn wagons from the Stores Depot at Montreal to La Chine, were conveyed up the St. Lawrence River by the military batteaux establishment to Brockville, and were transported inland to Perth on horse-drawn wagons on a bush road, and over a ferry crossing of Rideau Lake, for over 42 miles to Perth. Fresh produce was purchased by the Commissariat in the market towns on the St. Lawrence Front for transport inland to Perth.

The settling of the assisted-emigration Scots in the Rideau Military Settlement greatly increased the administrative and transport burden of the Commissariat Department, and all of the costs which were associated with the military settlement for both the military and civilian settlers were paid out of the Army Extraordinaries (the military chest). Moreover, the farming implements and domestic utensils appear to have been given to the Scots settlers free of charge by the Military Settling Department, rather than sold to them at prime cost. In addition, the provisions furnished to the Scots settlers far exceeded the standard military rations of the British Army, and included fresh beef which the Commissary Department secured by purchasing cattle on the St. Lawrence Front and driving them inland to Perth.[33]

In the British Army during the early 19th century, soldiers were accommodated in barracks and the daily military ration per soldier consisted of one pound of bread or flour, one pound of beef (or a half-pound of salted pork), a little butter and cheese, and a pint of beer, or rum. Vegetables had to be purchased by the soldier out of their pay of a shilling (12 pence) per day. Soldiers' wives and children generally did not receive rations or barracks accommodation.

According to Army Regulations, only six soldiers' wives per 100 men of a company were permitted to live in barracks with their children. The barracks' wives received a daily ration, and were employed in keeping the barracks clean, washing clothes and cooking for the soldiers in exchange for payment from them. When a regiment left England for foreign stations, the quota of barracks wives allowed was sometimes doubled, but the rest of the wives and children of the soldiers were left behind. Most were rendered destitute, and dependent on Poor Law relief in the parishes, and many returned to their home parishes for sustenance.[34]

In contrast, in the military settlements each military and immigrant Scots settler received a full ration, his wife received a half ration, and each dependent child a quarter ration, calculated on a per diem basis, and the provisions were issued on the 24th of each month from the Commissariat Depot in Perth. That cost was further increased as of the fall of 1816, when the military undertook to have a log cabin erected for each family in the settlement, and when the military provisioning system was extended until June 1817 to prevent starvation. Many of the civilian settlers had been located on their land for the prescribed six month period of provisioning support, but were not yet able to live off their land.

Despite the hardships of the first summer on the land, Colonel Christian Myers, the Deputy Quartermaster General, reported in October 1816 that twenty houses had been erected in the new village of Perth, and 250 cabins were constructed for the new settlers in the Rideau Military Settlement townships and were ready for occupancy before the winter. There were 840 men, 207 women and 458 children in the military settlement receiving the equivalent of 1,100 military ration provisions per diem; and an additional 200 rations would be required for settlers newly arrived in the settlement. Moreover, the Commissariat Department was providing 150 rations per day for the support of a number of discharged soldiers and their families who were settled on scattered lots in the surrounding townships of Wolford, Kitley, Bastard, Montague, and Oxford, along the Rideau River corridor where there were a few farm clearings, and several isolated hamlets established by Loyalist settlers in the pre-war period.[35]

The impact of the loss of cereal and vegetable crops during the freezing weather of the summer of 1816 was reflected in the prices that the Commissariat Department had to pay in importing provisions to the Rideau Military Settlement. As of the fall, flour was selling at $70 per barrel at Quebec, and potatoes at a penny a pound. Between the spring of 1816 and of 1817, the price of wheat soared from $1.50 to $2.87 per bushel, and corn from $1.12 to $1.78 per bushel in the New York market. Only the price of meat declined as farmers in the older areas of settlement flooded the market with cattle and pigs that they were unable to feed over the winter owing to the crop failures. Beef dropped in price from $15.50 to $7.75 per barrel, and pork from $26.00 to $16.00 per barrel.[36] In addition to paying for provisions, the Commissariat Department absorbed the heavy cost of transporting the provisions inland to the military settlement.

Despite the cost and provisioning difficulties that were being experienced in establishing the Rideau Military Settlement, during the winter of 1816-1817 the Colonial Office extended the eligibility for land grants to soldiers who had served in Europe, to decommissioned officers of the British Army and Royal Navy, and to half-pay officers. As a result, during the summer of 1817, some 600 discharged soldiers from various British Army Regiments applied for land grants in Canada. That number comprised veterans who had served in Europe during the Napoleonic Wars, as well as those who had served in Canada during the War of 1812, but had chosen to be discharged in

England to be reunited with their families.

The discharged soldiers were given free transportation to Canada, with their families, a land grant according to their rank, rations for twelve months, an issue of a blanket, felling axe, cooking utensils, and agricultural implements similar what was provided to the earlier soldier-settlers. The military settlers were placed in several different strategic areas of the British North American provinces, and in each area a Commissariat Department depot was established. A number of the discharged soldiers were located in the Rideau Military Settlement, principally in Bathurst and Drummond townships.[37]

For the Scots and soldier-settlers who were already on the land, the summer of 1817 was a period of continuing hardship, and particularly so following the termination of their provisioning with military rations. Unable to purchase high cost provisions from distant markets, the settlers had to resort to boiling the buds and leaves of different plants and trees in a stew, and hunting and fishing. Nonetheless, it was reported in July 1817 that a good number of the families had managed to achieve self-sufficiency following the harvesting of their spring crops; and that they were "well satisfied" with their situation. Other families were less well off, and were reported as being reduced to a diet of wild leaks, which were found in profusion in the forest. To relieve what continuing distress there was in the settlement, the Commissariat Department authorized yet another extension of the provisioning system. Half rations were provided to the large families, and families most in need, through to the fall harvest of 1817.

In the Perth military settlement, the clearing of the land continued over the summer of 1817 despite an infestation of mosquitoes that tormented the settlers day and night. Potato seeds were imported from Nova Scotia, and various vegetable crops were planted. In the fall, there was a good wheat harvest. By the summer of 1818, there were 44 cows and 22 oxen distributed among the Scots settlers alone, and two of the new arrivals – an Army Surgeon of the 104th Regiment, and a Loyalist from the St. Lawrence Front – had erected a grist mill, and a grist mill and a saw mill, respectively, at waterfalls on the Tay River. The Village of Perth was also becoming well established with thirty houses, a general store, an inn, a tavern, and a distillery. The one-acre town lots were occupied by half-pay officers who preferred to erect a house in the village, rather than live on their township land grant.[38]

For bush farmers, a cow was of inestimable value in providing milk for the feeding of a family, as well as butter and cheese, and especially so in periods of food shortages in a community dependent on subsistence agriculture. Oxen likewise were of great value to a bush farmer. They greatly facilitated the clearing, grubbing, and farming of the land, and were employed – given the absence of concession roads, and the scarcity of horses and wagons – in hauling grain by sled in winter. The settlers transported grain over great distances on frozen rivers and snow-covered paths through the bush to the nearest grist mill for grinding, and returned home with their flour. New settlers, after harvesting their first crop, had to carry grain in a sack on their back and walk miles through the bush to the nearest grist mill, and then carry flour back home in the same manner.[39]

Although independent emigration from the British Isles to British North America increased dramatically each year in the postwar period, from less than a thousand in 1815 to more than 9,000 persons in 1817, there was no mass influx into the Rideau Military Settlement. The military authorities would not permit non-assisted immigrants to settle in the Rideau wilderness, unless they could afford to purchase at least a year's supply of provisions.

In extending the military rations system into the summer of 1817, Lt.-General Sir John Sherbrooke, the Commander-in-Chief/Governor-in-Chief of British North America, remarked that, "in most cases", it required almost eighteen months from the time of location for a British immigrant to become completely self sufficient on a farm clearing in the bush. He recognized as well that British immigrants who lacked provisions would be unable to find any means of subsistence in a wilderness. Hence, Sherbrooke directed that penniless immigrants arriving in Upper Canada were to be located on Crown Reserve lands in settled areas, where they could receive support and assistance from the established settlers.[40]

The Richmond Settlement

During the winter of 1817-1818, the Military Settling Department undertook to expand the Rideau Military Settlement through establishing another settlement nucleus in the Rideau wilderness about thirty miles north-east of the new Village of Perth. New townships were surveyed, and a second supply depot was erected at a newly-surveyed townsite – what became Richmond – on the Jacques (re-named the Jock) River tributary of the Rideau River. The new area of settlement was soon occupied by both Scots immigrants and discharged soldiers.

During the early summer of 1818, a party of Scots immigrants arrived at Quebec, and were given land in the Rideau military settlement townships in the vicinity of the new townsite survey. They had financed their own emigration, with some support from the Colonial Officer under yet another assisted-emigration programme which was designed to encourage prospective British emigrants to settle in Canada, rather than go to the United States.

Earlier, in February 1818, the Colonial Office had instituted a new assisted-emigration programme. It provided that any "capitalists" of means, and initiative, who organized a group of ten families to emigrate to Canada, would receive government transport for the group to their settlement area, and each family would receive a free grant of 100 acres of land. A £10 security deposit was required for each family, refundable after taking up their land grant, and no family was to have more than two children. Each family was required to pay for its own provisions en route from Britain to Quebec, and to supply their own clothing and blankets, as well as purchase their own utensils, seeds, and farming implements. In addition, once on the land they were to erect their own cabins, or employ axemen to assist them, and would have to sustain themselves through purchasing provisions until they managed to clear enough land to plant and harvest their first crops.

Under the £10 deposit scheme, a hundred Scots families (311 persons) took ship for Quebec from Greenock on two ships in the spring of 1818. The emigrant party was composed of tenant farmers, mostly Presbyterians, from Loch Earn and Loch Tay in Perthshire. Following their arrival at Quebec, some of the families migrated to Prince Edward Island while the main party was transported inland from Montreal by the Commissariat Department on its ox-cart and batteaux transport system along the St. Lawrence River navigation system, and up the Ottawa River. In June 1818, they arrived at the Chaudière Falls, opposite Wright's Town and were encamped in tents supplied by the Commissariat.

An advance party of axemen was hired by the military to blaze a trail twenty-one miles inland from the Ottawa River to the new Richmond survey. Subsequently the immigrant party carried their belongings, and walked inland along the blazed trail to the new survey where they were located on their lots. The Scots settlers were placed in the Beckwith Township area of the Rideau Military Settlement, just to west of the Richmond townsite which was situated in Goulbourn Township.[41] In the late fall, the Scots immigrants were joined by soldier-settlers.

The new settlers comprised 167 discharged officers and men of the 99th Regiment of Foot (Prince Regent's Dublin Regiment of Foot), which was formerly the 100th Regiment of Foot prior to a re-organization in 1816 of the line regiments. The regiment was discharged at Quebec in July 1818, and provided with transportation for the men and their families to the new Richmond settlement. The former 100th Regiment of Foot was an Irish Ulster Protestant regiment. It was comprised mostly of former weavers and labourers who had been recruited in northern Ireland almost a decade earlier. During the war, the regiment had fought at Sackett's Harbour, in the raids on Buffalo and Black Rock, as well as at the capture of Fort Niagara in 1813, and at the Battle of Chippawa and at the Siege of Fort Erie in 1814.[42]

In late August 1818, the discharged veterans of the newly-designated 99th Regiment of Foot arrived at the Chaudière Falls on the Ottawa River. They were encamped with their families in tents at Bellow's Landing (now LeBreton Flats), while construction proceeded on the opening of a wagon road – the Richmond Road – inland twenty-one miles through the bush from the Chaudière Falls to the Richmond survey. They were joined by discharged soldiers from other regiments, and by the end of November, 400 military families were located on land grants in Goulbourn, Huntley, and Nepean townships in the vicinity of the Richmond depot.

Each military family in the Richmond settlement was furnished with a cabin which was erected for them on their lot, and the supply depot of the settlement was well provisioned from the Wright's Town settlement on the Ottawa River. Moreover, already there were seven or eight half-pay officers living in the new village of Richmond, as well as the Superintendent of the Richmond Military Settlement, a Pension Agent, a Commissary Paymaster, and several Clerks of the Commissariat Department who were employed in the stores depot and in the distribution of the military rations.

Thereafter, Lt. Colonel Francis Cockburn, Deputy Quartermaster- General for the Canadas, expended over £300 in employing eighty men for almost four months to open a good wagon road over a distance of 32 miles between Richmond and Perth. The extension of the Richmond Road was intended to encourage the development of trade and the spread of settlement between the two interior settlements, as well as to serve a military function. What Cockburn envisaged was a future additional extension of the Richmond Road from Perth to Kingston. When build, it would provide a military road communication from the Ottawa River through the Rideau interior to Lake Ontario, for use until the projected Rideau navigation could be constructed.[43]

The lots which were granted to the discharged soldiers in the Richmond settlement varied in acreage according to their rank, in keeping with the established practice in the Rideau Military Settlement. Similarly, each family was to receive the standard twelve months of military rations to aid in their transition onto the land. However, in drawing on the knowledge that had been gained from supporting the Scots settlers in the Perth settlement, the Military Settling Department sought to fully equip the soldier-settlers of the Richmond settlement to successfully engage in bush farming.

In addition to engaging French Canadian axemen from Wright's Town to construct a cabin on the lot of each new arrival, the Military Settling Department saw to it that the soldier-settlers were well equipped with tools and farming implements that would be needed in the process of establishing a bush farm. Each head of a family was furnished with a felling axe, a broad axe (squaring axe), mattock, pick axe, spade, shovel, hoe, scythe, drawing knife, hammer and hand saw, two scythe stones, and two files, as well as a camp kettle, a bed tick (mattress canvas) and a blanket. In addition, each group of five families was provided with a crosscut saw and a whipsaw (rip saw), and a grindstone, and the Richmond settlement depot was also equipped with two complete sets of carpenter's tools for use by the settlers. The Department also issued twelve panes of glass, one pound of putty, and 12 pounds of wrought iron nails in three different sizes for each settler, for the use in constructing the log cabins.

The education and spiritual welfare of the new settlers was not neglected. A provision was made for the payment of a salary for a schoolmaster, and arrangements were made for the Society for the Propagation of the Gospel (Anglican), to provide a clergyman for the settlement.

No expense was spared by the Commissariat of the British Army in transporting, provisioning, and equipping the discharged soldier-settlers and their families, to help them succeed in settling onto the land. As such, the soldier-settlers were much better prepared to meet the demands of bush farming than the Scots immigrants who arrived earlier in the Richmond settlement under the £10 deposit, limited assistance, programme of the Colonial Office. For the most part, the Scots settlers who were permitted to settle in the Rideau Military Settlement, were tenant farmers who had owned livestock and property in Scotland. They had arrived in Canada with some capital to purchase provisions during the initial settlement phase until several acres of land could be cleared, and their first crop planted and harvested. However, in the late fall of 1818, some of the £10 deposit Scots in the Richmond settlement were struggling to survive, and, with winter coming on Lt. Col. Cockburn reported that it would be cruel to deny them army rations.[44]

Regardless of the tools, implements, rations, and accommodation that might be furnished to a prospective settler, whether an immigrant succeeded in establishing a bush farm in a heavily-forested wilderness depended on one's character and the support of a family unit. In sum, any success in clearing the land and establishing a self-sufficient bush farm depended on a strength of mind, perseverance, a willingness to work hard, and a commitment to patient labour in a seemingly endless struggle to clear the forest. In addition, the degree of success depended on how quickly the settler adapted to the demands of bush farming, and on his being wise enough to choose a lot with good soil.[45]

Subsequently, the Scots settlers and soldier-settlers of the Richmond settlement were joined, during the period 1819-1820, by large groups of Irish Protestants who immigrated to Canada at their own expense, without receiving any aid from the British government. They included some families from North Tipperary, but were mostly from the Wexford and Wicklow counties of southeastern Ireland. These emigrant groups were part of a chain migration from Ireland to Upper Canada by Irish Protestants in the post-Napoleonic War period. This postwar Irish migration comprised mostly of Anglo-Irish Anglicans, but included as well a small number of Wesleyan Methodists. These independent Irish settlers established the towns of Morphy's Falls (Carleton Place) and Shipman's Mill (Almonte) on the Mississippi River in Ramsay Township, and Franktown in the adjacent Beckwith Township on the Richmond Road.

The Wexford and Wicklow Protestants comprised families of English origin who were settled in Ireland under the Stuart monarchy during the early 17th Century. They were prosperous yeoman farmers of some means, who owned large improved farms, spoke English, and had a varied diet rather than being dependent on a potato monoculture. The Anglo-Irish yeoman farmers – who had been settled in Ireland for well over two centuries – were known to be industrious men of excellent character, who were strong adherents of the United Church of England and Ireland (Anglican Church) and were loyal defenders of the Crown.

Although the Irish Protestant yeoman farmers of Wexford and Wicklow were economically well off in Ireland, their situation in that country had become precarious. The fierce fighting, and atrocities committed by both sides during the abortive Irish Rebellion of 1798, had left a legacy of hatred and ill-will between the Catholics and Protestants. In such a situation, the Anglo-Irish Protestant minority felt threatened and unsure of their future prospects in Ireland. Given that situation, and in the face of a rapidly increasing population and the onset of a post-Napoleonic War depression, thousands of Irish Protestant yeoman farmers were anxious to emigrate to Upper Canada to purchase land and establish a more secure future for their children. From the viewpoint of the military authorities in Canada, the Anglo-Irish yeoman farmers were ideal settlers for the Rideau Military Settlement based on their character, work ethic, loyalty, and ability to pay their own transport and settlement expenses.

The Anglo-Irish from Wexford and Wicklow were followed, in the period 1820-1822, by smaller groups of Irish Protestant families who settled in Goulbourn and Huntley townships, as well as in western Nepean and March townships on the upper Ottawa River. The Irish Protestants of this continuing migration were from North Tipperary and, for the most part, were yeoman farmers of English descent who sold their farms to emigrate on their own. Included among this influx were a number of Irish Protestant Army and Royal Navy Officers on half-pay, and Irish Protestant tradesmen of some means. These Irish immigrants possessed anywhere from £20 to £300 in capital per family, and were self-supporting. They were placed in the Richmond settlement and, once located on the land, received little, if any, assistance from the Military Settling Department.[46]

Despite the increasing numbers of non-assisted British immigrants arriving in Canada, the Colonial Office as of the early 1820s introduced two additional assisted-emigration programmes that brought immigrants to the Rideau Military Settlement. The first programme was intended to enable underemployed, or unemployed, Scots weavers from Lanark and Renfrewshire to emigrate to Canada, and the second programme was intended to enable impoverished Irish Catholics tenant farmers from southern Ireland to emigrate and settle in Canada in the Rideau Military Settlement.

In contrast to the earlier assisted-emigration programmes, these latter efforts did not originate in a desire by the British government to augment the British character of Upper Canada. They were initiated in response to severe economic distress and social-cum-political unrest in the British Isles. Yet, there was one constant. The Commissariat Department was to provide the support which would be promised the new settlers by government, and, in doing so, the Commissariat officers would continue to go well beyond their basic instructions in seeking to enhance the wellbeing of the new immigrants during their transition onto the land.

The Lanark Settlement

As of 1819 -1820, a postwar depression in Great Britain was

reaching its nadir with trade, commerce, and manufacturing
at a near standstill, widespread unemployment, and outbreaks
of social unrest, which gave rise to public demands for radical
political reforms, and for the government to establish emigration
programmes to relieve unemployment.

In Scotland, unemployment was particularly severe among the
handloom weavers who were subsisting on earnings of as little as
5s. per week after paying for their accommodation and the rent
of their looms. Many were unable to find any work at all and
were becoming destitute. In response, the weavers of counties
of Lanark and Renfrewshire organized emigration societies to
help unemployed weavers to emigrate, and forwarded petitions
to parliament requesting government support in aid of their
emigration efforts. Faced with widespread political unrest, and
members of parliament speaking out in favour of the efforts of
the Scottish emigration societies, the British government agreed
to work with the Glasgow Emigration Society – an umbrella
organization representing the local emigration societies – to aid
underemployed weavers to settle in Canada.[47]

In Canada, the Commissariat Department, and the Military
Settling Department, were instructed to provide support
for the assisted-emigration Scots to enable them to settle in
the Rideau Military Settlement. This time, the government
settlement operation would be under the overall command of a
Scot, Sir George Ramsay, Lord Dalhousie, the newly-appointed
Commander-in-Chief/Governor-in-Chief of the British North
American provinces. Once again, the military officers would be
exceptionally generous in interpreting the instructions from the
Colonial Office with respect to the support promised the new
immigrants, and the officers would go beyond their prescribed
duties in providing additional aid to individual families in need.[48]

In Britain, the Tory government agreed to assist the weavers, and
their families, to emigrate by providing each head of family with
a grant of 100 acre of land in Canada, free of survey fees, as well
as transport from the port of Quebec to the settlement area upon

their arrival. Once located on a lot, the settler was to be provided with seeds and farming implements by the government at prime cost. In lieu of providing rations, it was agreed that once a family was settled on the land, the government would advance £8 to each head of a family in three installments – £3 upon arrival in the settlement, £3 after three months from the date of arrival, and £2 at the end of six months – for the purchase of provisions until the first crops could be harvested.

The cash advances were to be repaid to the government within ten years, at which time the settler would receive title to the land. The ocean transport costs were to be paid by the emigrant families, with the assistance of the Emigration Societies, and the emigrants were expected to purchase their own provisions en route from the port of Quebec to the place of settlement.

The Glasgow Emigration Society gathered the names of the families who were interested in emigrating, chose the families to be assisted by drawing names, and took deposits of money from the selected families towards the cost of chartering and provisioning of ships to transport them. Once chartered, a ship had to be provisioned in keeping with government passenger ship regulations which prescribed the provisions and fresh water were to be taken on each ship, based on the number of passengers and a voyage of 84 days length. Such a voyage was considered more than sufficient in an era when sailing ships customarily took an average of fifty days to make an ocean crossing, but could take several weeks longer in the face of ocean storms and contrary winds.

The rations, which were issued each week to every person on board ship, varied according to the age of the recipient. Passengers over eight years old were to be issued: 1½ lbs of beef or pork, 3½ lbs of biscuits, 11 lbs of oatmeal, ½ lb of barley or pease, 1/4 lb of butter and ½ lb of molasses, each week. Children from two to eight years old were required to receive two-thirds of the prescribed adult rations per week, and infants under two years old were to be provided for by their parents. The emigrants were permitted to take on board whatever quantity of potatoes they wished, and were to supply themselves as well with porter, tea, coffee, and sugar, as well as domestic utensils.

Furthermore, government regulations determined the quantity of fresh water to be put on board, and served out daily, and the ship charter agreement between the Glasgow Emigration Society and the ship owners specified the number of cooking furnaces to be assembled on deck for the use of the passengers, and the number and type of berths to be provided on each vessel based on the number of emigrants on board.[49]

Almost immediately a critical problem emerged. Many of the unemployed Scots weavers, who were selected to participate in the assisted-emigration programme, were unable to bear their full share of the cost of chartering and provisioning a ship for the ocean voyage. This forced a delay in the sailing of the ships until July 1820, while monies were raised through public subscriptions in Scotland and London, and through a contribution of £766.7s.4d. from the British government. Once the financing was in place, the Glasgow Emigration Society was able to charter and provision several ships to send out 1200 emigrants – men, women and children – to Canada during the summer of 1820, and a further 1,883 emigrants – men, women and children – on four ships in the spring of l821. All sailed from Greenock for the port of Quebec, and almost all of the emigrant families were settled in the newly-opened Lanark settlement in Upper Canada.[50]

To open land for the settlement of the Scots weavers in Upper Canada, the Military Settling Department surveyed a new townsite – Lanark – on the Clyde River, about 14 miles northwest of Perth, and constructed a bush road to connect the new settlement with the Village of Perth. A commissariat depot was established in Lanark for the supply of the seeds, farm implements and provisions which were to be sold at prime cost to the new settlers, and survey work was completed in running concession road allowances and lot lines in three townships – Dalhousie, Lanark, and Ramsay – in the wilderness at the back of the Perth settlement townships. Each of the newly-surveyed townships was ten miles square.

In laying out the town of Lanark, ten acre lots were reserved around the town survey for granting to "mechanics" to facilitate the development of a self-sufficient village. Each of the mechanics was also to be granted a further 90 acres elsewhere in the settlement, which they were expected to clear and farm when not employed as an artificer in the village. In being far removed from the marshes and wetlands along the shores of Rideau Lake, it was expected that the new settlement would be free of the fever and ague which was present in Perth.[51]

Upon arrival at the port of Quebec, the Scots weavers were fortunate in having the cost of their transportation from the port of Quebec to the Lanark settlement covered and all their transport arrangements taken care of by the Commissariat Department. Upon the ships arriving at Quebec, the new immigrants were provided with passage by steamboat to Montreal. At that city, horse-drawn wagons were furnished for transporting their baggage overland to Lachine, with the men, women, and children walking the entire 8 ½ mile journey alongside the wagons. At Lachine, batteaux and Durham boats were provided for transporting the immigrants upriver, but given the large number of families, some had to wait as long as four days to secure a place in a boat.

During the passage upriver, three major rapids had to be surmounted: the Long Sault Rapids, the Rapide Plat Rapids, and the Galop Rapids. At each set of rapids, the baggage was transhipped into ox carts for carriage over a long portage, while the men helped the crews to haul the boats up through the fast flowing water, and the women and children walked over the portage, preparatory to re-embarking and continuing their voyage upriver. The trip upriver took six days, during which they had to sleep out of doors on the river bank en route to Prescott where wagons were engaged by the Military Settling Department to take the immigrant families beyond to the Lanark settlement. However, some families had to wait as long as three weeks to secure a place on the farm wagons, given the magnitude of the transportation task with some 1,000 persons, and their baggage, arriving in Prescott and in need of transport. Once the wagons were assembled, the Scots immigrants were taken by road for six miles upriver to Brockville, and inland for almost sixty miles along a muddy bush road to the Lanark settlement. The journey from Prescott to Lanark took a minimum of three days, or longer depending on the state of the road, and nights were spent in the clearings of isolated bush farms along the road.

Upon arrival at the Lanark townsite clearing, the Scots immigrants were sheltered in tents which were provided by the Military Settling Department. Once on site, each family was given a choice of two lots, and three days to decide on their location. Guides were provided for hire to take each family head to view the proffered lots before a decision was rendered; although the latter arrivals each year had to take what remained in the survey being settled.

The new arrivals suffered greatly from the intense heat of the day, and the cold night. However, in penetrating into the bush to establish a bush farm, they enjoyed the guidance and support of the Military Settling Department officers who were stationed at the Lanark depot, as well as the benefit of neighbours in the Perth settlement, at some distance, and in Lanark Township, who were experienced in bush farming. Moreover, upon arrival the new settlers received a prompt payment of the first installment of their promised cash advance.[52]

The Scots weavers of the assisted-emigration programme were located in the new Dalhousie and Lanark townships, as well as among the earlier settlers of the £10 deposit, assisted-emigration Scots and the independent Irish Protestant immigrants in the adjacent Ramsay Township. Some of the Scots weavers were also settled in the smaller Township of North Sherbrooke.[53]

The seeds which were provided for each settler comprised 15 bushels of potatoes, 20 bushels of oats, 20 bushels of Fall Wheat,

20 bushels of Spring Wheat, 1/4 bushel of Indian Corn, and small quantities of beans and "grass seed". Farm implements and tools were also made available to the Scots weavers by the Military Settling Department. The type of implements and tools differed somewhat from what the Commissariat had furnished to the earlier soldier-settlers and assisted-emigration settlers in the Rideau Military Settlement. The changes were made in response to the knowledge that had been gained the officers of the Military Settling Department as to the particular implements and tools best suited for clearing the land and establishing a bush farm.

Each family was allotted a felling axe, a hand saw, an iron wedge, pitch fork, two gimlets, two files of different sorts, a chisel, an augur, a scythe and a sickle, a spade and shovel, a pickaxe, a broad hoe and a narrow hoe, a carpenter's hammer, an adze, a drawing knife, brush hook, a plane, and nine harrow teeth. In addition, a broad axe (squaring axe), a grindstone, a crosscut saw and a pit saw, and a grind stone were provided for every 15 settlers in an area, and a set of blacksmith's tools was placed in each township. Moreover, each family also received an iron pot, a frying pan, two blankets, and an additional blanket for each child, a single paillasse (mattress), and an additional paillasse for families having more than one child.

Assistance was given the new immigrants in erecting a cabin. The building materials, which were furnished to each family, comprised two door hinges, and a lock and key, 18 panes of glass (each 7½ " x 8½"), and 1½ lbs of putty, as well as twelve pounds of wrought iron nails of various sizes. Moreover, for the first time in supplying the Rideau Military Settlement, each family was to be provided with 1,000 feet of pine boards which were purchased by the Commissariat from the sawmill in Perth.[54]

Presumably, the pine boards were to be used for flooring and roofing the log cabins, and for an interior partition. Earlier in the founding of the Perth settlement, the log cabins had only a single room, a packed earth floor, a fire backed by several large stones piled on the earth floor, and a hole in the roof to let out the smoke. These primitive cabins had either a sloping shed roof of 'scooped' basswood logs, or a pitched roof of split logs sealed with clay or moss in the gaps and covered with large sheets of peeled tree bark. Some cabins had a roof of roughly-split cedar boards. The early cabins had only a single wall opening – a door for entry and light – or a door, and a small window opening covered with an oiled paper.

Among the first improvements in the construction of log cabins were the introduction of an interior partition wall to form two rooms, a wood floor of split logs, and a fireplace and chimney, and sometimes a verandah. The fireplace was constructed of field stones, and the chimney of small tree branches, laid horizontally, notched at the corners, and covered on the inside with a thick layer of clay. The cabins were single storey structures, with but a few exceptions, and the more substantial structures could be large as 18 feet by 22 feet. The gaps between the horizontal logs of the walls were filled with clay and/or moss, and once a lime kiln was built in a community, with lime mortar.[55]

Following the establishment of a water-powered sawmill in Perth, a good number of the log cabins in that town were clapboarded; wood floor boards were installed; and the roofs were replaced with boards covered with cedar shake shingles. Moreover, the commercial buildings which were being constructed in Perth by this time, and the town houses of the half-pay officers of some means, were of a wood-frame construction, with a clapboard siding and a cedar shingle roof, and had several windows with glass panes.[56]

The log cabins in the Lanark settlement were constructed in the new manner. They had shingle roofs constructed of fir shakes, and had several windows. The provision of glass panes and lumber to the new immigrant settlers, by the Military Settling Department, was clearly a response to the introduction of more advanced building technologies into the Rideau Military Settlement.

The cost of provisions in a pioneer community fluctuated greatly depending on the settlement cycle. Initially, the entry of a large number of immigrants into a new survey in a wilderness area would result in high-priced provisions with no local food supply available, and heavy transport costs involved in importing food from a distance. However, once the first crops were harvested, and each settler became self-sufficient on his bush farm on a clearing in the woods, food prices would drop to a low level with no market being available in which to sell the local surplus produce. Thus, the government commitment to providing provisions to the Lanark settlers at prime cost – exclusive of transport costs – until their first crops could be harvested, was a major boon to the new settlers.

Initially, in the Lanark settlement, the price of produce sold on the open market was very high as it had to be transported from Perth. In 1821, flour sold for $7 a barrel, pork at 6d. per pound, and beef and mutton at 4½ to 5d. per pound, butter at 1s. per pound, eggs at 1s. per dozen, and a laying hen cost 15 d., and a quarter loaf of bread sold for 11d. Moreover, the nearest mill for grinding grain was in Perth, and the nearest market for selling farm produce was in Brockville, almost sixty miles away through the bush. There was also a scarcity of horses and oxen in the new Lanark settlement for clearing the land. A good work horse cost as much as £7 to £10, and a milk cow $20 to $22 [£5 to £5.10s.].

Nonetheless, the Scots who were located in Ramsay Township were even more fortunate in being settled amongst the earlier settlers, who were already growing potatoes and Indian corn, as well as some wheat and barley. Moreover, in all of the new townships the streams were full of fish, and gooseberry and raspberry bushes were found in profusion in the forest, as well as some black current bushes and plum trees, and wild game.[57]

During a two-year period, 1820 and 1821, it was the Military Settling Department that was responsible for the establishment and administration of the new Lanark settlement, and for the logistics of supplying the Lanark depot with the hardware items and provisions that were made available to the settlers for

Figure 12. "Bush farm near Chatham, ca. 1838", Lieutenant Philip John Bainbrigge, Royal Engineers, watercolour. A typical bush farm clearing, planted with corn, in a deciduous forest area of south-western Upper Canada. The Rideau Military Settlement townships in the north-east of the province, were in a mixed conifer and deciduous forest area with a somewhat less dense tree growth. (Library and Archives Canada.)

purchase. To that end, hardware items were transported inland to Prescott on the St. Lawrence military transport system, and salt pork and produce were purchased from farmers on the St. Lawrence Front. From Prescott, convoys of hired wagons carried the hardware and provisions to the Lanark settlement. Wagons were employed as well in bring fresh produce from Perth. Cattle were driven inland from the St. Lawrence Front to provide fresh beef. It was a daunting task which only the British Army Commissariat, in drawing on its organizational resources, was capable of performing in support of the Military Settling Department and the carrying out of its duties and responsibilities. Presumably cabins were also constructed for the new settlers; although that has not been documented.

In the Lanark military settlement, the officers of the Military Settling Department went beyond their prescribed duties in responding to the needs of the immigrant settlers. The original agreement between the Glasgow Emigration Society and the Colonial Office had stipulated that the immigrants were to purchase their own provisions en route to the new Lanark settlement, with the government providing only the transport. However, when some of the Scots weavers of the 1820 migration arrived penniless at the port of Quebec, or immediately expended whatever money they had in purchasing clothing, the Commissariat responded to their plight. Rations were provided for the destitute families – from military stores depots – during their passage from Quebec to the Lanark settlement. The initial intention, in providing free rations to the needy families en route to the settlement, was to have them reimburse the Commissariat, upon receipt of their first cash installment at Lanark. However, once the destitute families reached the settlement, it was recognized that the money was needed for them to purchase provisions. Hence, they were given their cash installment.

Thereafter, a number of changes were introduced in the support provided to the Scots weavers by the Military Settling Department. When some of the poorer families of the 1820 migration were found to be struggling to survive on their land, the cash installment payments system was altered. Installment payments were made to all the members of a family, rather than just to the head of the family as originally planned, to enable the struggling families to purchase additional provisions from the depot. Further aid was given to the poor immigrants in August 1820 when the Commissariat distributed 1,239 lbs of "damaged flour", free of charge, to the families in distress in the settlement.[58] When many of the immigrants were unable to pay for the farming implements, domestic utensils, and buildings materials that the Military Settling Department had imported for their benefit, the articles were dispensed to all of the assisted-emigration settlers free of charge. However, the settlers were still expected to repay the cash installments at the prescribed future date.

Thereafter, when 700 independent Scots immigrants arrived in the Lanark settlement, the Military Settling Department also provided support for them. They were not entitled to receive any benefits under the assisted-emigration programme, but were furnished with farm implements, tools, utensils, building materials, and blankets, free of charge. Such items were all but impossible to purchase on the open market in a new settlement in a wilderness environment. On the other hand, the independent settlers were not dependent on the Lanark Depot for provisions.

The independent Scots immigrants, who arrived in Canada with some capital or even substantial capital in some cases, were able to pay the high cost of their passage from Quebec to the Lanark settlement, the cost of purchasing a lot, the land fee costs, the cost of hiring axemen to erect a cabin, and the high prices demanded in the open market for produce transported to Lanark from the Perth settlement. Presumably the hardware items were given to the independent Scots out of a sense of fairness, and a desire to avoid social unrest in the Lanark settlement where the assisted-emigration Scots were already receiving the hardware items free of charge. There were also some discharged soldiers – half pay officers – amongst this group of independent immigrants.

While the immigrants were being settled on their lots in the townships around the Lanark townsite, the foundation of a village was being laid. As of the fall of 1820, three stores were established by merchants at the Lanark townsite, and at least a dozen respectable houses had been erected in the nascent village, in addition to the Commissariat Depot.[59]

The experience with settling the assisted-emigration settlers on the land in the fall of 1820 made it clear that poor immigrants were unable to settle in a wilderness without a great deal of support. Out of a concern for the wellbeing of future immigrant settlers, Captain William Marshall, the Superintendent of the Lanark settlement, wrote to the Glasgow Emigration Society during the winter of 1820-21. He advised the Society that the ships for the 1821 emigration ought to sail early in the spring to enable the families to be well settled on their land before the onset of winter, and that, for their own good, the emigrants should be well provided with clothing before leaving Scotland, and should not arrive penniless in Canada.

In response to the advice received from Captain Marshall, and reports received from the new settlers in the Lanark settlement, the Glasgow Emigration Society arranged for the four ships of the 1821 emigration to sail early in the spring, and changed the system for selecting the emigrants to be sent out to Canada. Where previously the emigrants had been chosen by lot from among the families who wanted to emigrate, they were now chosen on the basis of their ability to pay for the cost of their ocean transport, and for the purchase of provisions en route from Quebec to the Lanark settlement where they would receive their first cash installment payment. It was known by this time that the Military Settling Department was providing the farming implements, tools, domestic utensils, blankets, and provisions, free of charge to the assisted-emigration Scots immigrants upon their arrival in the Lanark settlement.

An effort was also made by the Glasgow Emigration Society to facilitate the acculturation of the new immigrants to the demands of living in the bush. Families who were seeking to join the assisted-emigration programme were advised to teach their children skills that would facilitate their survival on the land in Upper Canada. Girls were to be taught how to knit stocking of coarse wool, as well as how to spin woollen and linen yarn, and how to cut cloth for making clothes. Boys were to be taught how to make fishing nets and fishing tackle, to help support the family by fishing the rivers and lakes of the Lanark settlement, which were reportedly full of fish. The previous year's emigrants also advised prospective new emigrants to bring out lots of coarse woollen plaid for making clothes, as cotton would easily burn from the sparks of the fires which were employed in burning the underbrush and trees in clearing the land.[60]

The Glasgow Emigration Society was also anxious to promote the spread of education and religious devotion in the new pioneer society. By the existing agreement with the Colonial Office, the government paid for the salary of a teacher in the new settlement, and an arrangement was made for the provision of a clergyman. In addition, the new emigrants were encouraged to take books with them from their private libraries, and were admonished to maintain their daily worship of God, to honour the Sabbath, and to bear their hardships with Christian fortitude until, "with the blessing of God", they would prosper in the new land. An arrangement was made as well for the British and Foreign Bible Society to provide each family with a Bible, free of charge, on the boarding of their ship.

Once again the ships, which were chartered to carry the new emigrants to Canada, were inspected for their sea worthiness, for the number and suitability of the berths on board, and for the quality and quantity of the provisions and water stored for the voyage. There was also a concern to safeguard the health of the families. A surgeon was engaged to sail with each ship, and before boarding a ship, parents were required to provide proof that their children had been inoculated against smallpox.[61]

The emigrants who were sent out from Greenock in the spring

of 1821 were of a "most respectable appearance", and were much better off financially than the Scots weavers of the previous year. Indeed, the monies subscribed by the emigrants to pay for the charter and provisioning of the ships, amounted to a greater sum than the actual cost, and the surplus money was returned to the emigrants – once on board – proportional to their original contribution. Most of the new emigrants were country people – farmers – from outside of the town centres; although a significant number of artificers, such as smiths and joiners, were included to provide support for the new Lanark agricultural community in Upper Canada.[62]

In sum, the emigrants sent out in 1821 by the Glasgow Emigration Society were much better prepared, and had greater financial resources, than many of the hand loom weavers of the 1820 assisted-emigration Scots settlers. Nonetheless, even the poorest of the Scots immigrant settlers who had arrived in Lanark settlement a year earlier were already established on bush farms, thanks to the support provided of the Military Settling Department.

One of the settlers from the 1820 emigration described the experience of his family as follows:

> "Government has been very honourable. Besides conveyance from Quebec to Lanark, and rations, (the rations consist of one lb. of bread, and one of pork for a man, one-half each for a wife, and one-third for a child above seven, and one-fourth for those under), I have got [farm implements, tools, building materials, etc.]. .... The gentlemen here, and all the way from Quebec, who had the charge of forwarding us, seemed to vie with each other in discretion and kindness. This is the most merciful action that ever I knew the British Government to perform: it affords many poor industrious families the means of obtaining the necessaries of life, who had no such prospect before."[63]

Overall, the officers of the Military Settling Department carried out their duties and responsibilities in the establishment of the Lanark settlement in an exemplary manner. However, they went far beyond their prescribed duties to ensure that the new settlers were properly equipped and supplied to succeed in establishing a bush farm, regardless of whether they could pay for what they were given or not. Moreover, to aid the destitute settlers among the 1820 settlers, the amount of the cash installments provided was increased. Such a generous support went far beyond the limited financial and logistical support which had been promised to the Glasgow Emigration Society by the Colonial Office in London. The additional aid was furnished by the officers of the Military Settling Department out of a concern to promote the wellbeing of the poorer immigrant families through facilitating their successful settling onto the land, and to prevent them from suffering from extreme hunger, and even starvation, in the bush before their first crops could be harvested.[64]

As of the close of the year 1822, Perth and Richmond in the Rideau Military Settlement were self-supporting and no longer in need of any support from the Military Settling Department. Both depots were closed in December 1822, and plans were in preparation to close the Lanark depot at the end of 1823, by which time the settlement was expected to be well established and completely self-sufficient. The Lanark settlement accomplished its purpose, but the paternalism practiced by the officers of the Military Settling Department in support of the assisted-emigration programme of the British government, was not without its costs.

Overall, a total of £11,832.11s.7d. was expended by the Military Settling Department during a two-year period in providing support to facilitate the assisted-emigration Scots in settling on their land grants in Lanark settlement. That expenditure included the cost of constructing roads to access the new settlement, the land surveys, the expense of transporting the immigrants from Quebec to the Lanark settlement, the cost of erecting

Commissariat buildings (and perhaps cabins), and the cost of furnishing seed and farming implements to the Scots weavers, as well as the payment of the salaries of a military superintendent, a clerk, a surgeon, and a schoolmaster for the settlement. In all, an average of £15 to £16 per assisted-emigration family was expended by the Military Settling Department in the Lanark settlement. In addition, to these settlement costs, which were paid out of the Army Extraordinaries (the military chest), an additional £22,000 was expended by the Military Settling Department in paying the cash instalments of the capital promised the settlers by the Colonial Office, in lieu of providing them with military rations during their first year on the land.[65]

The monies that were expended by the Military Settling Department were essential to the successful establishment of the Lanark settlement. The capital expenditures also contributed to the prosperity of the newly-established Perth settlement in providing a market for its farm produce, and employment for the saw mill and two grist mills established on the Tay River. A market was provided as well for the produce grown by the settlers in Ramsay Township, who had arrived two years earlier.

The 1821 settlers were the last to be sent out from Scotland under an assisted-emigration programme of the British government. In Scotland, the Glasgow Emigration Society, and its affiliated local emigration societies, voluntarily disbanded at the close of the year. Earlier, as of the spring of 1821, the severe unemployment problem amongst the hand loom weavers of Lanark and Renfrewshire counties had been ameliorate through the assisted-emigration programme of the previous summer and a lifting of the postwar depression. With trade and commerce recovering, there was work readily available for the weavers of the counties of Lanark and Renfrewshire in Scotland; wage rates were rising; and no longer was there any need, or justification, for a government programme of assisted emigration to deal with unemployment and social unrest in Scotland.[66] In the Lanark settlement in Upper Canada, however, the depot remained open, and the superintendent, a clerk, a surgeon, and a schoolmaster were maintained there until 1829.[67] The depot was used to provide support for a new influx of settlers into Ramsay township and the two adjacent townships, under another assisted-emigration programme introduced by the British government in Ireland.

The Irish Catholic Poor-Relief Emigrants

In 1823, the population of the Rideau Military Settlement was augmented with the arrival of Irish Roman Catholic immigrants under the direction of Peter Robinson, an Anglican Tory from a distinguished Upper Canadian Loyalist family.[68] This latter group was part of an experiment in Irish poor relief by the Colonial Office. Its aim was two-fold: to determine whether distress in Ireland could be alleviated, and disaffection allayed, through an assisted-emigration programme; and to see if the disaffected who were assisted to emigrate could be transformed into loyal subjects through farming their own land in self-sufficient communities that would not become a burden to the colony. To that end, Peter Robinson was instructed by the Colonial Office to recruit potential emigrants, preferably Roman Catholics, from the most disturbed areas of Ireland: the southern counties of Cork, Limerick, Tipperary, Waterford, and Kerry.

A total of 568 emigrants were selected, including single men as well as heads of families. Most were small tenant farmers and cottiers (farm labourers who generally possessed an acre of land for growing potatoes and grazing a cow). All were suffering deprivation owing to a steep decline in wheat prices after the Napoleonic Wars. A number of rural tradesmen of reduced circumstances were also included. Few possessed any capital at all, and none could afford to emigrate on their own.

Although impoverished, the Irish Catholic emigrants were by no means taken from among the destitute paupers and beggars that roamed the bog lands, towns, and roadways of Ireland in the post-Napoleonic War period, rather they were tenant farmers from the landed estates. They were recommended by their landlord, and some even had character references from both a Protestant and a Roman Catholic clergyman. Most of the emigrants selected for the poor-relief experiment were literate in English, knew the rudiments of arithmetic, and were able to furnish themselves with extra clothes and some supplies for the voyage. Robinson had wanted the assisted-emigration party to include only respectable Irish Catholic farmers who were known to be loyal to the Crown, but to secure the support of the local landlords he was forced to accept some pauper families of questionable loyalty and several single males who were reputedly 'troublemakers'. Twelve Irish Protestant families were also included in the assisted emigration programme by way of ensuring the Irish Catholic families that the emigration programme was not a scheme to transport them into indentured labour in North America.[69]

The Colonial Office was particularly generous to the Robinson Irish. A sum of £12,000 was voted by Parliament on the Colonial Office estimates for Peter Robinson to administer in carrying out the Irish poor-relief experiment. The emigrants were provided with a free passage, medical care and generous provisions on board naval transport vessels during the ocean crossing, as well as rations and medical care en route from the port of Quebec to the settlement area. They were transported inland from Quebec on the St. Lawrence River navigation to Brockville, and into the interior of the province on the military bush road – the Brockville Road – through Perth and Lanark to their assigned lot locations.

Most of the Irish poor-relief immigrants were settled in Ramsay Township, amongst recently established Presbyterian Scots and Anglo-Irish Protestant immigrant settlers, and in contiguous areas of the adjacent Beckwith, Pakenham, and Huntley townships. Parts of Beckwith Township were settled as early as 1817 by Presbyterian Scots immigrants from Perthshire and Anglo-Irish immigrants (Anglicans and Wesleyan Methodists) from Wexford and Carlow counties in south-eastern Ireland. Both groups were part of chain migrations from their home counties to Canada. The first settlers in Huntley Township were Anglo-Irish Protestants who migrated there from the Richmond settlement in

1819, and they were joined in 1822 by an influx of Anglo-Irish Protestants immigrants. In Pakenham Township, the first settlers were Scots immigrants who settled around Shipman's Mills on the Mississippi River tributary of the Ottawa River in 1820.

Prior to the arrival of the Irish Catholic poor-relief immigrants, the families established on bush farms in Ramsay, Beckwith, Pakenham and Huntley townships were independent settlers who had paid for their own transport and settlement costs without receiving any government assistance. In contrast, the Irish poor-relief immigrants received a great deal of government assistance, not only in their transport to the settlement but also in settling on the land.

Each male, over eighteen years of age, received a location ticket for a grant of 70 acres of land, the patent of which could be secured by clearing and fencing 3 ½ acres of land, and erecting a cabin measuring at least 16 feet by 20 feet within a two year period. In addition, an adjacent thirty acres was reserved for ten years for potential purchase by the settler for the sum of £10. The poor-relief emigrants were also provided with provisions for a year, which Robinson purchased for them, presumably through a Commissariat supply depot that was established at Shipman's Mill (Almonte), and the depot established earlier at Lanark in the Lanark settlement.

Once on the land, the Irish poor-relief immigrants were issued bedding, cooking utensils, carpenter's tools, and farming implements from the Commissariat depots at Lanark and at Shipman's Mills. The hardware supplies that were issued the Irish Catholic settlers were consistent with what the Military Settling Department had provided earlier to the discharged soldiers and assisted-emigration Scots in the Rideau Military Settlement, with just a few minor variations. Otherwise, the Robinson Irish were treated more generously in being provided with shoes, cloth for making clothes, and a milk cow. The farming implements, domestic utensils, and blankets were purchased from the Commissariat by Peter Robinson, and distributed to the immigrant families.

A small family – man, wife and one child – received two blankets, two pair of shoes, and an iron pot, a felling axe for cutting down trees and a bill hook for clearing brush, together with a file for sharpening them, and a wedge for splitting wood for fence rails and shingles. The carpentry tools which were issued to a small family comprised a gimlet, two hammers, and a saw, with some families receiving a pound of nails as well for distribution. The farming implements consisted of a hoe, an auger, a pickaxe, spade, and sickle. In addition, each family received six quarts of wheat seed, and five bushels of potato seeds; and, if they remained on the land to the following spring, a cow.

A large family of eight, with two adult males would receive seven blankets, five pair of shoes, an iron pot, a kettle, and a frying pan, as well as a bill hook, two axes, and a cross-cut saw, as well as four sharpening files and two wedges. Such a large family would also receive additional carpentry tools, comprising a drawing knife for making shingles, three gimlets, a handsaw, a hammer, and six pounds of nails. The farming implements consisted of two hoes, two spades, two pickaxes, an auger, two sickles, and one scythe. In addition, a large family with two adults would receive nine quarts of wheat seeds, fifteen bushels of potato seeds, and, if they remained on the land until the following spring, two cows.

In keeping with the practice adopted in the fall of 1816 by the Commander-in-Chief for the Rideau Military Settlement, Robinson paid axemen to erect a log cabin on the lot of each of the Irish poor-relief immigrants. In addition, each family was furnished with two bolts of cotton serge and flannel. The Irish settlers were also fortunate in that they arrived in the autumn during a period of exceptionally good weather, and did not have to contend with either heavy rains, or the black flies and mosquitoes, that had plagued the earlier settlers upon their arrival in the Rideau Military Settlement.

Overall, during the course of twelve months in 1823-1824 a total of £12,539 was expended on the Irish poor-relief experiment for the destitute Irish Catholics and the several Irish Protestant families. That sum was the equivalent of £35 for each man, £25 per woman, and £14 for each child located on the land. Two towns were established by the Robinson Irish settlers: Teskeyville in Ramsay Township where the Teskey family – one of the Protestant Irish families – erected a saw and grist mill; and Pakenham Mills in Pakenham Township where Robert Harvey, an Anglican entrepreneur from Brockville on the St. Lawrence Front, came to erect a saw mill and potash works.

With the exception of several families who were settled in rocky areas of Parkenham township, the Irish Catholic poor-relief immigrants, and the several Protestant families amongst them, were settled for the most part on good land in a settlement area where their neighbours had already successfully adapted to the demands of farming in the bush. As such they were far more fortunate than the earlier immigrant groups in the Rideau Military Settlement who had penetrated into the wilderness under far more trying conditions, and some of whom were settled on rocky or swampy land that had proved unsuitable for farming.[70]

Cost -Benefits: The Rideau Military Settlement

Under the military settling/assisted-emigration programmes, great difficulties were encountered in settling the discharged soldiers and assisted-emigration British immigrants who were unaccustomed to the North American environment, into a virtual wilderness. Indeed, the very survival of the earliest groups depended solely on the paternalism of the officers of the Military Settling Department.

On first entering on uncleared land in the wilderness interior of the newly-surveyed military settlements, the new settlers were totally dependent on their military rations for survival. Moreover, it soon became apparent that British immigrants, inexperienced in coping with the demands of living and working in a wilderness environment, required almost 18 months to become self-sufficient. Thus, the military provisioning support for the first settlers was extended for an additional year beyond the original termination date, and then again for an additional several months, when the 1816 potato crop was destroyed by frost and the wheat damaged by rust during the "summerless summer". In that instance, the extension of the military provisioning system saved the soldier-settlers and assisted-emigration Scots settlers of the Rideau Military Settlement from starvation. Similarly, the paternalism practised by the Military Settling Department in going beyond their instructions to provide extra support for the Scots weavers and Irish poor-relief immigrants were instrumental in greatly facilitating their settlement onto the land.

Although the military settlement programme was well on the way to accomplishing its objective by the mid-1820s, the settlement experience was not completely successful. A large number of the soldier-settlers, and a significant number of the assisted-emigration settlers, did not remain on the land once the period of provisioning ended.

Despite extensive aid, only half of the soldier-settlers remained on the land past the support period. Those who left were primarily single men from the British Army units, and the foreign mercenaries from the DeWatteville Regiment. Among the soldier-settlers, the DeWattevilles had the poorest settlement record. One contributing factor was that the regiment was located on what turned out to be poor rocky soil in Burgess Township, where only 20% completed their settlement duties through remaining on the land for three years, erecting a house, and clearing four acres of land to qualify for their land patent.[71]

In contrast, all but one of the Scots emigrants stayed on the land in the Perth settlement, and within two years many had cleared as many as ten acres of land. Within five years of settlement, the more industrious among the Scots of the Perth settlement, and the Canadian settlers of the two fencible regiments who stayed on the land, had anywhere from 20 to 30 acres cleared, and possessed a yoke of oxen, several cows and hogs and, in rare instances, several sheep.[72]

The Lanark settlers, with military support and direction, also adopted well to their environment, in taking readily to the use of the axe in clearing their land. Approximately 61% completed their settlement duties within the required three years, and the vast majority of the settlers remained on the land and would have anywhere from ten to twenty acres cleared within seven years. By that time, the more successful possessed a yoke of oxen, as well as several cows and pigs.[73] The independent Scots and Irish Protestant immigrants who settled on the comparatively rich soil of Ramsay Township, also stayed and prospered. As of 1826, the military settlements in the back townships of the Rideau were producing a significant surplus crop of potatoes, grain, and turnips, lacking only a major market to encourage them to further production.[74]

The Irish poor-relief experiment in settling destitute Irish tenant farmers and rural tradesmen – primarily Irish Catholics – in the back townships, yielded a poor return. Of the 182 heads of families and individuals located in the back townships by Peter Robinson in 1823, only 120 were working the land two years later. Fully a third of the Irish poor-relief settlers had departed, with many of them leaving on the ending of the rationing system to seek work elsewhere in the settled areas of the province, or in the United States. Subsequently 83 families, or roughly 45%, completed their settlement duties and remained on the land.[75]

Heavily represented among those who failed were the tradesmen and the young single men, who had proved to be a highly unruly element in the Robinson settlement.[76] For the Irish Catholic poor-relief immigrants, whether ownership of their own land, equality before the law and political rights in Upper Canada, and freedom of religion, and the aid that they had received from the military in settling on the land, would awaken feelings of loyalty to the British Crown remained to be seen.[77]

Overall, the military settlement and assisted-emigration

programmes succeeded in establishing settlements to the rear of the Rideau River that would be able to contribute substantially to the construction of a future military water communication through the interior wilderness of Upper Canada. As of the close of 1822, there were over 10,700 self-supporting settlers who had been placed on the land in the townships to the rear of the projected Rideau Canal route; and that number included 3,570 males, inclusive of 1,307 discharged soldiers and 2,263 immigrants.[78] Moreover, that number increased further with the settling of the Irish Catholic poor-relief emigrants in 1823.

As of the spring of 1826, when the Board of Ordnance in London decided to undertake the construction of a military canal – the Rideau Canal – through the interior of Upper Canada, the securing of manpower and provisions for such an undertaking in a wilderness environment was no longer a seemingly insurmountable problem. The new villages of Perth, Richmond, and Lanark, and the farm clearings in the surrounding townships to the rear of the planned canal route were counted on to contribute substantially to the manpower and draught animals needed to construct the canal, and to supply the food and fodder that would be needed to sustain a large workforce living and working in what had been a veritable wilderness.

In the Rideau Military Settlement experience there was but one rather ominous development. A strong resentment, and animosity, was in evidence among the independent Scots and the Irish Protestants of Ramsay, Huntley, and Beckwith townships, towards the poor-relief Irish Catholic immigrants over the generous support that the latter had received during their emigration to Canada and settlement on the land. On April 23, 1824, a major riot erupted during a militia muster – the 'Ballygibblin Riots' at Morphy's Falls (Carleton Place). One man was killed, and several wounded, before the magistrate could assert his authority and end the conflict.[79] Such an occurrence did not bode well for the employment of a multi-cultural workforce on the projected Rideau Canal construction project.

From the Rideau Military Settlement experience, it was readily apparent that the degree of difficulty and success experienced in adapting to the demands of living and working in a wilderness environment and establishing a bush farm, depended on a number of factors. Among them were: marital status, as single men did not make good settlers; the previous occupation of the immigrant settler, whether yeoman farmer, tenant farmer, tradesman or soldier; and the degree to which the individual immigrants (both men and women) possessed adaptable skills in addition to their primary occupation. Other factors were the character of the individual immigrant settler, and the cultural values of the immigrant group formed within their particular ethnic and/or religious community in the old country.[80]

Conclusion

The initiatives taken by the officers of the Military Settling Department – under the command of the Commander-in-Chief of the Forces/Governor-in-Chief – in establishing the Rideau Military Settlement, provides yet another example of the practice of paternalism on the part of the British military in Canada during the early 19th Century. Time and time again, actions were taken by the officers of the Military Settling Department to alleviate the hardships being experienced by the immigrant settlers and to promote their wellbeing as their particular needs became known. The military provided support for the soldier-settlers and the assisted-emigration settlers that went far beyond what was promised them by the Colonial Office. Through the practice of paternalism, the immigrant settlers were saved from severe suffering in the wilds of Upper Canada and, in one instance, even from starvation under extremely adverse conditions. Where the Irish-Catholic poor-relief immigration experience was concerned, Peter Robinson, an Upper Canadian Anglican Tory, was equally paternalistic in responding to the needs of the immigrant settlers, and did so with the support of the Commander-in-Chief and the officers of the Commissariat Department of the British Army who continued to facilitate the settling of British immigrants onto the land in going beyond their prescribed duties and responsibilities.

End Notes

1. The effort of the Tory Loyalists of Upper Canada to support Lord Bathurst's policy through a policy of excluding American settlers from entering Upper Canada in the postwar period, is extraneous to this current treatment of military paternalism in the Rideau Military Settlement. The best treatment of that legislative effort to exclude American settlers, and the resulting Alien Question controversy, can be found in: Patrick Brode, *Sir John Beverely Robinson, Bone and Sinew of the Compact* (Toronto: University of Toronto Press, 1984). Brode provides an excellent analysis of the evolution of the provincial legislation, and of Tory aims, as well as a penetrating exposure of the fallacious opposition rhetoric.

2. LAC, MG11, CO43, Vol. 23, B-841, 122-123, Lord Bathurst to Sir George Prevost, 29 October 1813. The Scots who were anxious to emigrate were from the counties of Sutherland and Caithness in the far north of Scotland.

3. LAC, MG11, CO42, Vol. 355, B-296, 120-121, Sir Gordon Drummond to Prevost, 19 February 1814.

4. Helen I. Cowan, *British Emigration to British North America, The First Hundred Years* (Toronto: University of Toronto Press, 1961), 41-42; and CO42, Vol. 164, B-133, Young to Transport Board, 25 April 1814. Prior to the onset of the postwar depression, there was a strong opposition to emigration in Britain. In England, landlords feared the loss of their tenant farmers, industrialists wanted to keep a large labour pool, and the government was opposed to the emigration of artisans. In Ireland, there was opposition by the governing authorities and the Established Church of Ireland to the emigration of Irish Protestants to North America. In contrast, in Scotland the Highland clearances were generating a surplus population, and some clan chiefs were encouraging their displaced clansmen tenants to emigrate.

5. LAC, MG11, CO43, Vol 23, B-841, 178-179, Bathurst to Drummond, 31 May 1815; Eric Jarvis, "Military Land Granting in Upper Canada following the War of 1812", *Ontario History*, Vol. 67 (3), 1975, 121-123; and Hitsman, *The Incredible War of 1812*, 123-124. Fencible Regiments were raised in both

Upper and Lower Canada during the war, and were composed of volunteers recruited solely for the defence of Canada during wartime. The men enlisted for a two or three year term, or until six months after the conclusion of a peace. The fencible regiments were commanded by regular army officers, received army pay according to rank, and were organized and equipped the same as regular army regiments. During the War of 1812, the fencible regiments fought alongside the British Army regiments in most of the major battles.

6. LAC, MG11, CO43, Vol. 23, B-841, 174-175, & 180, Bathurst to Drummond, 10 March and 13 June 1815.

7. LAC, MG11, CO42, Vol 356, B-296, 69-72, Major-General Sir Frederick P. Robinson, Provisional Governor of Upper Canada, to Lord Bathurst, 29 July 1815. Ultimately, the discharged soldier settlers were located on the Rideau River in Upper Canada, on the St. Francis River in Lower Canada, and on the Crown Reserves in Glengarry on the upper St. Lawrence River, and in the Bay of Quinte on Lake Ontario. A small number of the discharged soldier-settlers were also located along the Timiscouasta Portage Road between New Brunswick and Lower Canada.

8. LAC, RG7, G1, Vol. 58, reel ? . 4-5. Bathurst to Francis Gore, Lt. Governor of Upper Canada, 8 January 1816. Gore was on leave in England during the War of 1812, but returned to his position as Lt. Governor in September 1815.

9. Jon Latimer, *1812, War with America* (Cambridge: Harvard University Press, 2007), 191, 223-224 & 269-270; and Donald E. Graves, "Why the White House Was Burned: An Investigation into the British Destruction of Public Buildings at Washington in August 1814", *The Journal of Military History,* Vol. 76, No. 4, October 2012, 1102-1112. The worst offenders in the looting and burning of the properties of the Tory Loyalist militiamen were the renegade American settlers of Upper Canada who joined the American invaders, and singled out the homes, farms, and mill properties of the loyal militia officers, and of the old Loyalist families, for destruction. The renegade American settlers formed a "Canadian Volunteers" corps attached to the American invasion army. The 'Canadian Volunteers' corps, which numbered as many as 164 men, was led by Joseph Willcocks, an Anglo-Irish immigrant place-seeker and pre-war political agitator in Upper Canada.

10. Robert W. Passfield, "Ordnance Supply Problems in the Canadas: The

Quest for an Improved Military Transport Ssytem, 1814-1828", *HSTC Bulletin, Journal of the History of Canadian Science, Technology and Medicine*, Vol. V, No. 3, September 1981, 187-191.

11. LAC, RG8, Series C, Vol. 38, C-2616, 129, Bathurst to Drummond, 20 October 1815. Subsequently, with the onset of a postwar depression, work on the projected Rideau batteaux navigation was postponed. As early as January 1816, the Lords Commissioners of the Treasury established the principle that the Canadian provinces were expected to pay half the cost of any canal project that served both a military and commercial purpose. See LAC, MG11, CO42, Vol. 180, B-142, 611, G. Manning, Treasury, to Henry Goulburn, Colonial Office, 6 January 1816. A decade later, however, the British government undertook to pay the entire cost for constructing the Rideau Canal.

12. LAC, MG11, CO42, Vol. 357, B-297, 41-42, Gore to Drummond, 23 February 1816; and ibid, 43-44, William Claus, Deputy Superintendent General for Upper Canada, Indian Affairs, to Captain Ferguson, Resident Agent of Indian Affairs, Kingston, 22 February 1816. The Indian Affairs department was engaged on behalf of His Majesty's Government in purchasing the lands in question, as well as several additional unsettled townships in the Rideau corridor, from the "Chippawa and Mississaguay Nations".

13. LAC, MG 24, A 12, Dalhousie Muniments, reel A-525, 123, "Memorandum Relative to the Water Communication between Upper Canada and Lower Canada"; LAC, MG 13, WO 44, Vol. 19, B-1294, 9, Henry Goulburn to George Harrison, 20 November 1817; and Eric Jarvis, "Military Land Granting in Upper Canada following the War of 1812" (*Ontario History*, LXVII, 1975): 122-134. See also Jean S. McGill, *A Pioneer History of the County of Lanark* (Toronto: T.H. Best, 3rd printing, 1970): 11, 15, & 19. The Rideau military waterway was initially conceived as a batteaux navigation of a two foot depth, which was to include several portages, and small number of low-head dams and locks to step past waterfalls and rapids. When construction work commenced in September 1826, the intention was to construct a uninterrupted gunboat canal with locks 20' x 108', and a five foot depth of water, but Lt. Col. John By, the Commanding Royal Engineer, Rideau Canal, recommended that the canal be enlarged to accommodate steamboats.. In June 1828, a senior Committee of Royal Engineers decided to construct the Rideau Canal as a steamboat navigation with locks 33' x 134', and a minimum five-foot depth of water, for the accommodation of river steamboats.

14. Cowan, *British Emigration*, 42. According to Cowan, the initial group of Scots emigrants were farmers and labourers, and largely from Edinburgh, Glasgow, Paisley, Knoydart, Glenelg, and Callander.

15. James Hunter, *Scottish Exodus, Travels Among a Worldwide Clan* (Edinburgh & London: Mainstream Press, 2007): 105-158. Hunter focuses on the emigration experiences of the Clan MacLeod, but the historical context and immigrations pattern applied to all of the Highland clans. The 'tackman' of an estate looked after the horses and cattle where communal farming was the norm, and was responsible for collecting the rents from the tenants for the Laird. The tackman was a sort of estate overseer responsible directly to the Laird.

16. Cowan, *British Emigration*, 42-43; and McGill, *A Pioneer History*, 6. All male children on attaining the age of 21 were likewise to receive a grant of 100 acres of land. Cowan states that the Colonial Office in its "Liberal Encouragement to Settlers" notice, published in Edinburgh on 25 February 1815, promised that axes, ploughs and other implements would be furnished to the assisted-emigration settlers at half cost; whereas the Commissariat actually supplied these items free of charge to the Scots settlers in the Rideau Military Settlement.

17. Marianne McLean, *The People of Glengarry, Highlanders in Transition, 1745-1820* (Montreal & Kingston: McGill-Queens University Press, 1991): 153-155.

18. McGill, *A Pioneer History*, 7; McLean, *The People of Glengarry*, 155; Campey, *Scottish Pioneers*, 35-36.

19. McGill, *A Pioneer History*, 10-11; McLean, *The People of Glengarry*, 199; and Smith, *Perth-on-Tay*, Addendum, 233-234, copy of Sidney Beckwith, Quartermaster General to Lt. General Drummond, 21 November 1815, and Beckwith to William Henry Robinson, Commissary General, 29 December 1815.

20. McGill, *A Pioneer History*, 12-15 & 22. The new Brockville-Perth Road was an extension of an existing road that ran 21 miles inland from Brockville in a northerly direction before turning north-westward to Stone Mills on the headwaters of the Gananoque River. The new military road continued the existing road straight north from the 21-mile point to Rideau Lake, and was

constructed a farther six miles from the mouth of the Pike River on Rideau Lake to the Perth in the Rideau Military Settlement. The total length of the new road was 42 miles, inclusive of the original 21 mile section.

21. McLean, *The People of Glengarry*, 196-201; and McGill, *A Pioneer History*, 11-12. In addition to the Highlanders, thirteen Lowland families of the Scots assisted-emigration group were settled in Glengarry County; and forty veterans of the Glengarry Light Infantry Fencibles received 100 acre land grants in the County at the end of the war under the military settling programme. Earlier, during the War, Drummond had shared Bathurst's view that the assisted-emigration Scots should be located on the unsettled lands in Lower Canada along the 45 parallel border with the United States. (LAC, MG11, CO42, Vol. 355, B-296, 118-119, Drummond to Prevost, 12 July 1814.)

22. McGill, *A Pioneer History*, 15-17 & 42-43; and Smith, *Perth-on-Tay*, 5 and Addendum, 239, copy of letter Lt. Governor Gore to Lt. General Sherbrooke, 15 October 1816. McGill also lists a "rasping hook" among the tools furnished each family of settlers, which is puzzling as no reference to such a tool has been found in the literature pertaining to pioneer farming tools and implements.

23. Marianne McLean, 'In the new land a new Glengarry': Migration from the Scottish Highlands to Upper Canada, 1750-1820, PhD thesis, University of Edinburgh, 1982, Chapter 10, Post-war Emigrants, 260-297. See Josephine Smith, *Perth-on-Tay, A Tale of the Transplanted Highlanders* (Merrickville: Mortimer Co.   Printers, 1901, reprinted 1987), "Addenda", 233-235, Extracts from Quarter Master General's Office correspondence of 21 November 1815 and 29 December 1815.

24. McGill, *A Pioneer History*, 230, Appendix B, "Statistical Data on the Scotch Line Settlers Interviewed by Robert Gourlay in July 1817".

25. McGill, *A Pioneer History*,17-22. On the De Watteville Regiment see: René Chartrand, "Louis de Watteville", *Dictionary of Canadian Biography*, vol. VII. When the regiment sailed for Canada in April 1813, it comprised over 1500 men of all ranks, 45 wives and 38 children. The number who chose to settle in the Rideau Military Settlement has not been ascertained. See also McLean (*The People of Glengarry*, 199), on the veterans of the Glengarry Regiment who settled in the Rideau Military Settlement.

26. McGill, *A Pioneer History*, 17; and Smith, *Perth-On-Tay,* 242, Christopher Myers, to Deputy Quartermaster General's Office, 4 May 1817; 246, D. Daverne, Secretary, Settling Department to Superintendent's Office, 17 October 1818; 247, "Hardware Supplies Furnished the Settlers"; and 243, Captain Samuel Romilly, Commanding R.E. for Upper Canada, J.W. Clarke, Deputy Commissary General, and Jonathon Hare, Assistant Storekeeper, "Board of Enquiry on Axes", to Colonel Addison, Military Secretary to the Commander-in-Chief, May 1819.

27. Hunter, *Scottish Exodus*, 144; and Harry & OliveWalker, *Carleton Saga*, (Ottawa: Carleton County Council, 1968 , 9; M'Donald, Emigration to Canada, 21-23; and Guillet, *The Pioneer Farmer and Backwoodsman*, Vol. I, 87-88.

28. Http://en.wikipedia.org/wiki/year_without_a_Summer; and Keith C. Heidorn, *Eighteen Hundred and Frozen to Death, The Year There was no Summer* (2004). Apparently the sun light was blocked by volcanic dust ejected into the upper atmosphere by a colossal eruption of the Mount Tambora volcano in Indonesia, April 5-15, 1815, which disturbed weather patterns worldwide, and destroyed crops and caused famine in areas as widespread as China, India, Northern Europe, and north-eastern North America. Over the previous four years, three other volcanic eruptions in East Asia and one in the Caribbean had contributed to the buildup of volcanic ash dust in the upper atmosphere, and to impact of the 'volcanic winter' of the summer of 1816. During the cold waves, cereal crops in Canada and New England were devastated, and poor harvest were recorded as far south as Pennsylvania and Virginia.

29. *Ibid*. Although the weather records cited by the above two sources are incomplete, and focus primarily on New England, the weather patterns for Upper and Lower Canada can be deduced from these accounts. In the Canadian provinces there may well have been even more nights of severe frost, but the cold wave patterns would have been the same. See also Walker, *Carleton Saga*, 1975, 36-37; and *Quebec Gazette*, June 6, 8 & 27. At Quebec on June 6th some of the snowflakes were up to 2" in diameter. During the June 22nd -24th heat wave temperatures over 90 degrees Fahrenheit were recorded in Massachusetts. In many of the northern and low lying areas of New England, there were localized famines by the fall of 1816; and presumably that appears to have been the situation more generally in the Canadian provinces.

30. Walker, *Carleton Saga*, p. 37; *Quebec Gazette*, 27 June 1816; and W.L. Smith, *The Pioneers of Old Ontario, the Makers of Canada* (Toronto: George N. Morang, 1923), "Gananoque", n.p. Smith describes what the Loyalist settlers ate earlier during an earlier 'year of scarcity' in 1788, but his observations apply equally to the bush farmers in Upper Canada during the summerless summer of 1816.

31. "A Proclamation", *Quebec Gazette*, 11 July 1816; and LAC, CO42, vol. 166, B-135, 183, Sherbrooke to Lord Bathurst, 23 September 1816.

32. Smith, *Perth-on-Tay*, Addendum, 241, Colonel Christian Myers, Quartermaster of Militia to Deputy Quartermaster General's Office, 13 October 1816, and 239-240, Lt. Governor Francis Gore to Lt. General Sir John Sherbrooke, 15 October 1816.

33. LAC, MG11, CO42, vol. 167, B-135, 63-67, W. H. Robinson, Commissary General, to Lt. Col. Addison, Military Secretary, 27 July 1816; and Smith, *Perth-on-Tay*, Addendum, 237, George Fowler, Superintendent, Rideau Military Settlement, to Lt. Col. Addison, 24 September 1816. Robinson objected to the Commissary Department having to support the assisted-emigration Scots out of the Army Extraordinaries (the military chest), without any financial contribution from either the Colonial Office or the provincial governments in Canada. In addition to Perth, as of 1816, the Commissary Department in Canada was maintaining stores depots for provisioning discharged soldiers and the assisted-emigration Scots settlers in Glengarry County, and on the nearby Raisin River (future Lancaster), as well as at the Carrying Place on the Bay of Quinte and on the St. Francis River in Lower Canada for provisioning discharged soldier-settlers.

The Army Extraordinaries account was distinct from the Army Estimates, which the War Office submitted to parliament each year to secure a grant to support the Army establishment and to cover the projected expenditures of the Army service departments. In contrast, the Army Extraordinaries account (the military chest) was not a specific parliamentary grant based on an estimate. It was a lump sum voted each year by parliament to cover colonial military expenditures (and often the civil establishment costs in a colony), as well as the cost of specific colonial projects sanctioned by the Lords Commissioners of the Treasury during the course of the year. At the close of the year, the Paymaster of the Forces would present a general statement of the Army Extraordinaries account to parliament. On that basis, a repayment grant would be made by parliament to cover any expenditures that had been made in the colonies in excess of the annual lump sum voted for the military chest for that year. As of the 1820s, parliament was voting a lump sum of anywhere from £800,000 to £900,000 for the Army Extraordinaries account each year, but was customarily voting as much as £2,000,000 to top up the military chest to cover the actual expenditures at the close of each year. See Henry Parnell, *On Financial Reform*, 3rd. ed. (London: John Murray, 1831), 129-130.

34. Myna Trustram, *Women of the Regiment, Marriage and the Victorian Army* (New York: Cambridge University Press, 1984):86-88.

35. Smith, *Perth-on-Tay*, Addendum, 240-241, Col. C. Myers, Deputy Quartermaster General, to Deputy Quartermaster General's Office, 13 October 1816.

36. Walker, *Carleton Saga*, 37; and Heidorn, *Eighteen Hundred and Frozen to Death*, n.p.

37. Jarvis, "Military Land Granting", 124, 128-131; and Cowan, *British Emigration*, 74. One group that was ignored by the Colonial Office in seeking to reward soldiers with land for their wartime service, was the loyal militiamen of Upper Canada. During the war they were promised land for their military service, but after the war were offered only 50 acre grants, which most refused. In 1818 the grant offer was increased to 100 acres, but on scattered lots across the province. No tract of land was set aside for them, and they were not permitted to settle on the Crown Reserves. Yet, it was the militiamen – mainly second generation Loyalists and the sons of pre-war British immigrants – who were acculturated to living in a pioneer society, and had the knowledge and skills needed to succeed in bush farming. Moreover, the Upper Canadian tories who fought in the loyal militia, and who had risked their lives and property during the war in fighting against the American invaders, would have been the first to suffer from any American conquest and annexation of Upper Canada.

38. Lanark County Genealogical Society website, Mary B. Campbell, "Early Days of the Perth Settlement", 17 February 1896 (manuscript); Walker, *Carleton Saga*, 37; Gates, Land Policies, 86 & 91; and McGill, *A Pioneer History*, pp. 21-23, 28, 41-44, 54-56, and 236-231, Appendix: "Statistical Data on Scotch Line Settlers interviewed by Robert Gourlay in July 1817".

39. Smith, *The Pioneers of Old Ontario*, n.p.   One American immigrant family settling in the Upper Canadian wilderness in 1794 was able to survive solely on their own until their first crops were harvested, on milk from their cow, on game and fish, and a half bag of flour that they had brought with them. The cow foraged for itself in the woods in the summer, and was tethered and fed sprouts from young trees by the children in the winter. Only experienced bush farmers, however, were capable of surviving on their own resources during the first months of settlement until a lot could be partially cleared and planted, and crops harvested. Most of the American settlers arriving in Upper Canada, however, had money in hand,and were well supplied with provisions, in having sold their farms in the United States to emigrate to Upper Canada.

40. MG11, CO42, Vol. 175, B-139, 130-131, Sherbrooke to Bathurst, 10 November 1817, and 132-135, Sherbrooke to Administrator of Upper Canada, 27 August 1817.

41. Cowan, *British Emigration*, 44-46, 74-75, 78 & 119; and McGill, *A Pioneer History*, 32-35. The £10 capitalist assisted-emigration programme of 1818 also attracted two other parties. They comprised an English party of 19 families that sailed from Whitehaven in June 1818, and were assisted to settle in the Rice Lake area in Smith Township, Upper Canada, and an Anglo-Irish party of 172 persons that sailed from Cork in May 1818, and were assisted to settle at London on the Lake Erie Front of Upper Canada. At Lachine, 31 members of the newly-arrived Anglo-Irish immigrants left their party to settle in the Rideau Military Settlement.

42. Eric Jarvis, "Military Land Grants in Upper Canada following the War of 1812", *Ontario History*, LXVII, No. 3, September 1975, 120-127; Walker, *Carleton Saga*, 51; and Wikipedia, "100th Regiment of Foot (Prince Rupert's County of Dublin Regiment)". In 1807 then Colonel Isaac Brock observed of the regiment: "the men were principally raised in the north of Ireland, and are nearly all Protestants". In 1816, the 100th Regiment of Foot was re-numbered as the 99th Regiment of Foot. (*ibid*).

43. Walker, *Carleton Saga*, 11, 51-54; and LAC, MG11, WO44, vol. 19, B-1294, 11-12, Lieutenant Colonel Cockburn, "Report on the Military Settlement in the neighbourhood of the Rideau, pointing out the Communication which may be established in that direction between La Chine and Kingston", 26 November 1818. Among the initial 400 soldier-settlers in the Richmond Settlement were a number of discharged soldiers, and their

families, from the 37th (North Hampshire) Regiment of Foot, and the 99th (Prince of Wales County of Tipperary) Regiment of Foot (re-numbered the 98th).

44. Jarvis, "Military Land Granting", 122-134; Bruce S. Elliott, *Irish Migrants in the Canadas, A New Approach* (Kingston & Montreal: McGill-Queen's Press, l988):120-127; and Cowan, *British Emigration*, 52-53. See also, William McElroy, "The Richmond Settlement", The McElroy Family of Richmond, Ontario, Canada, 1923 (Internet posting).

45. John M'Donald, *Emigration to Canada; Narrative of a Voyage to Quebec and journey from there to New Lanark in Upper Canada* (London: Andrew Jack, 1825), 17.

46. Cowan, *British Emigration*, 75-80; McGill, *Pioneer History*, 30-39; and Elliott, *Irish Migrants*, 66, 76, 86-87, 98, l0l, & 122-123. See also Gates, *Land Policies of Upper Canada,* 91-92; and Michael S. Cross, "The Age of Gentility: The Formation of an Aristocracy in the Ottawa Valley", *Canadian Historical Association, Historical Papers*, l967, 105-117. See also, Glen J. Lockwood, Beckwith, Irish and Scottish Identities in a Canadian Community (Carleton Place, Ontario: By the Author, 1991), 52-64.

47. Robert Lamond, Secretary & Agent, A *Narrative of the Rise & Progress of Emigration from the counties of Lanark & Renfrew t the New Settlements in Upper Canada on Government Grant: comprising the Proceedings of the Glasgow Committee for directing the affairs and embarkation of the societies, with a Map of the Townships, Design for Cottages, and a Plan of the ship Earl of Buckinghamshire. Also, Interesting letters from the Settlements.* (Glasgow: Chalmers & Collins, 1821, reprint 1978), 6; and Cowan, *British Emigration*, 59-61. The British government had good reason to fear public unrest. Earlier, in August 1819, over 60,000 persons had gathered on St. Peter's Field in Manchester to demand radical political reforms – universal suffrage, vote by ballot, and annual parliaments – and the repeal of the Corn Laws to let cheaper foreign wheat into the home market. The participants in the protest were attacked, and dispersed, by a cavalry unit. In the so-called "Peterloo Massacre", a dozen protesters were killed, and as many as 400 were injured.

48. The Earl Dalhousie had served in the Peninsular War under the Duke of Wellington, and rose to the rank of General, before undertaking a postwar career as a colonial administrator. In July 1816, he was appointed Lt.

Governor of Nova Scotia in which position he responded to the plight of penniless immigrants by providing them with land, military rations, seed, and farming implements, to relieve their suffering and aid them to settle on the land. Like the Anglican Tory officers, he believed in a paternal government authority, and favoured public enterprise in constructing land and water communications. He was also a promoter of education, and was instrumental in the founding of Dalhousie College. In April 1820, Dalhousie succeeded the ill-fated Duke of Richmond, as Commander-in-Chief/Commander-in-Chief. (Peter Burroughs, "Ramsay, George, 9th Earl of Dalhousie", *Canadian Dictionary of Biography Online*, Vol. VII.) With respect to the practice of paternalism, attention has been drawn to the cultural values of the English officers who were Anglican Tories, but clearly the Scottish lairds and their younger sons, who served as officers in the British Army, shared a good many of the same cultural values.

49. Lamond, *A Narrative*, 20-21, "Aid granted by Government to Emigrants from the West of Scotland, and 20-21, 45-48 & 55-57; and Gates, *Land Policies*, 91. The Lamond statement of "aid granted " records what was actually given to the Scots weaver immigrants in 1820 by the Military Settling Department in Upper Canada. Hence, it states that the money payments were made to each immigrant. However, the original agreement with the British government provided for only the head of each family to receive the prescribed cash payments, and the cash benefit was extended to each immigrant by the Military Settling Department officers, with the approval of the Commander-in-Chief, to address the need of the immigrants for additional monies to purchase provisions.

50. Lamond, *A Narrative*, 13-15, 25-26, 29-34, and 61-64.

51. Cowan, *British Emigration*, 84-89; McGill, *A Pioneer History*, 61-62; and Lamond, *A Narrative*, 52.

52. M'Donald, *Emigration to Canada*, 3- 15; and John Climie letter, Dalhousie, 8 February 1821, and James Gilmour letter, Lanark, 1 August 1821, in Lamond, *A Narrative*, 90-91 & 97-98. M'Donald describes the difficulties encountered by the 1821 immigrants who arrived in the spring of the year at Quebec, rather than in the fall which was the case previously with the 1820 immigrants. The 1821 immigrants were conveyed inland during a period of incessant rainfall, which brought them a great deal of misery. At Montreal, they were given a day of rest to dry out their clothes, but were

caught in heavy rainfalls again during the rest of their journey. Those who lacked a change of clothes had to remain in damp clothing throughout. As a result of being exposed to the elements, and a change in diet, sickness prevailed amongst them with some afflicted with fever and ague, and "the bloody flux' (dysentery). Presumably, the sick were treated by the surgeon who accompanied each ship, and the military surgeon at the depot in Lanark upon their arrival. During the 1821 travel from Quebec to the settlement, several adults died en route as did a number of children.

53. *McGill, A Pioneer History, 62-78.*

54. Lamond, *A Narrative*, 21-23.

55. Edwin C. Guillet, *The Pioneer Farmer and Backwoodsman*, Vol. I (Toronto: University of Toronto Press, 1970), 52-58. The later wood frame houses were erected on rubble stone masonry foundation walls, and the sill logs of the log cabins were placed on flat stones to prevent damp penetrating the wood from the ground.

During a visit to the Rideau Canal in October 1832, Captain James Alexander, 42nd Royal Highlanders, found that the cabins of the artificers settled along the Rideau Canal corridor – or the cabins of the Scots artificers in particular – had two interior rooms of the traditional Scottish "but and ben" layout. He described one of these cabins as having an ante room containing the kitchen, parlour, and bedroom, and an inner room that had a carpenter's bench and tools, and a hand loom, as well as pork, flour and salt barrels. See, Captain J.E. Alexander, *Transatlantic Sketches, comprising visits to the Most Interesting Scenes in North and South American and the West Indies with Notes on Negro Slavery and Canadian Emigration*, Vol. II (London: Richard Bentley, 1833), 86.

56. Andrew Bell letter, Perth, 17 May 1819, in Lamond, *A Narrative*, 74; and M'Donald, *Emigration to Canada*, 20-21. See also, McGill, *A Pioneer History*, 63. The basswood logs were split, and scooped out lengthwise, and placed in rows lengthwise down the slope of the roof so that the scooped logs overlapped with the trough of each log alternately facing up and down. The wood-frame houses of the well-do-do in Perth were often painted white, with a blue roof, and green window shutters; whereas the stores and clapboarded cabins were painted all blue, with some yellow and several red buildings. M'Donald noted also that some of the more recently erected cabins in Perth were constructed of squared logs. Cedar shakes were the common roof cover in Upper Canada,

but M'Donald states that the roof shingles in Lanark were of fir.

57. M'Donald, *Emigration to Canada*, 23-26. In contrast at Montreal, in a long-settled, market economy area, flour sold for 19s a barrel, beef at 5d to 6d a pound, butter at 1s per pound, cheese at 7½ d per pound, and eggs at 1s per dozen. In the old British currency, one pound (£1) comprised 20 shillings (20s), and one shilling (1s) was worthy 12 pence (12d).   In the Lanark settlement a Canadian dollar circulated at five shillings. Thus, one pound (£1) would have traded at $4.00 Canadian; although there are several published travelogues that mention the pound sterling as circulating as high as $4.50 in Canadian dollars at that time.

58. Lamond, 51-53 & 56; and ,Smith, *Perth-on-Tay*, 247. It appears also that the total of the installment payments was increased to £10. There are references to that new amount in several primary and secondary sources.

59. Gates, *Land Policies*, 91; and Lamond, *A Narrative*, 101 & 50. On the high cost of transport from Quebec to the interior settlements, and the cost of land fees, as well as the capital possessed by many independent Scots emigrants upon arrival at Quebec, see Cowan, *British Emigration*, 58, 57, and 53. Bush lands sold for 5s per acre, or £25 for an 100 acre lot. (Henry, *The Emigrant's Guide*, 332). Hence, immigrants upon arrival in Canada had to possess some capital in order to settle on the land, unless they were participants in a British government assisted-emigration scheme.

60. Lamond, *A Narrative*, 51-54, 28 & 88.

61. Lamond, *A Narrative*, 28-29, 60, 47 & 41. The Emigration Society also produced a number of fanciful designs for cottages considered suitable for erection in Upper Canada to house the new settlers, together with instructions as to how they should be constructed *(ibid,* 66-69).

62. Lamond, *A Narrative*, 59 & 61.

63. John Toshach, Lanark Settlement, to Alexander Sinclair, Wright Calton, Glasgow, 11 September 1821, in Lamond, *A Narrative*, 105-106. From the viewpoint of the poor Scots weavers, the Lanark settlement was a godsend, as one of the assisted-emigrant weavers reported. He and his father each had 200 acre lots, and the land was "pretty good". After a year on the land, the two of them had a total of seven or eight acres in crops, and were expecting a yield of

six hundred bushels of potatoes. Where previously, in Glasgow, they had to work 16 to 18 hours a day, and after they paid rent for their accommodation and loom, were left with as little as six or seven shillings a week to live on; whereas in the Rideau Military Settlement they could now work half as long each day, and gain everything they needed to prosper. Moreover, they were working in a healthy environment, rather than a damp shop. (A. Boag, Lanark, Upper Canada, to His Sister in Scotland, 24 August 1821, in Lamond, *A Narrative*, 103-104.) See also, William Miller, Perth, to his Father in Scotland, 3 October 1820 (*ibid*, 79).

64. The leaders of the Glasgow Emigration Society also were paternalistic in acting to protect and enhance the well being of the suffering artisans through ensuring that they were placed on seaworthy ships, with good berths, and plentiful good food and water, and in concluding an agreement with the Colonial Office for their transport and settlement on the land once in Canada, as well as in providing for their spiritual well being. The practice of paternalism on the part of those in authority contrasts greatly with the laissez-faire liberal political philosophy which would come to prevail later among the political and economic elite of the Victorian era.

65. Cowan, *British Emigration*, 60-63; Gates, *Land Policies of Upper Canada*, 91-92; and McGill, *A Pioneer History*, 61-7.

66. Lamond, *A Narrative*, 64-65. Earlier, the Colonial Office had agreed to extend the 1820 assisted-emigration agreement to provide support for a further 1800 Scots weavers to be settled in Upper Canada in 1821   It was the final agreement between the Colonial Office and the Glasgow Emigration Society. (*Ibid*, 18).

67. Cowan, *British Emigration*, 63.

68. Historians have treated the Irish poor-relief emigration program of 1823 as a separate subject from the Rideau Military Settlement programme. In sum, the purpose of the two programmes supposedly differed markedly in that one had a social and political purpose and the other had a military purpose. The Irish poor-relief immigrants were located on the land by the provincial government of Upper Canada at the behest of the Colonial Office, and the Irish poor-relief settlement programme was under the direction of Peter Robinson, rather than the Military Settling Department. However, it was John Beverley Robinson, the young, Anglican Tory, Attorney General of Upper

Canada, who suggested the Irish poor-relief scheme to Robert Wilmot Horton, the Undersecretary for the Colonies, and Robinson's motive was to strengthen the Rideau Military Settlement, and to promote its continued economic development through securing British government expenditures in support of new settlers.

In addition, the Irish poor-relief immigrants were conveyed to Canada on Royal Navy transports, were transported and provisioned on their inland journey by the Commissariat Department of the British Army, were settled in the Rideau Military Settlement townships, and were provided with farming implements, domestic utensils, and blankets from the Commissariat depot at Lanark and a new depot established at Shipman's Mills (Almonte). Moreover, by settling the impoverished Irish Catholics on their own land in Upper Canada, the Colonial Office hoped to transform them into loyal subjects who would contribute to the future defence of the province. Hence, herein the Irish Catholic poor-relief programme is treated as an extension of the Rideau Military Settlement experience.

69. Wendy Cameron, "Selecting Peter Robinson's Irish Emigrants", *Histoire Sociale/Social History*, Vol. 9, no. 17, May 1976, 24-46; Cowan, *British Emigration*, 102-103 & 115; and Donald MacKay, *Flight from Famine, The Coming of the Irish to Canada* (Toronto: Dundurn Press, 2009, 52-79. The role of John Beverley Robinson, the Attorney General of Upper Canada, in the establishment of the Irish-poor relief project is set forth in the following source. (MacKay, *Flight from Famine*, 52-53). One presumes that the original intention of the Robinson brothers was to assist Irish farmers of English descent to emigrate from southern Ireland to Upper Canada to strength the British character and loyalty of the province.

70. McGill, *A Pioneer History*, 89-94; Verna Ross McGiffin, *Pakenham, Ottawa Valley Village 1823-1860* (Pakenham: Mississippi Publishers, 1963), 23-63, 17 & 73; and MacKay, *Flight from Famine*, 64-68. The clothing, cooking utensils, carpentry tools, farming implements and seed furnished each Robinson Irish family are listed in McGiffin, 35-36. Peter Robinson purchased a felling axe for each family at Montreal on their travel inland, but otherwise the farming implements, bedding and blankets, and domestic utensils, were provided by the Commissariat Department, for which Robinson would have paid the 'prime cost" and, likewise, he would have paid the cost of the provisions purchased for the Irish poor-relief settlers during their first year on

the land.

To help repay the British government for the cost of the Irish poor-relief emigration programme, Willmot-Horton had stipulated that the 70-acre land grant would be subject, after a five-year initial period of settlement, to an annual quit rent of 2d per acre for twenty years; and that a similar quit rent would apply to the additional 30 acres for twenty years, if purchased. The quit rents, however, were never collected and, ultimately, were abolished by the British government with the result that the poor-relief Irish immigrants who remained on their land, received a free title to their lot. (Gates, *Land Policies*, 96,)

71. Jarvis, "Military Land Granting", 129-130; McGill, *A Pioneer History*, l8; and Gates, *Land Policies*, 93.

72. Cowan, *British Emigration*, 73; and Smith, *Perth-on-Tay*, Addenda, 255-256, & 262, Settler's Testimonials, c. l827.

73. McGill, *Pioneer History*, 77-78 & 124-125; Mactaggart, *Three Years in Canada*, Vol. II, 242-243; and Gates, *Land Policies*, 93-94. The best axemen among the British immigrant groups were reputedly the Ulster Protestant linen weavers whose manual dexterity, and ambidextrousness, facilitated learning how to effectively handle an axe. See A Backwoodsman, [Dr. William Dunlop], *Statistical Sketches of Upper Canada, For the Use of Emigrants* (London: John Murray, 1832), 7-8.

74. [Dunlop], *Statistical Sketches*, 67. In 1826, Bathurst township was producing 4,826 bushels of potatoes, 21,469 bushels of grain, and 11, 145 bushels of turnips. Ramsay township produced 2/3s of that quantity, and the other back townships – Huntley, Goulbourn, Pakenham, Beckwith, and Lanark – produced somewhat less than 1/10 of the Bathurst township totals (McGill, *Pioneer History*, 100).

75. Gates, *Land Policies*, 95-96; and Cowan, *British Emigration*, 105-107. This number has to be qualified for in one township, Parkenham Township, where some of the Robinson Irish were located on the poor rocky ground of the Canadian Shield. That factor contributed greatly to the high failure rate of the assisted-emigration settlers in that particular township (see McGiffin, *Pakenham*, pp. 30-31, & 63). The adaptation of immigrants from various cultures to the demands of the North American bush farming environment is

a complex subject that has been little studied. One excellent study, compares three Irish Catholic settlement areas in British North America: the Avalon Peninsula (1810-1835); the Miramichi (1815-1835); and Peterborough (1825-). See John T. Mannion, *Irish Settlements in Eastern Canada: A Study of Cultural Transfer and Adaptation* (Toronto: University of Toronto Press, 1974).

76. Cameron, "Selecting Peter Robinson's Emigrants", 35. After assessing the failings of the 1823 experiment in settling destitute Irish Catholics in the Rideau back townships, Robinson narrowed his selection criteria for the next assisted emigration effort: the 1825 Peterborough settlement experiment in Upper Canada. For the Peterborough experiment, large families with farming experience, preferably with older boys, were selected, and single men and tradesmen were excluded. Several heads of families over 45 years of age were also included to add stability to the emigrant group (*ibid*, pp. 35-39).

77. In Upper Canada, Irish Catholics enjoyed equality before the law and full political rights including the right to vote and to stand for election. Indeed, the personal, political and religious freedoms that they enjoyed in Canada were in marked contrast to the life in Ireland under the old Penal Laws, and greater even than in the United States where some State governments had laws discriminating against Irish Catholics well into the 19th century.

78. Gates, *Land Policies*, pp. 91-92.

79. Cameron, "Selecting Peter Robinson's Irish Emigrant", 35; and McGill, *Pioneer History*, 94-98. The leader of the Catholic Irish faction was Bartholomew Murphy, a 22 year old single man from Clogheen, Cork. The other leaders were from Ballygibbon Parish in North Tipperary (*ibid*). See also J.K. Johnson, "Colonel James Fitzgibbon and the Suppression of Irish Riots in Upper Canada", *Ontario History*, Vol. LVIII, 1966, 142-145; and Glenn J. Lockwood, *Beckwith*, 100-111.

80. To date, Canadian historians have not provided any comparative analysis of the degree of acculturation achieved by various groups of immigrant settlers of widely different cultures in Canada with respect to their relative success in adapting to the demands of the Canadian settlement frontier and in integrating into the Canadian community. Some revisionist history has been written concerning the settlement experience of the Irish Catholic immigrants in an attempt to discredit negative stereotypes that were introduced in the 19th Century, but even that is distorted by treating the Irish settlement experience

as a monolith. If such studies are to be undertaken from a cultural values perspective, then the settlement experiences of the Anglo-Irish Protestants, the Anglo-Irish Catholics, the Ulster Presbyterian Scots-Irish, and the Gaelic Irish Catholics need to be differentiated.

Where the degree of acculturation and adaptability are concerned, it appears that the Irish immigrants who were most successful in settling on the land – whether Protestant or Catholic – were the yeoman farmers, tenant farmers, and tenant farmer/artisans of some means from an anglicized, enclosed farming, market economy background. In contrast the less successful, or those who failed to establish themselves on the land, or managed to do so only with a great deal of government support, were the Irish immigrants from areas of backward husbandry, and subsistence communal/familial farming, who were products of an impoverished peasant culture. In sum, those who struggled to settle on the land in Canada were the Gaelic Irish Catholics from the impoverished southern and western counties of Ireland. In Ireland, they failed to adapt, or were unable to adapt, to the movement towards agricultural improvement, agrarian individualism, capitalism and the market economy which developed in Ireland in the late 18th and early 20th centuries. Having failed to adapt in Ireland, they were ill-prepared and ill-adapted to establish themselves on the land as independent farmers on the North American settlement frontier.

———————————

BIBLIOGRAPHY

Primary Sources - Archival

Douglas Library, Queen's University, Kingston, Rev. William Bell Diaries

Library and Archives Canada
MG13, WO44, War Office, Department of Ordnance, Canada
MG l3, WO 55, War Office, Ordnance Miscellaneous, Engineering Papers
RG5, A1, Upper Canada Sundries, Civil Secretary Correspondence
RG7, G1, Despatches from the Colonial Office
LAC, RG8, Series C, British Military and Naval Records
LAC, MG 24, Al2, Dalhousie Muniments/George Ramsay, 9th Earl Dalhousie Fonds
LAC, MG 24, D8, Philemon Wright & Family Fonds
LAC, MG 24, H12, John Burrows, Fonds
LAC, MG 24, I9, Hill Collection, Dr. A. J.C. Christie Correspondence

Provincial Archives of Ontario
Baird Papers, Reel 1.

Primary Sources - Published

Alexander, Captn. J.E., 42d Royal Highlanders, *Transatlantic Sketches, comprising visits to the Most Interesting Scenes in North and South America and the West Indies, with Notes on Negro Slavery and Canadian Emigration.* Vol. II (London: Richard Bentley, 1833).

A Backswoodsman [Dr. William Dunlop], *Statistical Sketches of Upper Canada, For the Use of Emigrants*, London: John Murray, l832.

The Albion, or British Colonial and Foreign Weekly Gazette (New York), 24 and 31 March 1827, "Rideau Canal".

Barker, Edward John. M.D. *Observations on the Rideau Canal*, Kingston, Upper Canada: Kingston Whig Office, 1834.

Bathurst Independent Examiner (Perth), 11 September 1829, "Daring Outrage", 15 January 1830, "Wanted", and 22 January 1830, "Daring Outrage".

Brockville Recorder, 11 May 1830, A.J.C. [Dr. Christie], "Memoranda taken during a tour through the line of the Rideau Canal from Kingston to Bytown, in February 1830", and 18 May 1830, "Rideau Canal".

de Beaumont, Gustave. *Ireland, Social, Political and Religious*, ed. & translated by W.C. Taylor, Cambridge: Harvard University Press, 2006, (1st ed. in French, 1839).

Farmers' Journal and Welland Canal Intelligencer, St. Catharines, 9 January 1828, "Bytown City".

Frome, Edward, Lt, R.E. "Account of the Causes which led to the Construction of the Rideau Canal, connecting the Waters of Lake Ontario and the Ottawa", in Great Britain, Corps of Royal Engineers, *Papers on Subjects Connected with the Duties of the Corps of Royal Engineers,* London: John Weale, 2nd ed., 1844, Vol. I. This paper is reprinted in George Raudzens, *The British Ordnance Department and Canada's Canals 1815-1855*, Waterloo, Ontario: Wilfrid Laurier University Press, 1979, 155-185.

The Gleaner, (Niagara), 17 March 1827, "Rideau Canal".

Graham, Thomas John. M.D., *Modern Domestic Medicine: or A Popular Treatise illustrating the Character, Symptoms, Causes, Distribution, and Correct Treatment of all Diseases incident to the Human Frame,* (3rd. ed., London: Published by Author, 1827.

Hall, Captain Basil, R.N.. *Travels in North America in the years 1827 and 1828,* Vol. I, Edinburgh: Cadell and Co.,1829.

Henry, George [George Henry Hume]. *The emigrants' guide, or Canada as it is: comprising details relating to the domestic policy, commerce, and agriculture of the upper and lower provinces; comprising matter of general information and interest, especially intended for the use of the settlers and emigrants.* Quebec: W. Gray, n.d. Subsequently reprinted under the author's name, George Henry Hume, with a similar title under the imprint, New York: Stodart, 1832.

Houston, Cecil J. & William J. Smyth. *Irish Emigration and Canadian Settlement Patterns, Links & Letters.* Toronto: University of Toronto Press, 1990.

K*ingston Chronicle*, 6 April 1827, Letter of Lt. Col. John By.

Lamond, Robert, Secretary & Agent. A *Narrative of the Rise & Progress of Emigration from the counties of Lanark & Renfrew t the New Settlements in Upper Canada on Government Grant: comprising the Proceedings of the Glasgow Committee for directing the affairs and embarkation of the societies, with a Map of the Townships, Design for Cottages, and a Plan of the ship Earl of Buckinghamshire. Also, Interesting letters from the Settlements.* Glasgow: Chalmers & Collins, 1821 (reprint 1978).

Lett, William. *Recollections of Bytown and its Old Inhabitants.* Ottawa: Citizen Printing and Publishing Company, 1874 (reprinted as *Lett's Bytown*, Ottawa: Bytown Museum, 1979).

Mactaggart, John. *Three Years in Canada: An Account of the Actual State of the Country in 1826-7-8 comprehending its resources, productions, improvements, and Capabilities and including Sketches of the State of Society, Advice to Emigrants, etc.,* Volumes I & II, London: Henry Colburn, 1829.

McGregor, John. *British America,* vol. I, Edinburgh: W.

Blackwood, 1832.

Montreal Gazette, 12 & 19 February 1827, "Government Contract".

Montreal Herald, 13 September 1828, reprint of article "Upper Canada, Niagara".

The Albion, or British Colonial and Foreign Weekly Gazette (New York), 24 and 31 March 1827, "Rideau Canal".

U.E. Loyalist, (York), 24 February 1827, "Rideau Canal".

Williams, C.W. *A Speech on the Improvement of the Shannon, Being in Continuation of the Debate in the House of Commons, 12 May 1835, Giving a Comparative View of the Navigation of the Rideau Canal, in Canada and the River Shannon, in Ireland with Observations on the value of a connection by steam packets, with British America*, London: J. Bain, I. Haymarket, 1835.

Secondary Sources - Articles

Bleasdale,"Class Conflict on the Canals of Upper Canada in the 1840s", *Labour/Le Travailleur*, Vol. 7, Spring 1981, 9-39.

Cameron, Wendy. "Selecting Peter Robinson's Irish Emigrants", *Histoire Sociale/Social History*, Vol 9, no. 17, May 1976, 24-46.

Cross, Michael S. "The Age of Gentility: The Formation of an Aristocracy in the Ottawa Valley", *Canadian Historical Association, Historical Papers*, 1967, 105-117.

Cross, Michael S. "The Shiners' War: Social Violence in the Ottawa Valley in the 1830s", *Canadian Historical Review*, Vol. LIV, No. 1, March 1973, 1-26.

Elliott, Bruce S. "The famous Township of Hull: Image and Aspirations of a Pioneer Quebec Community", *Histoire Sociale/Social History*, Vol. 12, No. 24, November 1979, 339-367.

Fingard, Judith. "The Winter's Tale: The Seasonal Contours of Pre-Industrial Poverty in British North America, 1815-1860", *Canadian Historical Association, Historical Papers*, 1974, 65-94.

Jarvis, Eric. "Military Land Granting in Upper Canada, following the War of 1812", *Ontario History*, LXVII, No. 3, September 1975, 122-134.

Le Goff, T. J. A. "The Agricultural Crisis in Lower Canada 1802-12: A Review of a Controversy", *Canadian Historical Review*, Vol. LV, March 1974, 1-31.

Lockwood, Glenn J. "Irish Immigrants and the 'Critical Years' in Eastern Ontario: The Case of Montague Township, 1821-1881", in Donald H. Akenson, ed., *Canadian Papers in Rural History*, Vol. IV, Gananoque, Ontario: Langdale Press, 1984.

Passfield, Robert W. "Ordnance Supply Problems in the Canadas: The Quest for an Improved Military Transport System, 1814 - 1828", *HSTC Bulletin, Journal of the History of Canadian Science, Technology and Medicine*, Vol. V, No. 3, September 1981, 187-209.

Russell, Peter A. "Wage Labour Rates in Upper Canada, 1818-1840", *Histoire sociale-Social History*, XVI, no.31, May 1983, 61-80.

Wylie, William N.T., "Poverty, Distress, and Disease: Labour and the Construction of the Rideau Canal, 1826-1832", *Labour/Le Travailleur*, Vol. 11, Spring 1983, 7-29.

Secondary Sources - Books & Reports

Akenson, Donald H. *The Irish in Ontario: A Study in Rural History.* Montreal/Kingston: McGill/Queens, 1984.

Akenson, Donald H. *Being Had, Historians, Evidence, and the Irish in North America.* Port Credit, Ontario: P.D. Meany Publishers, 1985.

Brault, Lucien. *Ottawa: Old and New.* Ottawa: Ottawa Historical Information Institute, 1946.

Bush, Edward F. *Builders of the Rideau Canal, 1826-32* (Smith Falls, Ontario: Friends of the Rideau CD Book, 2009). This is a reprint of an earlier work of the same title and content: Parks Canada Manuscript Report No. 185, 1976.

Campey, Lucille H. *The Scottish Pioneers of Upper Canada, 1784-1855, Glengarry and Beyond.* Toronto: National Heritage Books, 2005.

Coleman, Terry. *The Railway Navvies, A History of the Men who made the railways.* London: Penguin Books, 1981.

Connolly, T.W.J. *The History of he Corps of Royal Sappers and Miners.* Longman, Brown, Green and Longmans, London, 1855, Volume One.

Cowan, Helen I. *British Emigration to British North America, The First Hundred Years.* Toronto: University of Toronto Press, 1961.

Elliott, Bruce S. *Irish Migrants in the Canadas, A New Approach.* Kingston & Montreal: McGill-Queen's Press, 1988.

Elliott, Bruce S. *The McCabe List, Early Irish in the Ottawa Valley.* Toronto: The Ontario Genealogical Society, 2002.

Fortescue, J.W. *A History of the British Army,* Vol. VII. London: Macmillan, 1912.

Gates, Lillian F. *Land Policies of Upper Canada.* Toronto: University of Toronto Press, 1968.

Guillet, Edwin C. *The Pioneer Farmer and Backwoodsman*, Vol. I. Toronto: University of Toronto Press, 1970.

Heagarty, John J. *Four Centuries of Medical History in Canada, and a Sketch of the Medical History of Newfoundland*, Vol. I. Toronto: Macmillan Company, 1928.

Hirschman, Albert O. *The Passions and the Interests, Political Arguments for Capitalism before Its Triumph*, 10th ed. (Princeton: Princeton University Press, 1997).

Hunter, James. *Scottish Exodus, Travels Among a Worldwide Clan*. (Edinburgh & London: Mainstream Press, 2007).

Lee, David. *Lumber Kings & Shantymen, Logging and Lumbering in the Ottawa Valley*. Toronto: James Lorimer & Co. Ltd., 2006.

Legget, Robert F., *Rideau Waterway*. Toronto: University of Toronto Press, 1958.

Lockwood, Glenn J. *Beckwith, Irish and Scottish Identities in a Canadian Community 1816-1991, An account of two transplanted cultural communities, their adjustment to Upper Canadian frontier farming, their response to demographic constraints and industrialization, and the transformation of their identities between 1816 and 1991. Carleton Place: by Author, 1991*.

Lower, Arthur R. M. *Great Britain's Woodyard, British America and the Timber Trade, 1763-1867*. Montreal: McGill-Queen's Press, 1973.

Mannion, John J. *Irish Settlements in Eastern Canada: A Study of Cultural Transfer and Adaptation*. Toronto: University of Toronto Press, 1974.

MacKay, Donald. *Flight from Famine, The Coming of the Irish to Canada*. Toronto: Dundurn Press, 2009, 1st printing 1990.

McGiffin, Verna Ross. *Pakenham, Ottawa Valley Village, 1823-1860*. Pakenham: Mississippi Publishers, 1963.

McGill, Jean S. *A Pioneer History of the County of Lanark*. Toronto: T.H. Best, 3rd printing, 1970.

McKenna, Katherine M.J., ed., *Labourers on the Rideau Canal 1826-1832: From Work Site to World Heritage Site.* Ottawa: Borealis Press, 2008.

Mika, Nick & Helma. *Bytown, The Early Days of Ottawa.* Belleville, ON: Mika Publishing, 1982.

Miller, Kerby A. *Emigrants and Exiles, Ireland and the Irish Exodus to North America.* New York/Oxford: Oxford University Press, 1985.

Ouellet, Fernand. *Lower Canada l791-1840, Social Change and Nationalism.* transl. Patricia Claxton. Toronto: McClelland and Stewart, l980.

Palmer, Bryan D. *Working-Class Experience, The Rise and Reconstruction of Canadian Labour, 1800-1980.* Toronto: Butterworth & Co., 1983.

Palmer, Bryan D. *Working-Class Experience: Rethinking the History of Canadian Labour, 1800-1991.* Toronto: McClelland & Stewart, 1992.

Parnell, Henry. *On Financial Reform*, 3rd. ed., London: John Murray, 1831.

Passfield, Robert W. *Building the Rideau Canal, A Pictorial History.* Don Mills, Ontario: Fitzhenry & Whiteside/Parks Canada, 1982.

Pentland, H, Clare, *Labour and Capital in Canada*, 1650-1850. Toronto: J. Lorimer, 1981.

Ross, *A.D.H, Ottawa: Past and Present.* Toronto: Musson Book Company Ltd., 1927.

Sabine, George H. *A History of Political Theory.* 3rd. ed. London: George G. Harrap & Co. Ltd., 1963.

Shortt, Edward, ed.. *Perth Remembered*. Perth: Mortimer Ltd., 1967.

Smith, Josephine. *Perth-on-Tay: A tale of the Transplanted Highlanders*. Merrickville: Mortimer Co. Printers, 1987 reprint. (First printing, 1901).

Smith, *W.L. The Pioneers of Old Ontario, the Makers of Canada*. Toronto: George N. Morang, 1923.

Walker, Harry and Olive Walker. *Carleton Saga*. Ottawa: Carleton County Council, 1968.

Watson, Ken W., *Engineered Landscapes, the Rideau Canal's Transformation of a Wilderness Waterway*. Elgin, Ontario: Ken W. Watson, 2006.

Way, Peter. *Common Labor, Workers and the Digging of North American Canals, 1780-1860*. Baltimore: John Hopkins University Press, 1997.

Theses

Ball, Norman R. "The Technology of Settlement and Land Clearing in Upper Canada prior to 1840", Ph.D. Thesis, University of Toronto Institute for the History and Philosophy of Science and Technology, 1979.

McLean, Marianne, 'In the new land a new Glengarry': Migration from the Scottish Highlands to Upper Canada, 1750-1820, PhD thesis, University of Edinburgh, 1982.

Appendix

Marxism, Cultural Values and Military Paternalism

Although not all Labour historians are Marxists, nonetheless
the interpretation of the "working class experience" on
Canadian canal projects of the early 19th Century has tended
to be treated within a Marxist framework of interpretation. It
is an interpretation that draws on Marxist assumptions and
tenets pertaining to dialectic materialism, class conflict and
worker exploitation, worker alienation, and class consciousness.
However, such an interpretation ignores cultural factors, distorts
the history of labour relations during the early canal construction
era, and disparages the practice of paternalism. Moreover,
historians employing a Marxist interpretation of labour relations
have failed to appreciate the benefits that the workers received
due to the paternalism practiced by 'those in authority' during the
early period of canal construction in North America.

Marxist Canal Histories

A leading example of a Marxist interpretation of the working class
experience of canal workers is a study by Peter Way (*Common
Labor*, 1993), which focuses on North American canal projects
in the period, 1780-1860. Way applies a Marxist template of
interpretation to the working class experience of the unskilled
canal labourers, whom he refers to as "canallers".

In his interpretation of the 'working class experience' on canal
projects, Way sees the period of the canal building era, 1780-
1860, as the seminal period in the rise of industrial capitalism
and the modern class system in North America. It was a period
during which there as a significant accumulation of labour and
capital, and during which an hierarchical agrarian society –
comprised of farmers, merchants and workshop artisans linked
by personal relationships – broke down, and was gradually

transformed into an impersonal, market-driven, industrial capitalist order, which was based on wage labour and spawned new social, political, and economic relations.

In his treatment of the transition from an hierarchical agrarian society to a industrial capitalist order, Way discards the common labour history approach that focuses on the trades, the breakdown of the household and craft shop culture, and the emergence of the factory system. According to Way, the artisanal model with its focus on the separation of artisans from the means of production, their deskilling, and descent into wage labour – and the resultant development of a sense of alienation and a class consciousness – is not representative of the experience of the vast majority of workers in North America.

To the contrary, it is the experience of the unskilled canal labourers which is truly representative of the proletarianization of the majority of workers – the unskilled and unorganized workers – in their transition to the modern era of industrial capitalism. Indeed, according to Peter Way, the canal workers were in the vanguard of the transition to industrial capitalism in North America and were on "the leading edge of class formation". In North America, canal companies were the first large-scale industrial enterprises to accumulate great amounts of capital and to mobilize armies of wage earners and, as such, the working experience of labourers on canal projects "provides a paradigm for the emergence of the modern industrial class system". The proletarianization of the canal workers, however, did not involve a loss of skill and control over the means of production, but rather a significant decline in their material conditions.

According to Way, shortages of labour and limitations of capital, resulted in many of the early canal projects employing temporary labourers who returned to their farms or other employments when work ceased. That situation engendered a paternalistic system of production in which canal companies paid fairly good wages and provided the workers with food and shelter, and in which the contractors lived and worked alongside the workers in a personal and mutually beneficial, but unequal relationship. It was a system – "contractor paternalism" – that persisted while there was a shortage of labour.

The breakdown of the paternalistic system came with the economic depression of 1837 and the heavy Irish immigration of the 1840s. Faced with a fiercely competitive bidding process for canal work, a fear of bankruptcy, and a large labour surplus, contractors stripped away the benefits received by the canal workers under the earlier paternalistic system of canal construction. Workers were no longer provided with food and shelter; they had their wages cut to a bare subsistence level; and they were treated simply as wage labourers in an impersonal work relationship which was governed solely by market forces.

As a result, the class conflict and exploitation inherent in the capitalist wage relationship came to the fore. The canal workers were transformed into a working class that was isolated, cruelly exploited, and wholly alienated in a situation that gave rise to strikes, riots, work stoppages, and government repression through military force. Thereafter, when the economic situation improved, the canal workers remained part of a permanent working class in the impersonal 'cash nexus' economy of modern industrial capitalism. According to this interpretation, the canal workers of the 1840s were in the forefront of class formation in North America, but their own sense of class consciousness was slow to develop owing to their social fragmentation. In sum, they were transformed into a lumpen proletariat which was acted upon, but powerless to change an exploitative relationship.[1]

In *Common Labor*, Peter Way provides a comprehensive Marxist interpretation of the history of labour relations on North American canals during the canal building era. However, there are problems with employing a Marxist analytic framework and tenets to interpret labour relations during the 'contractor paternalism" period.

Marxist historians recognize that an ethos of paternalism existed during the early period of canal construction in North America in which labour relations were not governed solely by economic considerations. Indeed, Peter Way notes that "an entirely different set of social and economic relations" prevailed prior to the 1840s before the onset of the cash nexus market economy of industrial capitalism; and that much was lost by the workers in their transformation into a working class dependent solely on wage labour.[2] Yet, Marxist historians have not credited 'those in authority' for their paternalistic practices, or expressed any appreciation for the benefits that the practice of paternalism bestowed on canal workers. To the contrary, Marxist historians have denigrated the character of 'those who ruled', have attributed selfish and base economic motives to their practice of paternalism, and have denounced paternalism for delaying the development of a class consciousness on the part of canal workers.

For Marxist historians, paternalism grew out of a situation where there was a shortage of labour, wherein "those who rule" were forced to recognize the humanity of the men whom they relied on for labour. In doing so, the objective of the practice of paternalism – according to Marxists – was to mask the exploitation of the wage relationship, to obscure an inherently irreconcilable conflict of interest between the workers and their superiors, and to encourage the workers to accommodate themselves to inequality.

For Marxists, paternalism was a deliberate creation for selfish economic motives by 'those who ruled' – merchants, independent producers, and landed gentry. In Canada, it survived, and evolved, owing to the fragmentation of the producing classes, their "negotiated acceptance" of the role allotted to them, and the localized hierarchical political culture, and the social and economic isolation of many early Canadian settings. Overall, in keeping with the Marxist tenet of dialectical materialism, paternalism is condemned as a negative social and cultural force.

"Paternalism's ultimate significance, regardless of its character, lay in undermining the collectivity of the oppressed by linking them to their social superiors."[3]

Such an interpretation imposes Marxist concepts on the phenomenon of paternalism in early Upper Canada, and predisposes Marxist historians to view the practice of paternalism on Canadian canal construction projects in a negative light. From a Marxist perspective any social or cultural phenomenon that inhibits the transition to an industrial capitalist system, the alienation and exploitation of workers, and the emergence of class conflict, a class consciousness and class struggle, is to be disparaged. In sum, paternalism is seen as delaying the coming of the class struggle, social revolution, and the establishing of a classless society.

Yet another problem in writing the history of labour relations on North American canals from a Marxist perspective, is that it predisposes the historian to look for, and to magnify the significance of, any labour dispute or worker unrest as evidence of the emergence of a supposedly inherent class conflict. Any hardship experienced by the canal workers is cited as evidence of exploitation by their superiors, and an assumption is made that 'those who ruled' were motivated strictly by selfish economic motives and were indifferent – as a class – to the suffering of the workers.

This bias is readily apparent in a journal article – *Labour/Le Travailleur* , Spring 1983 -- that treats the labour situation on the Rideau Canal project from a Marxist perspective. Bald statements are made to the effect that the contractors and Royal Engineers saw canal workers as primarily an impersonal "instrument of production"; that the military showed no interest in the welfare of the workforce until disease threatened to drive workers from the project; and that, in a labour surplus situation, the canal workers were forced to endure low wages, poverty, disease, and dangerous working conditions to secure employment. Moreover, it is asserted that the two companies of Royal Sappers and Miners who were employed on the project, were used "above all as a quasi-police" to maintain order and suppress labour unrest. In sum, the emphasis is on a rudimentary class conflict between 'masters' and 'workers', and the canal labourers are depicted as being "an embryonic international proletariat."

Yet such a certainty of interpretation is strangely at odds with concurrent statements that a scarcity of documentary evidence makes it "difficult to generalize about the condition of the work camps"; and that "the information regarding labour conflict on the Rideau is sketchy". What is equally telling is a bald statement to the effect that the Commanding Royal Engineer on the Rideau Canal project, Lt. Col. John By:

> "was a man of his class. As an officer and a 'gentleman', he did not question the justice of a hierarchical social order or the inevitability of poverty".[4]

From a Marxist perspective such a statement is accepted as fundamentally true, but in reality it is highly biased. It is based on Marxist beliefs that the ideal society is an egalitarian, classless, society in which everyone participates in – and owns – the means of production; and that 'those in authority' in a capitalist system are motivated by the selfish economic interest of their class and indifferent to the welfare of the working class.

Whether class conflict and a class consciousness emerge naturally out of the wage labour relationship with workers becoming alienated from a lack of control over the means of production, is debatable. However, what is incontrovertible is that for a strong class consciousness to develop, it is necessary to have an exploiting class from whom the workers feel alienated, and by whom they are universally oppressed. In effect, such a work situation is needed to give rise to the recognition by the exploited workers that they have a shared interest as a collectivity, or as a class, in resisting their exploitation. However, that situation did not exist on the Rideau Canal project.

Lt. Col. John By and his engineering staff of Royal Engineers on the Rideau Canal project, were engaged in a public enterprise, which was to construct a military transport canal for the defence of the Province of Upper Canada and to facilitate its economic development. They were officers and 'gentlemen' of some family means, who had no personal or class interest motivating them to seek financial gain by exploiting canal workers. Had they been interested in pursuing personal wealth, they would not have entered into a military career in the Corps of Royal Engineers. [5]

They were Anglican tories, as well as officers, and as such had a strong sense of the duties and responsibilities of their social position towards God, King and Country, and towards those beneath them in the social hierarchy. In sum, any attempt to account for the practice of paternalism on the Rideau Canal project must take into account the character, cultural values, and worldview of the officers of the Royal Engineers, and seek to understand the "thought behind their acts".[6]

In their interpretation of historical events, Marxists historians invariably look for class conflict in keeping with their view of history as advancing by class struggle, and society as divided into classes based on their relationship to the means of production. From a Marxist perspective, the economic structure of a society determines the development of history (economic determinism), and each class in society – the bourgeoisie and the proletariat in an industrial capitalist society – has directly opposed economic interests, which are primary in the pursuit of its own interests and its self-preservation. Thus, Marxist historians interpret the practice of paternalism by canal contractors on North American canals, and by the military officers on the Rideau Canal project, during the 'contractor paternalism' era, solely in impersonal economic terms. It is explained away as something that was forced on the canal builders, against their class interest and inclinations, by a shortage of labour.

In sum, Marxist historians, in treating the working class experience on the Rideau Canal project, have failed to take into account that cultural factors can play a decisive role in the conduct of a 'ruling class', and that individuals in a position of authority can influence particular events. Such a statement is not intended to deny the Marxist tenet that the political culture, or ideology, which prevails in any society is a reflection of, and embodiment of, the interests of the ruling property class – the landed nobles in a feudal society, and the bourgeoisie, who own the means of production, in a capitalist society. Nor does such a statement deny that, at each stage of development, the prevailing ideology of society – the laws, politics, and morals – serves to legitimatizing the political power of 'those who rule', their control over the means of production, and their co-opting of the power of the Crown or the State for the protection of their property.

Cultural Values

Although economic forces are a major driver of great historical change, what needs to be recognized – in interpreting human conduct – is that the character, cultural values, and worldview of a community, or of an individual in a position of authority, can play a critical role in the unfolding of a particular historical event. Economic motives are not always the primary driving force in what transpires in an immediate situation.

There is also a need to recognize that not everyone within the social hierarchy of an industrial capitalist system can be categorized as a member of the bourgeoisie who acts in keeping with the tenets and values of the Lockean-liberal political philosophy of that class, and not everyone within the working class adheres to, or acts according to, the tenets of Marxism. Indeed, Marxists have recognized that the transformation in the forces of production does not proceed uniformly in any given country, or equally in comparing different countries. Remnants of the older economy, and its political culture, can continue to survive in the new stage of development, and can have an impact on events.[7]

In the period under study, both in England and within the agrarian commercial capitalist political culture of Upper Canada, there was a significant non-bourgeois cultural element. It was embodied in the Anglican toryism of the landed gentry in England, the character of the engineering officers of the Corps of Royal Engineers and the officers of the British Army units in Canada, and among the Anglican Loyalists settlers, High Church Anglican immigrants from Britain, and the political culture of the political leaders of the Province of Upper Canada in the post-War of 1812 period.[8]

It also needs to be recognized that spiritual values cannot be discounted as a factor in human conduct among Christians who continued to adhere to the faith of their forefathers, and particularly so, when spiritual values are intertwined with political values as in the Anglican tory political culture.

As a graduate student in history, the author became fascinated with the concept that 'ideas influence action'; and that history is much more than just a record of 'what happened' in a physical sense. What men actually did might be the result of accident, of compromise forced on them by events beyond their control, or the opposite of what they intended through their actions having unforeseen consequences.

To truly understand and relate what the leaders of a community were seeking to accomplish, the historian must penetrate into the mind of the leading historical actors to comprehend their particular worldview, and the matrix of political, cultural, moral and religious values that underlay their thought processes. In effect, the historian must understand the protagonists particular beliefs and values, their hopes and fears, and how they viewed their particular circumstance. What the leading actors in any historical action sought to achieve, and their approach to doing so, was ultimately guided and governed by how their particular situation was perceived and conceptualized within their own particular mental framework. This cultural values approach to the writing of history – which is advocated to gain an understanding of the motives for the actions of 'those in authority' in any given historical period – can be applied equally well for gaining an understanding of the motives for the actions of those who were acted upon, as articulated by their leaders.[9]

As an historian, the author has continued to be intrigued by the work of the American intellectual historian, and Professor of American Literature, Perry Miller (1905-1963), in his studies of the American historical experience from the beginning of settlement in New England. In particular the author was initially attracted to the assertion by Miller that the Puritans of New England had a coherent worldview, which guided and governed their actions; and that it was based on their theology. In sum, the history of the establishment of the Massachusetts Bay Colony was an effort by Puritans to work out their religious ideals in action.

For example, in *The New England Mind: From Colony to Province* (1953), Miller treats, in an historical narrative, the interaction of the religious ideals of the Puritans with the realities of the North American environment. He relates the history of the struggle which ultimately resulted in the godly "City upon a Hill" that the Puritan founders were striving to establish, evolving into a materialistic society contrary to their best intentions and efforts.

More generally, the author has found Perry Miller's declaration concerning his view of history to be quite compelling:

> "I have difficulty imagining that anyone can be a historian without realizing that history itself is part of the life of the mind; hence, I have been compelled to insist that the mind of man is the basic factor in human history."[10]

Moreover, R. G. Collingwood, an historian and metaphysical philosopher, has provided a sound philosophical argument for holding that: "All history is the history of thought". In *The Idea of History*, Collingwood concludes that the task of the historian "is to think himself into [the event], to discern the thought of the agent". In sum, "the object to be discerned is not the mere event, but the thought expressed in it. To discover that thought is already to understand it".[11]

In the research and writing of *Military Paternalism, Labour, and the Rideau Canal Project*, however, the author has focused strictly on the actions of Lt. Col. John By, the Commanding Royal Engineer, and his engineering staff. The objective was to examine the questionable assumption made by historians of a Marxist persuasion that Lt. Col. John By and his engineering officers were indifferent, as a 'ruling class', to the suffering of the canal workers on the Rideau Canal project.

Similarly, the actions of the officers of the Military Settling Department in the establishment of the Rideau Military Settlement, were examined to determine whether the paternalism practiced by 'those in authority' on the Rideau Canal project was simply a function of the character of the Commanding Royal Engineer, Lt. Col. John By, or was indicative of a wider phenomenon among the senior officers of the British Army who were in positions of authority over a civilian population. In sum, the practice of paternalism has been found to have prevailed both on the Rideau Canal project in alleviating the suffering of the workers, and in the assistance given the immigrants settling in the Rideau Military Settlement. Herein, it is suggested that the practice of paternalism was a natural outgrowth of the Anglican toryism of the British officer class at that time period.

No effort has been made to prove that 'ideas influence action' through a direct linkage of the Anglican tory beliefs of the military officers with their practice of paternalism, or to come to a better understanding of the phenomenon of paternalism by entering into an imaginative understanding of the mind of the military officer class. Nonetheless, the military officers were largely Anglican tories, and the basic beliefs, tenets, and cultural values of the Anglican tory political philosophy can be sketched herein by way of indicating the credibility of such a direct connection, and to promote a better understand of the motives for their actions. Indeed, the author has suggested as much in the brief biographical treatment of Lt. Col. John By, Commanding

Royal Engineer, Rideau Canal.[12]

Secondarily, the sketch of the cultural values of Anglican toryism is accompanied by a sketch of the cultural values of Lockean-liberalism, with the intention of aiding Canadian historians to see a cultural bias in much of the existing works on the history of the Province of Upper Canada.   R.G. Collingwood (*The Idea of History*) has pointed out that historians tend to view and interpret the past through their own value system and present postulates; and that it is a tendency which leads to the ignoring or disparaging of historical actors of a different mindset.[13] That is precisely what has transpired with respect the treatment of the Upper Canadian tories in Canadian historiography. Liberal historians and Marxist historians, with their progressive philosophies of history, have ignored the Upper Canadian tories, or dismissed them as reactionaries, or disparaged them as being – supposedly – selfish, self-serving, oligarchs.

Anglican toryism

The traditional Anglican-tory political philosophy in its social and political worldview encompassed a number of tenets and concepts derived from the ancient Greek philosophers – primarily Plato and Aristotle – within a Christian framework of beliefs. Among the concepts adopted, and adapted, from the Classics were those relating to the moral purpose of civil government, the common good, the good man-good citizen, the role of human reason and education in knowing 'the Good', the existence of natural law, and the concept of a harmonious hierarchical society based on function and aptitude, as well as the ethical state, rule by law, and constitutional government.[14]

Among the major figures in that intellectual process of integrating Greek philosophy, and social and political concepts, into a Christian teleology and eschatology were St. Augustine (*City of God*, written 413-416 A.D.) and Thomas Aquinas (*Summa theologica*, written 1264-1274 A.D.), both of whom worked within an universal (Roman) Catholic Church context, and the

Anglican divine, Richard Hooker (*The Laws of Ecclesiastical Polity*, written 1594-1597 A.D.), who worked within a national State-Church context. The synthesis achieved by Richard Hooker, as conceptualized in Anglican-tory political philosophy, was subsequently carried forward within the established Church of England in its teachings and traditions, through Anglican priests and laymen teachings in schools, through the family, and through the landed gentry serving in parliament, local government, and the judiciary.[15]

Anglican tories believed in a natural, God-ordained, social hierarchy based on function and aptitude, in which each order performed a vital function in the proper functioning and maintenance of a society of mutual dependence and benefit. Man was a social being by nature, and society had evolved to meet the social needs of man, which could not be met by a life of isolation. It was a natural organic society in which each order not only performed a vital function in God's creation, but wherein the members of each order filled vocational positions suited to their particular God-given aptitudes and abilities. Moreover, each order had its particular duties, responsibilities, and rights, which adhered to its social position in a naturally harmonious social hierarchy. The ultimate justification for the authority of those in power was that God had bestowed them with a superior intellect and the aptitude and ability to govern over their fellow man.

The members of each order were expected to contribute to the common good by striving to perform the duties and responsibilities of their particular station to the best of their abilities and knowledge. And all were expected to be loyal and supportive of the established natural social order. In particular, the natural rulers of society and government had a duty and responsibility to maintain social harmony, to promote the well-being of all orders of society, to maintain the rule of law, and to foster peace – only defensive wars were justified – and to maintain social peace and public order through providing good government and promoting the common good. All were subject to, and protected by, the rule of law.

The Anglican tories were strong supporters of the British constitution, and the existing polity, which they believed had evolved naturally to represent the interests of the various orders, or corporate entities, within society. In sum, it was held that government, in its origin, was a natural organic outgrowth concurrent with the formation of society, and that human or positive law had evolved to provide the rules which men would live by within society. In a legitimate government – non-tyrannical – human law was based on the law of reason, which man could know as a rational being and through public approbation over time. The law of reason, in turn, was a reflection of God's divine law as revealed in the Bible.

It was the human law, or what came to be called the 'common law' – which was held to be in accordance with the law of reason and divine revelation – that established the duties, responsibilities and rights of every man, set the standard of justice for the polity, and established the legal rights and liberties of each member of the commonwealth, whether king, lord, or commoner. All members of society and government were subject to the common law of the commonwealth. Even the king had his prescribed duties and responsibilities, and limitations established by law, constitutional traditions, and custom. There was no concept of a sovereign power in Hooker's political philosophy. All powers adhered to one's position rather than to one's person in a polity where the law was supreme and the power of the courts indefeasible under the rule of law.

In the Anglican tory political philosophy, there was no concept of royal absolutism or any justification for the same; nor, on the other hand, was there any recognized right of resistance by the people. The commonwealth was viewed as a self-sufficient corporate entity, with laws that bound all of its citizens as members of the corporation and, as a corporation, the commonwealth, once established, existed for all time.[16] All members of the commonwealth, including the king, were held accountable by the courts for their actions if they violated the law.[17]

For the Anglican tories, it was the representatives of the various orders of the realm acting in Parliament, not the mob in the street, which was responsible for holding the king accountable for his conduct. Parliament, was the highest court in the land for enforcing the laws of the realm, and it could act, as it did – during the Glorious Revolution of 1688 (long after the passing of Richard Hooker) – to remove a king who abused his powers.

Thus, the Glorious Revolution of 1688 was viewed by the Tories as a legitimate political act in deposing of the Roman Catholic monarch, King James II. The removal of the King was carried out by Parliament – the Lords Spiritual and Temporal, and the Commons – and its declared purpose was to preserve the Protestant religion and uphold the laws and liberties of the country against subversion by the King. In sum, the justification for proclaiming the removal of King James and the declaring of William and Mary, jointly as King and Queen, was set forth in a Declaration of Right (March 1689), and subsequently incorporated into a Bill of Rights, which was passed by Parliament in December 1689.

The Bill of Rights declared that King James II had "abdicated" in fleeing England, and that, during his reign, he had violated "the laws and liberties of this kingdom". The specific transgressions of King James were enumerated, and the Bill of Rights reiterated the "ancient rights and liberties" of the king's subjects, the established limitations on the Crown, and the prerogatives of Parliament.[18] Hence, what had transpired, in removing King James, was an adjustment in leadership to restore the proper functioning of a commonwealth based on law, rather than a revolutionary change in government or society. It was largely a conservative adjustment in the established polity in keeping with Anglican tory principles.

For Hooker, government had a moral purpose. It was responsible for promoting the common good of the citizens of the nation in an ethical state governed by law. Hence, the first charge on government was to render support to the true religion, Christianity, through a national church to which all citizens belonged in virtue of that fact that they were citizens of the country and subject to its laws, including ecclesiastical laws. Religious sects were to be tolerated, but the purpose of a national church was to teach men to know 'the Good'.

God was the creator of the universe, the maker of all things, and the source of order in all things. He was the source of all morality, all goodness, and of law and justice, which man could know through Church traditions, human reason, and the Scriptures. In a true polity, human laws were based on the law of reason, which was consistent with the natural law that governed all things of various types, and was in turn a reflection of the divine law in Scriptures. Indeed, all good laws were derivative from divine law as revealed in the Scriptures.

Moreover, as Christians the tories believed in Divine Providence, in the general sense of God the maker of the omnipresent natural law governing all things for His own purposes, and also in an immediate or active sense. Man had free will, and God rewarded – with his blessings – those who obeyed his commandments and loved Him, while those who turned away would suffer for their sins in this life as well as at the Day of Judgement.

In sum, 'the Good' could be perceived by man – through human reason, Church traditions and the Scriptures – but the living of the good life and the promoting of the common good was another matter.[19]   For Anglicans, 'the Good' was attained through living a Christian life of good works and charity in accordance with God's Will, but man in his natural state was morally and ethically corrupted. Only through baptism – in entering into Christ, receiving God's saving grace, and being empowered by the Holy Spirit – could the corruption of original sin be washed away and the citizen be enabled to live a moral life of good works, charity, and self-restraint, in keeping with God's Will.

In sum, the good citizen and the Christian were one and the

same, and the good citizen was expected to obey the ecclesiastical law of the Church and the civil law of the State; although the two were separate authorities. Anglicans were admonished to recognize and obey the civil magistrate where the temporal authority was "regularly and legitimately constituted", but it was held that the magistrate had no authority to interfere with "things purely spiritual".[20]

In sum, for Anglican tories, their belief in the ethical state and their God-given duty to promote the common good, made it incumbent on 'those in authority' to provide for the development of the moral character of the members of society through supporting a national Christian Church, the clergy of which had a responsibility for educating youth, as well as their religious duties. Those in authority also had a duty to promote the common good of the nation and the wellbeing of its citizen in all spheres of activity, and the responsibility to maintain the rule of law and harmony between the various 'natural' social orders. Economic development was to be fostered, to increase the power of the State, and to strengthen the economy and defences of the realm, for the benefit of the nation in maintaining peace, security, and public order. Hence, the Tories did not hesitate to regulate trade and commerce, to employ state enterprise in the construction of fortifications, roads, harbours and docks, and to undertaken other works for the common good of the nation.[21]

With respect to British military officers in Upper Canada, their tory principles can be seen in the promotion of the common good through the construction of fortifications, arterial roads and military canals to facilitate the defence of the colony and the promotion of its settlement and economic development. Their tory beliefs, as expressed by the concept of *noblesse oblige*, can be seen in the paternalism of the British military officers in providing assistance and support for impoverished British immigrants employed in constructing the military canals and those seeking to settle onto the land in Canada.

If, and when, the history of the Province of Upper Canada

is written through taking account of the cultural values and worldview of the different interests involved in the particular political issues and developments of that period of history, historians will need to keep in mind that there were two significant fragments of different ideologies present in the body politic of that era.

On the one hand, there was an Anglican tory cultural fragment. It was embodied in the Anglican Loyalists settlers who had fled the American Revolution, and the High Church British immigrants who settled in Upper Canada both before and after the War of 1812.[22]

The Upper Canadian Anglican tories favoured the maintenance of the British constitution and the Imperial relationship, a 'natural' hierarchical society, and an ethical church-state polity. Where the formation of the moral character of the province was concerned, they believed in an established Church as well as the establishment of a common school system open to all, under the superintendence of the 'national' Church. It was an educational system in which students were to be educated in moral precepts, the classics and practical subjects, and in which those who were blessed with superior God-given aptitudes and who excelled in learning and personal achievement, were to be identified and mentored in a system of higher education to take their rightful place as the natural leaders of society in the professions, government, the Church, and in education.

On the other hand, there was also a Lockean-liberal cultural fragment present in Upper Canada. It was embodied in the American settlers who had entered into the Province in large numbers in the two decades prior to the War of 1812, and among a goodly number of postwar British immigrants – from, one presumes, the commercial and industrial areas of Britain – who were largely religious dissenters. The American settlers were democratic republicans and proponents of individual freedom. They were opposed to a church-state polity, and many of them favored the annexation of the Province of Upper Canada to the new republic of the United States of America. The religious dissenters among the British immigrants favoured the maintenance of the British tie, and the British constitutional form of government, but were opposed to the church-state polity ideal of the Anglican Tories.[23] In effect, it was a society in which an Anglican corporate toryism was at odds with a Lockean liberal individualism.

Lockean liberalism

In the United States at the onset of 19th Century, a Lockean-liberal political philosophy prevailed among the public and defined the American political culture; whereas in Britain, a Lockean-liberal political philosophy prevailed amongst the commercial interests and an emerging middle class – the bourgeoisie – which was spawned by the growth of industrial capitalism. Moreover, the Lockean-liberal political philosophy was melded with a laissez-faire economic theory that shared a similar man-centred worldview and the same novel concept of 'the Good' as comprising the pursuit of one's individual self-interest. In Britain, the transition to industrial capitalism was well underway in a country where large amounts of capital – which had been accumulated under a commercial capitalist system – were being invested in establishing factories that employed unskilled wage labourers – men, women and children.

Lockean liberalism was basically a justification for the cultural values, worldview, and the particular constitutional beliefs of the Whig political interests in Britain, and their middle class supporters, as articulated and rationalized by John Locke (1632-1704), a medical doctor and public officeholder cum-political philosopher. Locke was a former close associate of the 1st Earl of Shaftesbury, who had founded the Whig 'party' and was its leading spokesman in parliament. Following the Glorious Revolution of 1688, Locke published several works that had a transforming impact on political thought during the 18th Century Enlightenment, and on the development of Whig-liberalism. Among his most influential publications were: *Two Treatises*

on Government (1689); *A Letter Concerning Toleration* (1689);
An Essay Concerning Human Understanding (1690); and *Some Thoughts Concerning Education* (1693).[24]

In his writings, Locke acknowledged that he was indebted to the "judicious Hooker" and, indeed, in many ways the political philosophy of John Locke appears to consist of a total re-working of the Christian worldview of the Anglican divine, Richard Hooker. Locke adopted the basic premises of Anglican toryism in its Christian belief in God as the Creator of all things and of the order of the universe, in man as a rational being, and in a law of nature that could be known by man and was a reflection of Divine Law as revealed in the Scriptures. However, Locke brought about a revolution in political theory through introducing a number of novel concepts.

Where Locke differed fundamentally from Richard Hooker was in their contrasting views of human nature, the purpose of government, and what constituted 'the Good'. Locke discarded the God-centred, 'ancient political philosophy' of Anglican toryism with its identification of 'the Good' with morality and the obeying of God's Will. He replaced it with a man-centred 'modern political philosophy' – bourgeois liberalism – that focused on individual rights and personal freedom, property rights, limited government, the separation of church and state, religious equality, and the pursuit of individual self-interest and personal happiness. Locke also set forth a different view of the purpose of education and political economy.

Where human nature was concerned, Locke discarded the Christian belief that the nature of man was corrupted by 'the Fall' and in need of redemption. He held that human reason alone was capable of knowing and understanding the natural law governing the universe – the universal standard of right and wrong – without any recourse to divine revelation; and that man was perfectly capable of living in accordance with the natural law without any recourse to the supernatural. Moreover, he asserted that each man, as an individual, was endowed by his Maker with certain inalienable and indefeasible natural rights; and that these natural rights comprised the right to life, liberty, health and property. The older belief of Richard Hooker in man as a natural social being with duties, responsibilities and rights that adhered to one's particular functional position in a natural, God-ordained, social hierarchy, was jettisoned in favour of inalienable and indefeasible natural rights pertaining to man as an individual.

For Locke, the state of nature was a place of peace, mutual assistance and good will, wherein each individual was free to follow his enlightened self-interest and to enjoy the fruits of his own labour and property. It was a state of nature wherein property was created by the labour that the individual invested in land to make it productive, and wherein there were no great social differences as the capacity of an individual to produce and consume perishable products was quite limited. In sum, man was completely free and self-sufficient in the state of nature. He enjoyed self-evident natural rights, and the natural law governing the world was readily known through human reason. However, there was a lack of security.

According to Locke, government was founded by the people to provide a better protection for personal security, the continued enjoyment of their individual rights, and the security of individual property rights. Here Locke introduced the concept of a social contract whereby free individuals supposedly consented to the establishment of a government to make and enforce law, as well as entered into society, for the better protection of their individual rights. In effect, the legitimacy of government rested on the consent of the governed, and the role of government was limited to establishing and enforcing positive laws – based on the natural law – for the protection of property and individual natural rights, and the enforcing of the sanctity of contracts. Government was viewed as a 'neutral judge', the necessity of which was to preclude any man being judge, jury, and executioner in defence of his individual rights and property.

Given the premise that government was based on the consent of the governed, Locke held that if a government violated the trust of the people through engaging in "a long train of abuses" of individual rights, then its right to govern would be forfeit. Power would revert back to the people. It was 'the people' who possessed the supreme power and who, when faced with a tyrannical government, had the right to install a new government. Hence, the power and prerogatives of government were strictly limited, and the people possessed a lawful right of rebellion to resist tyranny.

For the Whigs, the Glorious Revolution of 1688 was interpreted in keeping with Locke's political theory that power resided with the people; and they held that the rebellion against the king, and his overthrow, was justified because he had repeatedly abused the rights of the people. The Revolution of 1688 was also a victory for the Whigs in that it resulted in the establishment of the Whig principle of the supremacy of Parliament – the people's representatives – over the King, which was confirmed in a revised Coronation Oath. Equally important for the Whigs, and their middle class supporters, the revolution – in establishing the supremacy of parliament – secured the transfer of the taxing power of the state, the regulation of trade and commerce, and control over the national debt from the King to Parliament.

Based on his theory of individual freedom and natural rights, Locke totally rejected the Anglican tory concept of 'the Good' as the living of a moral life in obedience to God's Will. Moreover, there was no concept of an ethical state with a duty to promote the wellbeing of its members and to foster social harmony. For Locke, just or good laws were simply laws that protected the natural rights and property of the individual citizens of the state. God had established the natural law and endowed man with natural rights, and the state was simply a vehicle for enforcing natural rights, including the property rights, and for keeping the peace. If the state were governed by just laws that were in accordance with natural law in protecting individual rights and property, and man followed his enlightened self interest in his personal life, the common good would be promoted. The prosperity and harmony of society and the nation, and the happiness of the individual, would be assured.

The liberal political philosophy of John Locke was not strictly secular. He recognized God as the creator who ordered all things in the world, and did not deny that the Scriptures were the revealed Word of God. However, Locke did not believe in original sin, and saw no need for an established church or of revealed religion where the function of government was concerned. Human reason and natural law provided all that man required for guidance in government and life, and a church or sect was simply a voluntary organization which individuals joined of their own free will for public worship. Hence, Locke advocated the separation of church and state, and religious toleration, on the ground that human reason could not discern supernatural truths and, even if the 'true religion' could be known, any attempt to impose a religious uniformity on society would lead to social disorder and violence.[25]

For Locke, it was education that made the man, and he was strong advocate of education for young gentlemen of the landed estates and the sons of the middle class. He also believed that young women "of the genteel class" should receive basically the same education as young gentlemen. However, where education was concerned he rejected the classical curriculum and the study of Latin and Greek. He favoured a strictly practical education in the vernacular language, focusing on useful subjects. He also believed in physical exercise to attain 'a sound mind in a sound body'. The purpose of education was to produce a rational, thinking being, with a love of knowledge and of self-improvement who would question the authority of custom and accepted beliefs. For Locke, the virtuous man was the educated individual who followed what reason directed in controlling his passions.

The epistemology of Locke was based on an older Aristotelean theory that the mind of man was a blank slate – a tabula rasa – at birth, and devoid of innate ideas. For Locke, all knowledge came from experience – from sensation or reflection – and education had a critical role to play in the formation of the mind and the development of the reasoning power of the individual. Knowledge would lead to understanding. Hence, it was critically important that education commence at an early age for children; and that the child be exposed to ideas, language, and experiences, which upon becoming lodged in memory, would become in turn the materials with which the mind worked in developing broader associations. For Locke the impressions made on the youthful mind were of a lasting consequence throughout life.

To prepare young men for life, and to enter into government – and presumably for the middle class to enter into the professions and commerce – proper attitudes and civilities had to be taught: viz. self-denial, liberality towards others, truthfulness, good manners, courage and humility, as well as industry and a disdain for idleness, as well as the inculcation of personal self-esteem and respect for others. In effect, human nature could be moulded through education, and human reasoning power developed, to enable man to act according to his enlightened self-interest and the prescriptions of natural law. Man was what he was, for good or evil, depending on his experiences. Although the mind of man was held to be a blank slate at birth, Locke did not deny that children had innate aptitudes, talents and interests. He encouraged parents to closely observe their children to ascertain what they were best suited for in life.

In sum, for Locke individual freedom and knowledge were superior virtues, and virtuous conduct consisted of following one's enlightened self-interest, and the precepts of natural law which provided a sufficient rule for life. The purpose of education was to develop the reasoning power of the individual, and to inculcate civic virtues and useful knowledge. Virtuous acts on the part of individuals would lead to a universal virtue. The underlying and unspoken assumption, of course, was that the natural law was a reflection of Divine law by which a benevolent God had ordered the universe for the benefit and wellbeing of man. However, since the natural law could be known through reason alone, there was no need to acknowledge or resort to the Scriptures; or to compare

Locke's concept of the natural law with God's revealed Word in the Scriptures. The teaching of religion, ethics, and morality was not part of education, according to Locke. Such matters were best left to the individual, as well as his relationship to God. Man as a conscious, thinking being was capable of feeling pleasure and pain, and experiencing happiness or misery, and was responsible for his choices in life as a free individual.

With his novel political philosophy and epistemology, Locke rejected the cultural values and Christian worldview of the Anglican tories, the moral character ideal of man, the belief in a natural social hierarchy, in paternalistic government, and the pursuit of 'the Good'. He substituted a concept of man as a self-sufficient and self-interested individual, with natural rights and freedom of conduct, of a society composed of individuals, and of government as simply an enforcer of individual rights and a defender of the sanctity of property with no overriding moral or religious purpose.

In effect, Locke totally transformed the older concept of natural law. He removed its moral and religious context and its implied enjoining of the common good of society, and construed the natural law as a body of natural rights that sanctified individual liberty and property rights and placed them beyond any interference by government. The individualism and freedom championed by Locke also embraced a different economic outlook and attitude towards labour than previously prevailed. In sum, Locke was a man of the new bourgeois world of trade, of a growing middle class, and of commercial cum-industrial capitalism; and he expressed its values.

Locke believed in the labour theory of value. Indeed, the right of private property, which existed prior to government and society, was based on the labour expended upon it. In the state of nature, property accumulation was limited by the ability of the individual to produce and consume perishable products. However, with the introduction of money and the production of durable goods, it became possible to accumulate property, both fixed and moveable.

Locke was aware that there were great differences in the amount of property held by individuals in society, but he argued that the people by accepting the introduction of money as a medium of exchange – which made possible the accumulation of property – had tacitly consented to economic inequalities.

As exclaimed by Locke, "money answers all things", and it was the market – supply and demand – that determined the price of goods and labour.[26] In effect, wages would sink to a subsistence level in a period of surplus labour; prices would soar in a period of high demand and shortages of a particular product; and rents would fluctuate depending on the demand for accommodations and for land to lease. Such was the law of the free market, which was to function without interference from government. The concept that the price of a product should fluctuate based on supply and demand, constituted a complete rejection of the Christian notion – widespread during the 17th century – of a just price.

For Christians, a product had a recognized price under normal market conditions that took into account the cost of labour and materials, and the realizing of a reasonable return to the producer – sufficient to let him live comfortably according to his position in the natural social hierarchy. In sum, there was an intrinsic value that adhered to a product based on the common perception of its regular market price. To increase the price in times of high demand was unjust to the buyer, and to sell the product for less than it was worth in times of low demand was unjust to the seller. Justice consisted of a market exchange of proportional value between the purchaser and the seller, based on the traditional or common market values, rather than the fluctuations of supply and demand.[27]

Locke was a man of the new world of trade, mercantile capitalism, and the middle class, and his man-centred political philosophy – Lockean liberalism – with its emphasis on individual freedom and responsibility, and the primacy of self interest, fostered a different attitude towards labour and the poor. This can be seen in his report "On the Poor Law and Working Schools" (1697), which contains recommendations for putting the poor and their children to work so as to relieve the middle class of the tax burden of paying the poor rates for parish relief. For Locke, the poverty experienced by beggars and the labouring poor in receipt of poor relief, was not caused by a lack of employment opportunities in a time of a trade boom. It was due to the lack of industry and virtue on the part of the poor, and to their leading of a life of idleness, drink and debauchery. His solution was to put them to work in situations where they could be severely disciplined.

He recommended that all healthy beggars and layabouts between 14 and 50 years of age ought to be taken to the nearest seaport and impressed into the Royal Navy for three years at a soldier's pay, with deductions to pay for their victuals. All beggars incapable of serving at sea, or over 50 years old, were to be place in a House of Correction at hard labour for three years. When released, those who returned to begging were to be transported to 'the plantations' overseas under the same system as convicts. Females over 14 years old were to be returned to their parents, or Master, who would be held responsible for supporting them.

For child beggars, and the children of the labouring poor who were receiving poor relief, Locke called for the establishment of "Working Schools". All such children, from three to fourteen years of age, male and female, were to be placed in working schools where they would be schooled, given their daily bread, and put to work. Here what Locke had in mind was employing the children in spinning and knitting and other aspects of woollen manufacturing. He recognized that a three-year old would not produce enough work to pay for his/her keep, but over a decade at the working school would do so. The idea was that the working schools would be self supporting, without any need for the imposition of parish poor rates; and that the children would be fed, schooled at a basic level, and taught to be industrious, as well as inured to labour, in the working school. Locke also recommended that the children be taken to Church each Sunday, to inculcate in them a sense of religion and morality. Apparently the maintenance of social order required that those who were without a well-developed reasoning power, and an understanding of their enlightened self-interest, needed to be steeped in religion.

Once, the children reached the age of fourteen, they were expected to be able to live an industrious and sober life, and to secure gainful employment. To facilitate that process, Locke recommended that the boys, at 14 years of age, be apprenticed to master tradesmen and to farmers of some substance; and that Royal Navy captains be required to take on one boy each year, on a nine-year apprenticeship, for a career at sea.[28]

During the 'Enlightenment' of the 18th Century numerous public intellectuals in England, France, and Scotland, championed natural rights, human reason, individual property rights, the pursuit of self-interest, political equality, limited government, and ultimately the pursuit of economic self-interest. In the political, social and educational spheres, European intellectuals were heavily influenced by the writings of John Locke, and in the economic sphere Lockean liberalism melded well with new capitalist beliefs that the pursuit of economic self-interest, and laissez-faire government would promote the public good. In less than a century, concomitant with the growth of commerce and manufacturing, the development of commercial cum-industrial capitalism, and the growth of the urban middle class, the climate of opinion among the educated and increasingly secular elites of the urban centres of Europe was totally transformed. In the process, the traditional Christian sin of avarice – greed for material wealth – was turned into a public virtue in a totally new ideology.

The theorists who were the most influential in establishing the new attitude in favour of the pursuit of economic self-interest, were Montesquieu, a philosophe of the French Enlightenment, and Adam Smith, a moral philosopher of the Scottish Enlightenment. That new attitude had led in turn to an argument for laissez-faire government as developed by Adam Smith in drawing on the work of French economic theorists, the

Physiocrats.

Charles-Louis de Secondat, Baron de Montesquieu, in his *De l'esprit des lois* (1748, English translation 1750), was one of the leading political theorists of the Enlightenment. At a time when moral philosophers were struggling with the problem of whether human reason was sufficient to control the three traditional political passions – avarice, lust for power, and lust for glory – that brought political unrest and social disorder, Montesquieu offered a novel theory. If man simply followed his own individual interests, it would promote the public good. In effect, according to Montesquieu, there was a natural harmony of interest whereby everyone in society, in pursuing their own particular interests, contributed – unbeknownst to themselves – to the general good.

For Montesquieu, commerce was the very foundation of society, and had a transforming effect on human character and behaviour. He saw the 'spirit of commerce' as promoting public order and regularity, and personal frugality, moderation, and tranquility, as well as a work ethic. For Montesquieu the growth in material prosperity would spread through all social orders for the general benefit of society, and trade relationships would bind society together with common interests. International trade would also promote peace among nations engaged in mutually beneficial exchanges. Moreover, the growth of commerce and commercial agriculture would promote the cause of liberty through the growth of a middle class strong enough to resist oppression – a class that believed in individual freedom and natural rights.[29]

Montesquieu's views of the benefits to be gained by the spread of commerce and the pursuit of individual self-interest, constituted a powerful message with a great appeal to the bourgeoisie of the new middle class. And that message became even more powerful when Adam Smith introduced an economic theory to justify the pursuit of economic self-interest.

In *The Wealth of Nations* (1776), Smith argued that the dominant drive or passion of man was "to better his condition" in the world. It was a passion imbued by nature that was present at birth and governed human conduct throughout life. For Smith, the desire for betterment was so strong that, if left unrestrained by monopolies and trade regulations, it was sufficiently powerful to bring wealth and prosperity to all members of society, and to the nation, through everyone following his own private interest. According to Smith, merchants in following their own economic interests were "led by an invisible hand" to promote the best interests of society.

Hence, Smith argued that government ought to be limited to providing security of person and property, and to leave individuals free to follow their own economic interests. Once freed of restraint, the interest and passions of individuals would dispose them to employ themselves in the productive activities which were the most advantageous to society.

Thereafter, Smith's theory of economic individualism became associated with the 'invisible hand' concept, and with the "laissez-faire" belief in limited government popularized by the leading economists of France, the Physiocrats. They held that economic activities should remain free of government control and regulation; and that government ought not to intervene in the economic sphere.

Smith shared the belief of Montesquieu that commerce, as well as manufacturing, would foster good government and order in society and would transformed human behaviour, but not necessarily all for the better. Human folly would still lead to wars, and for Smith the growth of commerce and industry, and the division of labour, also brought the loss of the heroic spirit and moral virtue, and a denigrating of education in favour of the practical man.

Laissez-faire capitalism held a powerful appeal for the new urban middle class, spawned by the growth of commerce and industry and commercial cum-industrial capitalism. Moreover, it became an even more powerful ideology when fused with the

Lockean political philosophy to form what became known as "liberalism" or, in retrospect, "classical liberalism". Whether classical liberalism with its emphasis on the pursuit of individual self-interest in all aspects of life, laissez-faire government, and the pursuit of personal wealth, would benefit the labouring class and the poor, remained to be seen.[30]

Classical liberalism was a political economy theory that embodied the interests of the new bourgeoisie of the era of commercial capitalism and of a growing industrial capitalism. In England, it marked the discarding by the new urban middle class of the Anglican-tory synthesis of Christianity with the civic virtues of the Ancient Greeks in favour of a new worldview, new cultural values, and a new concept of human character as totally malleable. Classical liberalism posited a view of the mind of man as a blank slate at birth and susceptible to being taught the character values required to facilitate the optimum development of commerce and industry; and it held to a belief that the role of government was limited to protecting individual rights and property. Government had no right to interfere in the market.[31]

God was relegated to the periphery as a 'Clockmaker', who created the universe, established the natural law, endowed man with reason and inalienable natural rights, and whose creation supposedly ensured that individuals in following their own economic self interest would promote the general welfare and human progress towards material wealth and happiness here on earth. Such a political economy theory posed a major threat to the nascent Anglican-tory political culture of the Province of Upper Canada.

For the Province of Upper Canada in the post-War of 1812 years, the effort of the Loyalists and the Loyal of the War of 1812 to establish an Anglican-tory political culture, faced a more immediate threat. The neighbouring, democratic republic of the United States of America was based on a Lockean-liberal political philosophy as clearly enunciated in the Declaration of Independence.[32] Moreover, the new republic was committed to expansionism to extend its liberal democratic republican values throughout the North American continent. Thus, the subsequent history of the Province of Upper Canada, was one of a struggle for survival against the external threat posed by the United States and, within Upper Canada, it consisted of a constant struggle with Lockean-liberals over the future political culture of the province. Moreover, it was a struggle that was soon joined by a great influx of British immigrants who, in espousing classical liberalism, contributed strongly to the ultimate overwhelming of the fragile Anglican-tory political culture of the province.

Any effort to understand the paternalism in evidence in the treatment of labourers on the Rideau Canal project (1826-1832) and the severe exploitation of labourers on the canal projects of the 1840s in Canada, must start with examining the character, cultural values, and worldview of 'those in authority' over the workers on the respective canal projects. The growth of commerce and industry brought about not only a change in the relationship of labour to the means of production, but also a new 'spirit of capitalism' and a different mentality on the part of employers towards their workforce.

Endnotes

1. Peter Way, *Common Labor, Workers and the Digging of North American Canals, 1780-1860* (Baltimore: John Hopkins University Press, 1993), 1-17 & 265-274. Within a Canadian context, Way sees the severe exploitation of the canal workers by contractors on the Beauharnois Canal project (1842-1845), and the repression of the striking workers by government troops in June 1843, as marking "the emergence of industrial capitalism and the modern worker." (*ibid*, 11). Presumably Way is thinking in terms of the powerlessness of the workers; otherwise such a statement presents a very negative, dismal, and highly dubious stereotyping with respect to the condition of labour in general under an industrial capitalist system.

2. Way, *Common Labor*, 68, 105-106 & 273-274. One has to qualify the assumption that all of North America was undergoing the beginnings of a

transition from an agrarian commercial capitalism to industrial capitalism during the canal building era. In much of Upper Canada, during the early canal building era, the economy on the frontiers of settlement was still in a primitive barter stage with a prevalence of subsistence agriculture. Once constructed, it was the canals – in providing a transport facility for conveying bulk produce over great distances at relatively cheap rates – that opened up local markets and the export trade, which brought the frontier farmers into an agrarian merchant capitalist market economy.

3. Bryan D. Palmer, *The Working Class Experience, Rethinking the History of Canadian Labour, 1800-1991*, 2nd. ed. (Toronto: McClelland & Stewart, 1992), 41-48, and especially 41-42.

4. William N.T. Wylie, "Poverty, Distress and Disease: Labour and the Construction of the Rideau Canal, 1826-1832", *Labour/Le Travailleur*, Vol. 11, Spring 1983, 7-29. In this article, Wylie draws heavily, for interpretation purposes, on the work of Clare Pentland, an Economic historian, who employed a Marxist analytical framework, a Marxist concept of class, and a focus on labour, in his history of the development of capitalism in Canada. See H. Clare Pentland, *Labour and Capital in Canada 1650-1860* (Toronto: J. Lorimer, 1981).

5. In investigating working conditions on a canal project to determine whether workers were exploited or not, there is a systemic problem in applying a Marxist analysis. Orthodox Marxist hold that the wage labour relationship is exploitative by its very nature. In effect, any work performed beyond what the workers require for their own livelihood – work that yields a profit for the employer – is deemed 'surplus labour' taken from the workers, and hence, an exploitation of the worker. Moreover, according to Marxists, the wage relationship empowers the bourgeois to dominate and exploit the worker, the interest of each class is inherently different and in conflict, and the wage labour means of production has to be overthrown to usher in the socialist and classless society. Hence, Marxist historians see exploitation in the wage labour relationship itself, regardless of actual working conditions and pay levels on a construction project.

In the case of the Rideau Canal project, the wage labour relationship was mutually beneficial for the canal workers and for 'those in authority'. It provided the workers with the necessities of life in a situation where they would otherwise have faced destitution, if not starvation,, and the British

Government/Royal Engineers gained the means of realizing the construction of a canal for the benefit of the province as a whole.

6. The quoted phrase is borrowed from E.H. Carr, *What is History* (New York: Penguin Books, 1990 reprint), 24. Carr comments on "the historian's need of imaginative understanding for the minds of the people with whom he is dealing, for the thought behind their acts".

7. This understanding of Marxism – the economic, social, and political philosophy of Karl Marx and its elaboration by Friedrich Engels – is largely drawn from: George H. Sabine, *A History of Political Theory*, 3rd. ed. (London: Lowe & Brydone Ltd, 1963) 756-804.

8. On the concept of "cultural fragments", see Louis Hartz, *The Liberal Tradition in American, an interpretation of American Political Thought since the Revolution* (New York: Harcourt Brace, 1955), and Louis Hartz, *The Founding of New Societies: Studies in the History of the United States, Latin America, South Africa, Canada and Australia* (New York: Harcourt Brace & World, 1964, with various contributions). Hartz concludes that English Canada had a predominately Lockean-liberal political culture, but with a feudal fragment, "a tory touch", which was introduced by the Loyalists following the American Revolution. However, Gad Horowitz subsequently pointed out that toryism in English Canada was actually a quite significant component of the Canadian political culture; and that the 'point of congealment' was not necessarily at the time of the arrival of the Loyalists, given the heavy British immigration after the War of 1812. (See G. Horowitz, "Conservatism, Liberalism, and Socialism in Canada: An Interpretation", *The Canadian Journal of Economic and Political Science*, Vol. 32, No. 2, May 1966, 143-171.)

One might add that the heavy postwar emigration from Britain included a large number of Yeoman farmers and tenant farmers, as well as a significant number of half-pay officers of the Army. In contemporary England, Toryism was more than just a 'feudal fragment' in a predominately Lockean-liberal political culture. It was a major element in the English political culture with strong roots among the landed gentry in a country where a Lockean-liberal political culture predominated among the commercial and industrial interests.

9. Bryan Palmer (*Working Class Experience*, 1992, 13-14 & 19-20) has called for Labour historians to take into account cultural factors in seeking to appreciate and understand class formation; and he recognizes that "differences

of region, skill, gender, ethnicity and race silence class identity" in Canada. While holding that any reference to a common "working class culture" in Canada is somewhat far fetched, nonetheless he maintains that the concept still has some validity and value. However, that is highly questionable during the canal building era. At that time the labourers were immigrants, or recently settled immigrants, most of whom worked for only a short period of time on a canal project. Moreover, many of them were former tenant farmers from Britain, and many of the non-English-speaking Gaelic Irish immigrants were from a peasant culture. The identity and loyalty of the workers was to their ethno-religious group and place of origin, rather than to any common working class identity. Hence, any real understanding of the culture and consciousness of canal workers should commence by focusing on the cultural values and worldview of each particular ethno-religious immigrant group working on a canal, and its shared memories as a group of past experiences, both personal and historical. In aggregate, such studies would provide a good understanding of the consciousness of the canal workers, and would serve to identify any common consciousness in their response as workers to those in authority over them.

10. Perry Miller, *Errand into the Wilderness* (New York: Harper Torchbooks, 1954), Preface, ix. This entire passage is an almost verbatim reproduction of the author's earlier expression of his view of Perry Miller's approach to the writing of history, as published in: Robert W. Passfield, *Phips' Amphibious Assault on Canada – 1690* (Amazon.com, 2011), Acknowledgements, xiii-xiv. The other work referred to is: Perry Miller, *The New England Mind, From Colony to Province* (Cambridge, Mass.: Harvard University Press, 1962).

11. R.G. Collingwood, *The Idea of History* (Oxford: Oxford Paperbacks, 1963). The quotations are from 215, 213 & 214.

12. While a graduate student at McMaster University in the early 1970s, the author undertook to write a Ph.D. thesis on the subject of the Upper Canadian Tory Mind. The intention was to conceptualize the religious, educational, and constitutional beliefs of the leading Anglican tories in post-War of 1812 Upper Canada, and to show how their Anglican tory political philosophy underlay the positions that they took on the critical issues of the day. The argument to be developed was that 'ideas influence actions'; and that the political philosophy of the Upper Canadian tories embodied a true organic conservatism within an overwhelmingly Lockean-liberal ethos

in North America. In the event, the subject proved overly ambitious for a graduate student. With the thesis incomplete, the author embarked on a career as a public historian which required him to abandon intellectual history and pursue work in other fields of history.

13. Collingwood, *The Idea of History*, 153-155 & 321-330.

14. Sabine, *A History of Political Theory*: on Plato, 39-44, 48-49, 50-53, 54-56, 59-63, 68-70, 76-84, 86; and on Aristotle, 91-122 & 245. In the writings of Plato (427-347 B.C.), there are surprising similarities to Christian theology. Plato believed in the spiritual essence of man, in an immortal soul, in absolute moral values transcending time, and in a future state of rewards and punishments, and a Supreme God who created and ordered all things. Plato's God was also the fountain of all law and justice, and the embodiment of the ideal Form of "the Good" – absolute goodness and knowledge. Plato also believed that God's law – natural law – could be known through human reason. Indeed, the highest pursuit for man was to strive to attain goodness, to be God-like, and knowledge of 'the Good' could be gained, although imperfectly, through human reason and through the teachings of philosophers. The schools were to teach the idea of 'the Good", encompassing morality, religion and ethics, as well as mathematics, astronomy, and logic. For Plato, the system of education was to be regulated and supervised by the City-State, and religious rites were to be performed in public temples by authorized priests to avoid private allegiances and in recognition of the direct linkage between moral behaviour and religious belief.

Although the metaphysics of Plato and Christianity share a surprisingly similar eschatology and teleology, there were significant differences. Christians believed in Divine Revelation – the Bible – which revealed God's Will and was reflected in God's natural law. Christians also believed in Providence – in an omnipresent God, ever present in the material universe in actively rewarding those who obeyed his revealed Will while those who disobeyed would suffer for their sins. Also in Anglican toryism, Plato's ideal of man striving to attain 'the Good'– to be God-like in goodness and knowledge – was translated into a belief in man's duty to strive to be Christ-like in goodness and virtue – in the image of the Son of God – in living and acting in obedience to God's revealed Will and in exercising a Christian charity to those less fortunate. Moreover, God's Word, and Christian morality and beliefs, were to be taught by a national Church and by learned clerics serving as teachers in an educational system. In addition, Anglican tories rejected Plato's advocacy of communism and his call for abolishing the family, which he thought necessary to eliminate significant class differences, private loyalties and selfish interests within the ideal ethical state.

15. This is not to deny the inspired work of Archbishop Thomas Cranmer in formalizing the rites and doctrines of the established Church of England in *The Book of Common Prayer* (1549 A.D.). It merely attests that it was Richard Hooker who elaborated on the political philosophy inherent in the Anglican religion as it evolved from Roman Catholicism and the synthesis of Christianity and Platonism, and the incorporation of Aristotle on law and nature. Within the established Church, the concepts of Anglican toryism with respect to the nature of man and, society, reason and revelation, the common good, good works, the ideal state, obedience, and a national Church, were conveyed through sermons, Scriptural readings, the Homilies, and the prayers and creeds of *The Book of Common Prayer*, inclusive of the Thirty-Nine Articles.

16. Sabine, *A History of Political Theory*, 439-442 & 453. British tories believed that the natural rulers of society – those who were blessed with superior God-given aptitudes and abilities for governing – were found amongst the aristocracy and landed gentry. In contrast, Upper Canadian tories were adherents to the Platonic view that God-given talents and abilities were found throughout all orders of society. Hence, for Upper Canadian tories a common school system open to all was necessary to enable the gifted future leaders of government, the judiciary, the Church, and society, to be identified and selected for higher education. Moreover, the school system needed to be run by the Established Church to ensure that the future leaders of society would be men of a good moral character, who would be dedicated to promoting the common good of society. In effect, Upper Canadian tories believed in a meritocracy with careers open to all aspirants of superior talent, ability and education.

17. During the English Civil War (1642-1651), there was a faction among the Royalists supporters of King Charles I which believed in the divine right of kings as set forth by Sir Robert Filmer, *Patriarcha, or the Natural Power of Kings* (published posthumously in 1680). However, royal absolutism was a political theory that had no basis in Anglican toryism, and did not enjoy any widespread support in England.

18. See online, Yale Law School, The Avalon Project, "English Bill of Rights 1689, An Act Declaring the Rights and Liberties of the Subject and Settling the Succession of the Crown". In November 1688, Prince William of Orange, the Stadholder (chief of state) of the Calvinist Dutch Republic (Republic of the United Netherlands), landed in England with a Protestant army of 15,000 men at the invitation of several leading Tory members of the government and with the support of the Whig opposition. The purpose was to force a change in the royal succession from the new-born son of James II, who would be raised a Roman Catholic, to Mary, the daughter of James II. Mary had been raised a Protestant and was married to the Prince of Orange. After several minor battles, and with his support collapsing, King James fled to France in early December 1688, and was succeeded by the joint Protestant monarchs, King William III and Queen Mary II. Not only was Prince William a Protestant, but he was the leader of the Protestant powers of Europe who were engaged in resisting the expansionist policies of the Roman Catholic absolutist monarch, King Louis XIV of France.

19. Sabine, *A History of Political Theory*, 439-442.

20. Text of the Thirty Nine Articles (1571) online. Of course, the ultimate aim of Christians was to attain salvation and eternal 'felicity', but for Anglicans salvation depended on faith alone. Good works were the direct result of faith in Christ, but were not critical to salvation in and of themselves.

21. George Grant, *Lament for a Nation, The Defeat of Canadian Nationalism* (2nd. ed., Toronto: McClelland and Stewart Ltd., 1970, 14, 19, 65 & 71), has noted that it was Conservative governments who established Ontario Hydro, the CNR, and the CBC, and did so to protect the public interest – the common good. The present author would add a qualification to the effect that it was Tory conservatives who did so; and that the building of the transcontinental Canadian Pacific Railway is an example of a government enterprise – in conjunction with a private contractor – by a Conservative government motivated by a residue of tory beliefs. In sum, where the promotion of the common good or public interest by government is concerned, Tory conservatives have favoured joint public and private enterprises in a mixed capitalist economy. Gad Horowitz ("Conservatism, Liberalism, and Socialism in Canada") has denoted Conservatives who believe in public enterprise as "Red Tories", or conservatives with a socialist leaning. That is a completely ahistorical misnomer applied from a socialist perspective.

They are organic conservatives, and embody a residue of a formerly robust Anglican toryism in the Canadian political culture.

22. Grant (*Lament for a Nation*, 63), has noted that "many of the American Tories were Anglicans and knew well that in opposing the revolution they were opposing Locke. They appealed to the older political philosophy of Richard Hooker".

23. Among the Lockean-liberal British immigrants settling in Upper Canada during the post-War of 1812 period, were a handful of democratic radicals, and a greater number of Whig liberals of the new middle class of merchants and tradesmen. In Britain, both interests favoured an extension of the franchise: for the democratic radicals to universal male suffrage; and for the Whig liberals to a property franchise that would enable the middle class to be represented in parliament. The democratic radicals stood for democracy and espoused many different schemes aimed at social equality; whereas the Whig liberals were believers in individual rights, laissez-faire government, free trade, the supremacy of parliament over the king, constitutional government, the separation of church and state, and religious equality, but not social or political equality.

In sum, Upper Canada had a rich political culture, which Canadian historians have failed to recognize. They have neglected to enter, imaginatively, into 'the mind' of the leaders of the various different political interests in Upper Canada to determine their cultural values and worldview, not to mention to ascertain their particular character.

24. John Locke (1632-1704) was born in Wrington, Somerset, England, into a strongly Puritan, middle-class, household. His father John, a country lawyer and clerk to a Justice of the Peace, had fought on the side of the Parliamentarians, as a cavalry captain, during the English Civil War (1642-1651). In origin, as a religious community, the Puritans were Calvinist Anglicans who believed that the Reformation would not be completed until the national Church, the Church of England, was "purified" through the removal of its episcopal polity and other 'Papist' remnants of the liturgy and clerical vestments retained on the breaking away from the Roman Catholic Church.

25. On the other hand, as was made clear in a later anonymous publication by John Locke, *The Reasonableness of Christianity, as Delivered in the Scriptures*

(1695), he was not in favour of extending toleration to atheists. He believed that the maintenance of social order – presumably among the illiterate masses – was dependent on a belief in God. Moreover, although Locke has been seen as the founder of English Deism, he was not strictly speaking a deist. The deists believed that God could be known strictly from reason; and that God had created the world and its order, and then left man to live according to the natural law. The deist view of God was captured in the image of "God, the clockmaker". In contrast, Locke accepted revelation as a matter of faith and held that Christian doctrines, stripped of some – unspecified – supernatural elements, were reasonable and ought to be embraced by all men. For Locke the essence of Christianity was a belief in God and a belief in Christ as the Messiah. He rejected the deist belief that the existence of God could be known from reason and observation of the natural world alone without any resort to divine revelation; although he was in accord with the deists in rejecting church authority and traditions.

26. This entire section on "Lockean liberalism' is based on Sabine, *A History of Political Theory*, 517-519 & 523-541, and to a lesser extent on several thoughtful articles posted on wikipedia pertaining to: "John Locke "; and Locke on government, on education, on toleration, on the social contract, and on property.

27. The notion of 'just price' was set forth by Thomas Aquinas in the *Summa theologia*. It is not clearly defined, but was widely held by both Catholics and Protestants in the 17th Century. At present, the author is not prepared to attest that the Anglican tories of the early 19th century still adhered to the concept of a just price; although it appears that Lt. Col. John By adhered to a similar concept of a fair or just wage on the Rideau Canal project.

28. Internet, University of Texas (pdf), John Locke, "On the Poor Law and Working Schools" (1697). The Whig-liberal attitude towards poor relief, as expressed by Locke, led to the establishment of 'workhouses' in England, and ultimately to the passing of the "Poor Law Amendment Act" (1834) by a Whig government, which established a national system of 'workhouses'. These were the notorious workhouses of the 19th Century. The harsh treatment meted out in the workhouses was intended to force the poor to migrate to the industrial centres and to work in the factories at subsistence wages, rather than seek to sustain themselves on the older poor relief system in their parish.

29. Albert O. Hirschman, *The Passions and the Interests, Political Arguments*

for Capitalism before Its Triumph, 10th ed. (Princeton: Princeton University Press, 1997, 60-61 & 70-80. Montesquieu is considered a liberal for his political views in favour of liberty under the law, his theory of the balance of powers, and his belief in religious toleration, republican government, and in representative government; yet he did not share the 'laissez-faire' economic theories of the French Physiocrats and later of Adam Smith, or the rights-holder individualism and sanctity of property of Lockean-liberals. Montesquieu believed that government had a right to regulate property for the general good; and that government had a responsibility to ensure that all citizens had access to food and clothing, and the conditions necessary for a healthy life. (Internet: Céline Spector, "Montesquieu's The Spirit of the Laws in the History of Liberalism".) Nonetheless, Montesquieu's formulation of what became known as 'the invisible hand' had a major impact on the development of liberal economic theory.

30. Hirschman, *The Passions and the Interests*, 18-19, 39-40, 66, 100-112 & 120. On the relationship between Smith and the Physiocrats, see Hirschman, 93-100. For Smith, the "invisible hand' ensured that individuals in following their own economic interests were promoting, inadvertently, the public welfare in producing goods that were needed and in promoting a general prosperity. Subsequently, the concept of the "invisible hand" was interpreted as the self-regulating behaviour of a competitive market place.

31. The social cost of the freeing of liberal man to pursue his own individual economic interests and material wealth in the absence of moral and religious restraint, and of laissez-faire government with no commitment to promoting morality, the common good, and the well-being of society, did not take long to manifest itself. The heartless exploitation of factory workers in England by the "liberal manufacturers" of the new bourgeoisie during the early phases of the Industrial Revolution, is well documented by Frederick Engels in *The Condition of the Working-Class in England in 1844*, English translation, 7th edition (London: George Allen & Unwin Ltd., 1952).

32. See online text, The Declaration of Independence: "In Congress, July 4, 1776, The unanimous Declaration of the thirteen united States of America". The second paragraph of the Declaration of Independence reads:

"We hold these truths to be self-evident, that all men are created equal, that they are endowed by the Creator with certain inalienable Rights, that among these are Life, Liberty, and the pursuit of Happiness – that to secure these rights, Governments are instituted among men, deriving their just powers from the consent of the governed – That whenever any Form of Government becomes destructive of these ends, it is the Right of the People to alter or abolish it, and to institute a new Government, laying its foundation on such principles and organizing its powers in such form, as to them shall seem most likely to effect their Safety and Happiness......"

The entire American Declaration of Independence is based on the tenets of the Lockean-liberal political philosophy in its emphasis on inalienable individual rights, its view of the role of government as limited to securing and protecting individual rights, the concept of popular sovereignty and the right of rebellion, and its emphasis on the pursuit of personal freedom and happiness as the ultimate good and virtue in life. As such, the values expressed in the Declaration of Independence, and embodied in the American political culture, differ dramatically from the former Anglican-tory political culture of the Province of Upper Canada.

A Note About the Author

Robert W. Passfield was born and raised in St. Thomas, Ontario, Canada. He is a graduate of the University of Western Ontario (Honours BA, History, 1968), and McMaster University (MA History, 1969), and pursued Ph.D. studies at McMaster University where he read in a major field, Canadian History (Pre- and Post-Confederation), and three minor fields (Political Philosophy, Modern European History, and Diplomatic History). With his dissertation incomplete, he joined the Parks Canada Program of the Department of Indian Affairs and Northern Development in Ottawa as an historical researcher in the National Historic Sites Branch.

You become what you do: During a 30-year career as a public historian Passfield worked in a wide variety of fields: industrial archaeology; history of technology; public works history; and heritage conservation. He read widely in all of these fields and prepared numerous reports recording, documenting, and evaluating the heritage value of engineering works for Parks Canada, as well as reports in support of the Parks Canada heritage conservation mandate, and Agenda Papers and Submission Reports that documented and evaluated the historical significance of various prominent Persons, Places, and Events in support of the national commemoration mandate of the Historic Sites and Monuments Board of Canada.

While employed by Parks Canada, Passfield published a number of articles in professional journals, two books on heritage canals, and contributed chapters to several books in public works history. In 1987 he was awarded the Norton Prize (now the Robert M. Vogel Prize) by the Society for Industrial Archeology (SIA) for an outstanding article in industrial archaeology, and in 1996 the W. Gordon Plewes Award by the Canadian Society for Civil Engineering (CSCE) for a noteworthy contribution to Canadian engineering history. He has also received a Parks Canada Merit

Award and a Parks Canada Prix d'Excellence for his contributions to Parks Canada program initiatives. Most of his publications were an offshoot of research conducted in support of Parks Canada program needs, or in support of the Historic Sites and Monuments Board of Canada.

In retirement, Passfield has continued to be engaged as an historian in subject areas pertaining to his earlier work for Parks Canada. He has published several articles in the history of technology and heritage conservation fields, and a book that drew on his earlier historical research in support of a Parks Canada archaeological project: *Phips' Amphibious Assault on Canada – 1690 : Origins, Logistics, and Organization, The Attack and Aftermath, & 'Where Sovereignty Lay'*. In May 2012, he was awarded the Robert M. Vogel Prize by the Society for Industrial Archeology for "outstanding scholarship in the field of industrial archeology". Passfield is a member of the Society for the History of Technology (SHOT), the Society for Industrial Archeology (SIA), and the Canadian Science and Technology Historical Association (CSTHA).

www.passrob.com

——————————

Rideau Canal Publications
by the Author

During a thirty-year career as a public historian with the Parks Canada Agency, and subsequently in retirement, the author has published a number of works pertaining to the history and heritage of the Rideau Canal.

Articles & Books

"Swing Bridges on the Rideau Canal", in *IA: Journal of the Society for Industrial Archeology*, Vol. I, no. 2, 1976, 59-64. This article identifies the various types of moveable bridges extant on the Rideau Canal in the early 1970s, and comments on the different types of moveable bridges erected on the canal since its construction in 1826-1832. The article is illustrated with historic engineering drawings, and photographs of the extant moveable bridge structures

"Ordnance Supply Problems in the Canadas: The Quest for an Improved Military Transport System, 1814-1828", in *HSTC Bulletin: Journal of the History of Canadian Science, Technology and Medicine*, Vol. V, No. 3, September 1981, 187-209. This article comments briefly on the military transport problems experienced by the British Army during the War of 1812, and traces postwar efforts to develop a safe interior water communication independent of the St. Lawrence River. The efficiency and operating costs of rail, road, and canal, are compared in their contemporary state of technological development circa 1825, in an assessment of why the Board of Ordnance in London opted for the construction of a military canal through the interior of Upper Canada.

Building the Rideau Canal: A Pictorial History (Don Mills, Ontario: Fitzhenry & Whiteside/Parks Canada, 1982), 184 p., illus. This hardcover book, produced to mark the 150th Anniversary of the Rideau Canal, provides an overview history of the origins, construction, and operation of the canal in the context of its strategic, economic, and engineering significance, and is heavily illustrated with contemporary watercolours, pencil sketches, and historic engineering drawings. French edition: *Construction du canal Rideau: Histoire Illustrée* (Ottawa: Parks Canada, 1982), 184 p., illus. Subsequently the English edition was reprinted by Fitzhenry & Whiteside (1983); and by Friends of the Rideau (2003), with permission.

"The Role of the Historian in Reconstructing Historic Engineering Structures: Parks Canada's Experience on the Rideau Canal, 1976-1983", *in IA: Journal of the Society for Industrial Archeology*, Vol. ll, No. 1, 1985, pp. 128. This article comprises a case study of an historian's contribution to several lock reconstruction projects on the Rideau Canal. It documents the historian's role in the utilization of historical sources; in the planning and consultations process; and in the selection of treatment options for preserving and restoring historic engineering structures. (Following the publication of this article, the author was awarded the Norton Prize in June 1987 by the Society for Industrial Archeology "for outstanding scholarship in industrial archeology").

"The Rideau Canal Waterway", *in Water International, Official Journal of the International Water Resources Association* (IWRA), (Urbana, Illinois: University of Illinois), Special Canadian Issue, Vol. 12, No. 4, December l987, pp. 189-194. This article comments on the topography of the Rideau waterways system, its engineering structures, and its functioning as a water control system. It was prepared, at the invitation of the International Water Resources Association, as a contribution to a 'Special Canadian Issue' to mark the Sixth World Water Conference of the International Water Resources Association.

"A Wilderness Survey: Laying out the Rideau Canal, 1826-1832", in *Science, Technology and Medicine in Canada's Past* , Richard A.

Jarrell & James P. Hull, eds, (Thornhill, Ontario: The Scientia Press, 1991), 149-171. The laying out of a canal was one of the most difficult tasks that a 19th century surveyor could undertake, but even more so in a heavily-forested wilderness environment where traditional surveying methods were largely inapplicable and long lines of sight to known landmarks unobtainable. This chapter comments on the surveying systems employed in the British Army's topographical survey in Britain, and traces the adaptations that had to be made, and the bush surveying techniques that were adopted, in laying out the Rideau Canal through a tract of wilderness. It is a reprint of a paper that first appeared in the Canadian Institute of Surveying *Centennial Convention Proceedings* (Ottawa, April 1982), 291-313.

"Design Evolution: Reconstructed Timber Swing Bridges on the Rideau Canal", *in Canal History and Technology Proceedings,* Vol. XXVI, March 2007, 1-41. This article records and documents the provenance, the original design, and structural evolution of the Rideau Canal centre-bearing timber swing bridge from its introduction on the canal in 1866, through a succession of replacement-in-kind constructions at roughly 12 to 15 year, until 1972 when Parks Canada acquired the Rideau Canal under a mandate to preserve its historic structures. It also provides insights into the art of empirical engineering, and the traditional timber bridge building culture of the 19th century.

"Reconstructing Timber Swing Bridges at Parks Canada", *in Canal History and Technology Proceedings,* Vol. XXVI, March 2007, 42-76. This article treats the reconstruction of four timber swing bridges undertaken by Parks Canada in the period 1978-1986. It identifies and documents several departures introduced during the reconstructions; and assesses the historical accuracy of the reconstructions. In doing so, it compares two different approaches to reconstruction; and comments on the efficacy of 'ekki' – a West-African hardwood – in facilitating the attaining of a highly accurate reconstruction while permitting a doubling of the load carrying capacity.

"Evaluating Authenticity: Reconstructed Timber Swing Bridges", *IA: The Journal of the Society for Industrial Archeology*, Vol. 31, No. 2, 2005, 5-26. [Published in 2008.] When Parks Canada acquired the Rideau Canal in 1972 under a mandate to preserve its historic structures, there were five reconstructed timber swing bridges extant on the waterway. Subsequent research revealed that the design prototype for the timber swing bridges had been introduced on the Rideau Canal in 1866; that the bridges had evolved within a continuing traditional culture of conservation through replacement-in-kind reconstructions; and that the swing bridges had been reconstructed at 12- to 15-year intervals for more than a century.

This article examines and evaluates the authenticity of the five reconstructed timber swing bridges extant in 1972, and does so within the existing culture of replacement-in-kind conservation, to determine whether they were 'what they were purported to be' – an evolved integral form of the original timber swing bridge that conserved the genuine heritage values which conveyed the significance and character of the original structure within its setting. In so doing, the article adapts and applies the revised test of authenticity developed by the UNESCO World Heritage Centre at the Nara Conference on Authenticity (Nara, Japan, November 1994) to industrial archaeology, and provides a case study of a new approach to industrial heritage evaluation that recognizes reconstruction as a legitimate conservation approach.

Historic Bridges on the Rideau Waterway System, A Preliminary Report (Smith's Falls, Ontario: Friends of the Rideau/CD Book, 2009), 50p., illus. This is a published CD Book version of an earlier report of the same title: Parks Canada Manuscript Report Series, No. 212, 1976. This CD Book comprises an investigative survey level photo-recording of the historic bridges extant along the Rideau waterway in July 1974 within the newly-acquired Rideau Canal National Historic Site. It locates, dates, and describes the bridge structures, and identifies them according to their general type, configuration, and materials of construction, with a brief history of each bridge site and the bridge structure. A total of 26 historic bridges, both road and railway are treated, and illustrated with a photo of each structure and historic engineering drawings of several of the older types of swing bridges.

Canal Lock Design and Construction: The Rideau Canal Experience, 1826-1982 (Smith's Falls, Ontario: Friends of the Rideau/CD Book, 2010), 482p., illus. This is a published version of an earlier Parks Canada report of the same title in the Parks Canada Microfiche Report Series, No. 57, 1983. It comprises a structural history of the design evolution, construction, and evolution of the locks on the Rideau Canal. The design of the stone masonry locks is analyzed in terms of contemporary canal construction practice and empirical design formulas, and the design, construction materials, and methods of construction, are described and explained in detail. The CD Book is illustrated with over 90 period engineering drawings, historic photos, and contemporary photos, reproduced in high resolution images.

Addendum: A comprehensive list of publications pertaining to the Rideau Canal – inclusive of Parks Canada publications and reports – can be found in Ken W. Watson, *Engineered Landscapes, The Rideau Canal's Transformation of a Wilderness Waterway* (Elgin, Ontario: Ken W. Watson, 2006), 291-293. Among the more recent Rideau Canal publications of note are: Mark E. Andrews, P.Eng., *For King and Country: Lieutenant-Colonel John By, R.E., Indefatigable Civil-Military Engineer* (Merrickville, Ontario: The Heritage Merrickville Foundation, 1998), 239p., illus.; Edward Bebee, *Invisible Army: Hard Times, Heartbreak and Heritage* (Smith's Falls, Ontario: E. Bebee & Friends of the Rideau, 2010), 466p., illus.; Ken W. Watson, *The Rideau Route: Exploring the Pre-Canal Waterway* (Elgin, Ontario: K.W. Watson, 2007), 146p., illus.; and Ken W. Watson, *The Sweeney Diary: the 1839 to 1850 Journal of Rideau Lockmaster Peter Sweeney* (Smith's Falls: Friends of the Rideau, 2008), 198p., illus.

INDEX

American Settlers, 134, 190, 198, 236

Anglican toryism, v, 101,128, 225-226, 229, 230-235, 255
      Hooker, Richard, 230-231, 232

Army Extraordinaries (military chest), 153, 196-197

Board of Ordnance, 3, 29-30, 72-73
      Composition, 72-73
      Medical Department, Dr. John Webb, 30
      Rideau Canal Project, 3

Beckwith, Sir Sydney, 140

British Currency (conversions), 89, 202

British Emigration, 11-12, 15-16, 61-62, 74-75, 91
      Assisted Scots, 142-144, 158, 164,169,193, 194
      Irish Poor Relief, 203-204
      Glasgow Emigration Society, 166-167, 176-178, 180, 203
      Opposition to, 135 -136, 190
      Timber ships, 11, 16, 44, 74
      Unassisted, 162-163, 175

Bush farming, 14, 42-48, 61, 89, 91, 149-150, 157, 202

By, Lt. Col. John, 105-129
      Anglican Tory beliefs, 118-119, 121, 224-225
      Appointment, 3, 105, 115
      Biography, 105- 121
      Bridge design, 114, 125
      Character, v, xiii, 118, 120-121
      Paternalism, v, xiii, 17 -18, 26, 29, 46, 61, 68-69, 71, 101
      Quebec Model, 112- 113, 125
      Shernfold Park, 105, 111- 112, 124

Sickness, 37

Canals of the 1840s, 71, 98-99, 101

Careers open to Talent, 255

Christie, Dr. A.J., 18, 23, 24-25, 33

Chaudière Bridges, 23, 50, 117, 126

Clowes, Samuel, 117, 118

Cockburn, Lt. Col. Francis, 160, 162

Commissariat Department, 141, 147, 153, 154, 155, 156, 189

Dayworkers, xx, 81

Deism, 257-258

Drummond, Lt. General Gordon, 134, 140, 145

Duke of Wellington, 113, 116, 127

Economic Self-Interest
    Classical Liberalism, 249, 259
    God the Clockmaker, 249
    Montesquieu, 247-248, 259
    Physiocrats, 248, 259
    Smith, Adam, 247-248, 259
    Spirit of Capitalism, 248, 250, 259
    Spirit of Commerce, 246-249

Enlightenment of 18th C, 246-249

French Canadians, xii, 12-14, 24, 51, 57, 58, 76, 99

Good Works, 234-235

Glorious Revolution of 1688
      Bill of Rights, 233, 256
      Tory View, 233
      Whig View, 240

Grant, George, 256

Hamlets & Villages
      Merrick's Mills, 41
      Smith's Falls, 41
      Kemptville, 41

Historiography
      Carr, E.H., xviii, 252
      Collingwood, R.G., 228, 230
      Cultural bias, xv-xvi
      Cultural Fragments theory, 236, 252
      Cultural Values, v – vi, 226-230
      'Ideas influence actions', 227, 229
      Labour historians, v, xi, xiii, 68, 70-71, 99, 219
      Liberal historians, 230
      Marxist historians, v, xiv, 219-225, 251, 252
      Miller, Perry, 228

Horowitz, Gad, 252

Immigrants
      Army & Naval officers, 160, 164
      Immigration levels, 11, 14-15, 75, 90-91, 157
      Diet, 24, 166
      Gaelic-speaking Irish, xvii, 42- 43, 89, 79, 96, 207
      Health, 20- 21, 23-24, 25, 82, 91
      Anglo-Irish, 11, 43, 74, 77-78, 162-163
      Irish Catholics, 12, 20, 42, 43-44, 74-76, 86-89, 98
      Irish Catholic Poor Relief, 47, 181-185
      Protestant Irish, 11, 15-16, 42-47, 74, 162-166, 169, 187
      Scots, 43, 45-46, 142- 180
      English, 46

Just Price concept, 244, 258

Land
Clergy Reserves, 62
Crown Reserves, 62
Landless labourers, 47, 49, 82
Military grants, 8, 136-137, 148

Lockean liberalism, vi, 129, 226, 230, 237-244, 257
John Locke, 237-244, 246, 257-258
Working Schools, 245-246

Lord Bathurst, 134-135, 136, 139, 181

Lord Dalhousie, 19, 165, 199-200

Mactaggart, John, 33, 98, 116-117, 127

Mann, Lt. General Gother, 115

Marshall, Captain William,176

Military Rations
British Army, 153-154, 157
Rideau Canal, 25, 81
Rideau Military Settlement, 8-9, 56, 57, 167-170, 178

Military Settling Department, 7, 8-10, 35, 149, 153, 155, 178, 196
Establishment, 7
Expenditures, 179-180
Responsibilities, 8

Perth: 142-157
Cabins, 154-155, 202
Food Prices, 155
Military Rations, 148, 153, 156
Tools & Implements, 147

Surveys & Townships, 145, 157

Richmond: 158-164
Cabins, 160, 161
Clergyman, 161
Military rations, 161
Tools & Implements, 161-162
Schoolmaster, 161
Surveys, 160

Lanark: 164-178
Cabins, 170-171, 204
Clergyman, 177
Food prices, 171-172, 205
Cash advances/rations, 166, 159, 170, 174
Tools & Implements, 169-170, 174-175
Surveys & Townships, 167-168

Irish Poor Relief: 181-185
Cabins, 183, 204
Expenditures, 182, 185
Military Rations, 183
Purpose, 181
Quit rents (abortive), 205
Tools & Implements, 183-184
Surveys & Townships, 182- 183

Mill Sites: Rideau Military Settlement
Morphy's Mill (Carleton Place), 163, 188
Perth, 156-157
Shipman's Mills (Almonte), 163, 183

Myers, Colonel Christian, 154

Ordnance Surgeons
Michael Tuthill, 30-31, 33
William Kelly, 39

Paternalism (definition), xiii

Paternalism, military, 156,157-158, 165, 174-176, 179, 189, 235

Plato (427-347 B.C.), 254- 255

Provisions
        Cost on Rideau, 92-93
        Cost in Military Settlement, 155, 172, 202

Regiments
        Canadian Fencibles, 8, 147-148, 186
        DeWatteville Regiment, 8, 147-148, 186, 194
        Fencible regiments (definition), 190-191
        Glengarry Light Infantry of Fencibles, 8, 147-148
        99th Regiment of Foot, 8, 159-160, 198

Rennie, John C.E. (the Elder), 114, 115

Rideau Canal, 3-102
        Accommodations, 17-18, 19, 21, 25, 58, 81
        Acculturation, 41-52, 86-89
        Artificers/artisans, xx, 13
        Canal expenditures, 63
        Canal impact, 72
        Casual labourers, 27, 31
        Commencement, 11, 17, 18, 116, 117
        Commissariat, 20, 79
        Contractors, 3, 22, 25, 31, 54, 58, 68, 83, 93
        Contract system, 3
        Diet, 24, 53-56
        Drinking, 21-22, 25, 63-64, 80
        Ethnic differences, xvii, 65-68
        Employment levels, 14, 77
        Irish faction feuds, 65, 98-99, 101
        Food prices, 56, 93
        Hospitals, 18, 25, 36, 81
        Irish pauper immigrants, xvii, 20-24, 26-27, 41-45, 47,

58-59, 91-92, 97
    Land costs, 19, 46, 47, 58, 88-89
    Maintaining order, 22-23, 63-68
    Malaria/Lake fever & ague, 32- 41, 68, 69, 84
    Medical care, 17, 18, 24, 26, 33-41, 83
    Mortality rates, 32-33, 37, 39-41, 81, 85
    Multi-cultural workforce, xii
    Project organization, 4, 5, 7
    Purpose, xi, 139
    Provisioning, 17, 19-20, 35, 52-57, 78, 93
    Riots & brawls, 22-23, 80, 82, 138, 140
    Royal Sappers & Miners, 7, 23, 39, 40-41, 81
    Rock excavation, 3, 36, 68, 86
    Settlers, 4, 12, 14, 96- 97
    Sickness, 31- 41, 69, 84
    Slackwater system, 7
    Smallpox, 31-32, 82-83
    Steamboat waterway, 72
    Stoppage system, 29-31
    Surveys, 3, 13, 18
    Temperatures, 47
    Wage rates, 57-58, 80, 90, 94-95, 97
    Winter work, 25, 56-57, 59
    Work camps
        Bytown, 5, 18-19, 55
        the Isthmus, 3, 36
    Workforce composition, xii, xvi-xvii, 11-14, 77-78, 98
    Workforce well-being, 61, 63, 72

Rideau Military Settlement, 133-207
    Acculturation, 205-206, 207
    Axemen, 205
    Axe problem, 149
    Ballygibblin Riots, 188, 206
    Cost/Benefits, 185-188
    Crops, 205
    Ethnic animosities, 188
    Perth, 7, 157

Richmond, 7, 158-164
Lanark, 10, 164-178, 200-201
Land grants, 8, 161, 197
Population, 10, 188, 197
Scots, 9, 186
Soldier-settlers, 8, 155- 156,157, 191, 198
Summerless Summer, 150-152, 155, 195
Surveys & Townships, 192

Rideau route, 3-4

Roads
Brockville Road, 7, 140-141, 193-194
Perth- Lanark Road, 10, 41
Richmond Road, 7, 141, 160
Richmond-Perth Road, 10, 141, 160-161
Rideau Canal roads, 5

Robinson, Major-General Sir Frederick, 136-137

Robinson, Peter, 181-183, 189, 204, 206

Royal Absolutism, 255

Royal Gunpowder Mills, 109, 113-114

Royal Military Academy, 107-108

Sherbrooke, Lt. General Sir John, 152, 157-158

St. Lawrence Military Canals, 112,124-125, 138

Subsistence agriculture, 4-5

Timber Trade, 12-13

Towns
> Bytown, 41
> Kingston, 4, 41
> Lanark, 9, 168, 176
> Perth, 146, 156 - 157
> Richmond, 159, 160
> Wright's Town, 4, 12-13, 22, 50, 117
> York, 4

Upper Canada
> American immigration, 190
> British character, 134
> Loyalists, 137, 249
> Loyalty, 134, 136
> Struggle for Survival, 249-250

Upper Canadian Tory Mind, 253-254

Upper Canadian Tories, 236, 249-250

War of 1812
> American marauders, 137, 191
> American threat, 134, 139, 190
> Loyal militia, 137, 197
> Rideau waterway proposal, 139
> Treaty of Utrecht, December 1814, 135
> Wartime transport, 138-139, 153

Way, Peter, 219-221, 250

Whig liberals, 257

Working Class Culture, 252-253

Worker exploitation, 251, 259